To
Roger —

may all your hunts

be successful, and

good luck in the

deer woods —

Regards,

Jim Zumbo
aug 1, 89

Hunting America's Mule Deer

DAVE WADE

Hunting America's Mule Deer

Jim Zumbo

WINCHESTER PRESS
An Imprint of
NEW CENTURY PUBLISHERS, INC.

Printing code
        12   13   14   15   16
Library of Congress Catalog Card Number: 83−62028

ISBN 0-8329-3443-7
Printed in the United States

All photographs in this book are by the author unless
otherwise noted.

To a pair of special people—my in-laws,
DeMarr and Mada Dudley.

Acknowledgments

When Bob Elman, editor-in-chief of Winchester Press, gave me the go-ahead to write this book, I had no idea of the project I'd undertaken. As it turned out, I needed a lot of help from a lot of people, and I want to now thank them for their efforts.

Special thanks go to my wife, Lois, for rounding up the venison recipes in the Appendix (and testing them out on me and the kids); to my hunting buddy, Parker N. Davies, M.D., who helped me with the chapter, "Getting in Shape for Mule Deer Hunting"; to Joy Flora, production director of Winchester Press, who designed this book and had the remarkable tenacity and patience to work out the myriad of details to get it all together; and especially to Dave Wade, the talented artist who drew the frontispiece and painted the picture for the back of the book's jacket.

A note about Dave Wade. A couple of years ago, Dr. Huge Hogle, an eminent Salt Lake City surgeon, avid hunter, and connoisseur of wildlife art, told me he'd discovered a young artist whose big game paintings were the best he'd ever seen, particularly mule deer. I was skeptical, but when I saw Dave Wade's work I was quickly convinced. Of course, my book wouldn't be complete without a Dave Wade work, and I was delighted when he agreed to do the two pieces for it.

Thanks are also in order to the following people who provided photos or information: Dick Bolding, Murry Burnham, Kirt Darner, Professor Ray A. Field, Dan Gardner, Bob Good, Jerry Horgesheimer, Tim Irwin, Rich LaRocco, Andy Lightbody, Ray E. Lightbody, William H. Nesbitt, Tom Opre, Ed Park, Mike Perry, and Jesse Williams.

I'm also grateful to the following organizations, corporations, and agencies for helping with photos and information: Browning Co., Bushnell Optical Co., Boone and Crockett Club, National Rifle Association, Remington Arms, Wildlife Management Institute, U.S. Forest Service, U.S. Bureau of Land Management, and several state wildlife agencies.

Foreword

When Jim and I climbed to the top of a ridge along the Continental Divide, splitting Montana and Idaho, we could see our horses tied to a tree in a basin far below us. We still had several hours of daylight, so we continued to look for elk along the ridgeline. We were about 11 miles from our base camp in the Centennial Valley. But we weren't worried. Our horses would get us out of the mountains even in the dark. Jack Atcheson, a good friend and well-known outfitter, was hunting along a ridge parallel to us, and we planned to meet at the horses an hour before dark. Everything went according to plan...until we reached the basin. Our horses were gone! I plopped down in a foot of snow.

"What the hell do we do now, Zumbo?" I asked.

We walked, that's what we did. Or rather Jim walked and I gasped for air about 20 yards behind him. I'm an Eastern hunter whose idea of high-altitude hunting is a tree stand 12 feet off the ground. This was the first day of our elk hunt, and I'd come up from sea level to nearly 10,000 feet. My lungs felt like a brush fire. I'll never forget that hike out of the mountains with Jim. We shared some jerky and a candy bar. When we finished the water in our canteens, we ate snow and broke through stream ice to get at the water below. We reached camp about midnight. For the first time in my life, I fell in love with a sleeping bag.

Two days later, Jim's horse lost its footing while crossing a creek bed. It went down, panicked, and rolled on Jim's leg. It could have been serious, but Jim escaped with a painful limp that lasted several days. He couldn't lift his right leg higher than a few inches off the ground. Our streak of bad luck didn't stop there. The following day, while riding out of the mountains at night, I forgot to duck and ran a tree branch into my eye, scratching the cornea. It wasn't my shooting eye, however, so I figured my luck hadn't run out completely. But for the next several days, I hunted with an eye patch...and Jim hobbled along with me. I don't recall Jim complaining much, but I remember we laughed a lot.

At night in our log cabin bunkhouse, we built a wood fire in a converted drum stove and sipped Scotch whiskey iced down with snow. A drink never felt better going down. With elk racks wired to the lodgepole rafters over our heads, we'd talk for hours about everything and anything ...guns, fishing, our families, dogs, whiskey, and even women. Most of the time we talked about hunting, and this was when Jim seemed most happy.

We didn't get an elk on that trip, but that didn't seem important then and it doesn't now. Please don't misunderstand me. Jim and I are hunters, and we tried very hard to kill a couple of big bulls. But there's much more to a hunt than killing an animal. And if anyone disagrees with me, he should probably think about giving up the sport, because he didn't get the message.

Jim and I have worked together for many years as editors on the staff of *Outdoor Life*. I help put the magazine together in New York, but Jim's the lucky one. As one of our field staff, Jim hunts and fishes across the country. When he comes to New York, he doesn't stay long. I suspect the city makes him uncomfortable. He visits his parents in upstate New York, checks out the land at West Point where he worked as forester and wildlife biologist, then heads West where there is room to breathe and hunt big game.

Jim killed his first mule deer about 20 years ago, a giant buck dressing out at 232 pounds on grain scales. Since then, he has taken two or three bucks a year, keeping meticulous records of every kill. Jim may have cut his teeth on whitetails, but he has made a science of hunting mule deer.

There are probably many hunters who could write a book on deer hunting, but few could give a book the added dimension that only a wildlife biologist and forester can supply. Jim does just that. He doesn't limit his advice to when and how to hunt mule deer; he gets into the behavior of the muley, and he explains why this Western deer acts differently under a variety of conditions. You'll discover why the mule deer is sometimes predictable and sometimes not. In short, you'll learn everything there is to know about mule deer hunting.

Most hunters spend a couple of weeks a year hunting deer, but Jim has chalked up nearly 20 years of experience in deer country as a full-time wildlife biologist. His experience is day-to-day, and that makes him an expert. He has also worked as a forest ranger, timber cruiser, and forest fire fighter. Just about every job Jim has held has put him in close contact with deer.

Jim Zumbo knows mule deer; if a hunter doesn't learn something from this book, he just isn't paying attention.

Vin T. Sparano
Executive Editor,
Outdoor Life

Introduction

Picture yourself high in the Rockies, amidst towering firs and rimrock outcrops. You breathe with some difficulty in the rarefied air, and perspiration seeps down your arms and the small of your back. A whiskey jack flits to a nearby tree, cocks its head to one side, and flies to a rotted log on the forest floor where it eyes you quizzically.

Suddenly, you hear the clatter of rocks from a talus slope above. You look up and see a grand buck mule deer leaping across the boulders in great bounds. His heavily muscled body carries him swiftly as his huge antlers sway ponderously in rhythm with his stride. Resting your rifle across a log, you find him in the crosshairs and squeeze the trigger. The buck stumbles, wavers, and collapses in the rocks. The magnificent animal is yours.

Fact or fantasy? Have you ever tied your deer tag on a muley? If not, would you like to? Whatever your answer, this book was written for you. It explores the world of the mule deer, a creature that dwells in practically every Western environment.

Though the West is endowed with an enviable assortment of big game animals, the mule deer is the beloved quarry. His splendid antlers are cause for much fantasy among hunters, and his delectable flesh feeds millions of people each year.

Not many years past, truly big mule deer were unbelievably common. So much so, in fact, that the species was often considered to be less than wary; more plainly put—stupid.

But times have changed. Accelerated hunting pressure and increased access to the hinterlands have combined to shape a new breed of mule deer. Not in a biological sense, of course, but behavior-wise. Indeed, plenty of big bucks are out there, but few are easily taken.

And that is what this book is all about—to make you a better mule deer hunter. I wrote this book to inform, not to entertain. In it you'll learn how, why, when, and where to hunt mule deer—and only mule deer. Most books discuss all the deer species or big game species together, with little information on the mule deer. Not so in this book. The seven subspecies of mule deer, from the popular Rocky Mountain subspecies to the black-tail, are discussed thoroughly.

Because mule deer country is so vast, generalizing would not be of much help. Techniques that apply in one habitat might not apply in another. If you look down on the Western landscape from a jetliner, you see a mosaic of landforms, from Pacific coastal forests to the Badlands of the Dakotas, from greasewood desert thickets to alpine evergreen woodlands. Mule deer live in each of these environments, and also behave differently in each.

To focus closely on these varying habitats, I separated them into eight categories and devoted a chapter to each. For example, you wouldn't hunt muleys in a pinyon-juniper stand the same way you would in sagebrush, or in the rimrock or in agricultural areas. You choose techniques best for the area you're hunting and vary them accordingly. That's exactly what I tried to discuss in eight chapters, and I hope the information helps put meat in your freezer this fall. To demonstrate the effectiveness of various methods, I sprinkled the chapters liberally with anecdotes. It's easier to learn by reading about other people's successes and failures.

Another chapter tells you how to put together a mule deer hunt on your own, whether you've ever been west or not. And if you want someone to guide you, another chapter tells everything you need to know when selecting an outfitter. And how about your hunting vehicle? Will it stand up in the Western mountains? And how about public lands, where are they located and where do you write for maps? Answers to these questions and many, many more are in this book.

You'll read about rifles for mule deer, bowhunting gear, muzzleloaders, optical systems, and how to handle a horse. How about getting your deer home in a jetliner, in your pickup, or the trunk of your car? What are some ways to get a heavy buck from the mountains to your vehicle or hunting camp? These are details you need to know. How about the common fear of getting ill at high altitudes when you're used to sea level? A chapter by my friend, Dr. Parker Davies, Jr., tells you how to get in shape for your Western hunt.

Most hunters dream of a magnificent trophy that would look good over the fireplace or office desk. A chapter on trophies tells you what to look for, how to hunt, and where to go.

And what about the future for mule deer? Where will they be 10 years from now, and how about our chances of getting permits in rapidly grow-ing Western states? The final chapter evaluates where muleys are now and where they're heading.

When it comes time to feast on your mule deer, the Appendix contains a chapter by my wife Lois who describes recipes for many epicurean repasts.

The Appendix also details a comprehensive state-by-state directory of mule deer, from their history to their present status, as well as population estimates, recent harvest figures, hunter success rates, and where to go.

Join in my affair with this wonderful animal. There are few superlatives to describe his being, his existence. He is simply a marvelous creature, a symbol of wildness and all that is free.

Jim Zumbo
Vernal, Utah
1981

Contents

All About Mule Deer

Of all the big game species in the West, the mule deer is far and away the favorite among hunters. Antelope are speedier, elk and moose are bigger, sheep are classier, bears are tougher, but the muley is hunted with more zeal and enthusiasm than any other.

Surveys indicate there are about 8 million mule deer in the West, including blacktails. About a half million are harvested annually by America's hunters.

The term mule deer is a general name encompassing 11 separate subspecies, though biologists are in general agreement only on seven subspecies. They are the Rocky Mountain mule deer, desert mule deer, Columbian black-tailed deer, Sitka black-tailed deer, California mule deer, southern mule deer, and peninsula mule deer.

The Rocky Mountain mule deer is by far the most popular and widespread of the seven subspecies. Its range exceeds the ranges of all other subspecies combined. This deer lives in all the Rocky Mountain and intermountain regions, with populations as far north as the northern Alberta and British Columbia borders and as far east as Iowa, Minnesota, and Manitoba.

The desert mule deer inhabits the Southwest region of North America. It dwells in New Mexico, Arizona, Texas, and Mexico. The southern mule deer occupies the top half of the Baja Peninsula and extends somewhat into California, while the peninsula mule deer lives in the bottom half of Baja. The California mule deer ranges in central and southern California, from the coast up into the Sierras. The Columbian

I

black-tailed deer, popular among West Coast hunters, occupies central to northern California, western Oregon, western Washington, and western British Columbia. The Sitka black-tailed deer lives in western British Columbia and parts of coastal Alaska.

Obviously, interbreeding between these subspecies along their boundaries has caused confusion during attempted identification. Only trained biologists can tell them apart, and sometimes they can make only educated guesses.

Besides hybridization, disputes as to the correct nomenclature of the blacktail, even to the common spelling of its name, have been a problem. The prestigious Wildlife Management Institute, for example, refers to it as the black-tailed deer (with a hyphen). The Boone and Crockett Club, equally prestigious, calls it simply the Columbian blacktail, and lumps

Look at the massive body on this buck! He would probably weigh 325 pounds on the hoof. You need an adequate firearm to bring him down.

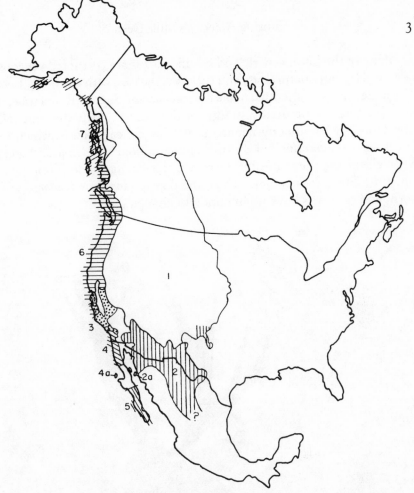

Map showing the geographic range of mule deer subspecies: (1) Rocky Mountain mule deer; (2) desert mule deer; (2a) Tiburon Island mule deer; (3) California
mule deer; (4) Southern mule deer; (4a) Cedros Island mule deer; (5) peninsula
mule deer; (6) Columbian blacktail deer; (7) Sitka blacktail deer. This map is
reprinted from *Mule and Black-tailed Deer of North America* (University of
Nebraska Press, 1981), edited by O. C. Wallmo. *(Courtesy of the Wildlife
Management Institute.)*

together as one the Sitka and Columbian subspecies. Early scientists
termed the blacktail a separate species, and labeled it *Odocoileus columbianus*. Today it is properly identified as *O. hemionus columbianus*.

All mule deer are classified *Odocoileus hemionus*. The first word,
Odocoileus, is the genus; the second word, *hemionus*, is the species. The
third word is the subspecies.

Many of the Latin generic and specific names are corrupted versions bestowed by early naturalists, and such was the case with the mule deer. The muley owes its scientific name to Constantine Samuel Rafinesque, a French-American naturalist. In 1832, he decided to classify the whitetail deer found in Virginia by naming it after its concave tooth, which in Greek was *Odontocoelus*, but the translation resulted in *Odocoileus*. Later, when classifying the mule deer, he gave it the specific name of *hemionus*, which in Greek means mule. Thus, the name *Odocoileus hemionus* was born, and scientists have no intention of changing it.

A nontypical buck. Note the unusual palmation and short tines.

Mule deer have distinguishing features that set them apart from whitetails. Their antler tines fork instead of growing off a main beam as on whitetails. Mule deer antlers, especially of the Rocky Mountain subspecies, are typically wide and massive on mature bucks.

Typical weights of the Rocky Mountain subspecies are from 150 to 225 pounds for bucks and 120 to 150 pounds for does. Blacktails, desert, and other subspecies are lighter in weight. Exceptional bucks of the Rocky Mountain subspecies may exceed 300 pounds dressed weight.

A mature buck stands 3½ feet at the shoulder and averages about 6 feet in length. Ears are about 10 inches long, hence the name "mule" deer.

Generally, the mule deer is far less nervous than the whitetail. Whereas the latter moves about constantly, jerking its head up to look for danger with tail twitching frequently, the muley carries itself calmly and steadily.

Because of the country in which it lives, the mule deer has been widely known to stand stupidly in the open while a hunter made an easy shot. Without question, muleys take safety in distance, but too often the distance is within striking range of a high-powered rifle. In recent years, mature mule deer have apparently learned to take shelter in timber and brush. With more backcountry opening up each year, big deer retreat from human pressure by hiding out in rugged country or dense thickets. Many observers see a "new" mule deer in the making, one that challenges the hunter every bit as much as the whitetail.

Since mule deer inhabit rugged country, they must cope with a variety of profound problems that would otherwise do them in. Starvation is a common problem, especially when winter ranges are in poor shape and deer are too numerous. In much of the West where winters are severe, deer must migrate from high elevations to lower altitudes to find adequate food. Sometimes, however, the quantity of food might be sufficient, but its nutritional quality is not. Commonly, mule deer range over vast areas in the summer, but move into restricted areas when winter sets in. Many winter range areas are 10 percent or less of the deer's habitat. Since deer are concentrated in winter, disease, starvation, and predation become important problems.

In the tri-state area where Utah, Wyoming, and Colorado join together, deer funnel into a long, narrow valley called Brown's Park which lies on the floor of the Green River. Deer from all three states migrate into the park, seeking sagebrush for winter forage. The park is a typical winter range because it's protected by mountains and receives comparatively light snowfall. In the mountains surrounding Brown's Park, snow depths can be 3 to 6 feet or more. Tagging studies there indicate some mule deer have traveled 60 to 80 miles to reach the park from the high country. While working in the park as a wildlife biologist, I often inventoried 1,500 or more deer in a single day. I also documented numerous predator kills from cougars and coyotes, as well as disease-related deaths.

Mule deer build up fat reserves quickly, starting in April and May when new forage appears. But, by the first of the year, they begin rapidly losing weight as they struggle with winter's grasp. Deer become weakened and are vulnerable as never before to all sorts of factors that normally would not bother them. Human disturbance on winter ranges can often be a major problem if deer are harassed. Snowmobilers are often responsible for deer mortality by unwittingly forcing weakened animals out of the valley bottoms and up into rugged terrain where feed is marginal. Many states forbid snowmobiling and other human intrusions into deer winter areas, and rightly so.

Most mule deer pictures are of big, pretty bucks. Here's what they look like at the age of 1 year. These bucks are skinny because they barely survived the severe 1978–1979 winter.

This deer is a classic fence victim. Thousands suffer a similar fate each winter when they're weakened.

Common range fences are killers in winter by ensnarling deer as they try to jump over. During other times of the year mule deer can easily jump a standard 3- or 4-foot fence, but in winter it's another story. When snows are deep and animals weak, they often fail to clear the top wires. In most cases, the hind legs miss the top wires and slip between the top two. The wires flip over, and the deer is hopelessly trapped to die an agonizing death. Along a particular stretch of fence that bordered BLM (Bureau of Land Management) land near the Utah-Colorado border, more than 50 deer were estimated to have been caught and killed within a fifteen year period. The controversial fence made news, and the agency restrung it so it would not trap deer. The fence problem is so common that the BLM made a study to design a fence that would be safe for mule deer, yet contain livestock, which is their exclusive purpose. The study resulted in a design that was implemented on all public lands. Most problem fences have been modified.

Several years ago Dan Gardner, who works as a wild horse specialist for the BLM, came across a doe trapped in a fence in northeast Utah. He carefully freed her, but she ran off a few yards and stood there, wobbling about with weakness and severe damage to her hind legs. Dan left her alone, and when he returned to the same area to check on her the next day, he found a few bones and bits of hair—and coyote tracks everywhere.

Domestic dogs take a large toll of wintering mule deer each year. Most states take a dim view of deer-running dogs, and wardens are usually empowered to shoot such dogs on sight. The problem has become serious with the growth of ski and winter sports areas on or near winter ranges. People bring their dogs with them, but aren't aware that Fido is off chasing and killing deer. The situation is especially serious in Colorado, where ski areas have attracted tens of thousands of people and their dogs. A game warden told me horror stories of dog-deer atrocities, and grimly related the number of dogs he kills each winter, sometimes totaling in the hundreds.

When deer are weakened and concentrated on winter ranges, disease can spread like wildfire. Entire herds can be wiped out in a matter of weeks.

Starvation is the primary problem in the winter, and accounts for perhaps the greatest losses during extremely severe winters. Unfortunately, people do not often understand the nutritional requirements of deer, and "kill them with kindness" by feeding them.

This deer died in a haystack with its belly full. Deer often are unable to digest unnatural food.

In a deer's stomach, plant fibers are digested by rumen microbes—bacteria that break down food into necessary energy. When deer are suddenly fed foods that are not "natural," stomach bacteria are often incapable of breaking down the fibers, and the deer dies with a full belly.

Marauding deer that attack haystacks in the winter are common victims of this malady. Hay is a foreign substance if the animal is subjected to it suddenly, and it can kill deer quickly. During the severe winter of 1978–79, which many observers call the worst of the century in the Rockies, thousands of deer died along haystacks and from handouts by well-meaning people. Biologists attempted emergency feedings in some states by formulating pellets made up of various ingredients. Some worked, some did not. I traveled extensively that winter, photographing deer and interviewing wildlife officers. A visit to Gunnison, Colorado, which was perhaps the hardest-hit region in the Rockies, was most sobering. I counted hundreds of dead deer, despite feeding efforts by the state wildlife agency. A trip to the Jackson Hole, Wyoming, area was even worse. Deer were dead and dying along highways where people had been throwing bales of hay in an effort to keep them alive. In the spring, after the snow thawed, I visited the Jackson Hole area again and was appalled at the carcasses everywhere.

Besides filling the deer with useless food, people who feed deer get the animals in trouble by concentrating them in areas where they're vulnerable to dogs, as well as diverting deer from natural winter ranges where they might be able to find adequate forage on their own.

Predators are always an important factor in mule deer country. Coyotes and cougars prey on deer extensively, but much controversy, as expected, surrounds the deer-predator relationship.

Dr. Maurice Hornocker, the nation's authority on cougars, says not enough is known about the cougar-deer relationship to draw conclusions. He said, "Lions (cougars) are known to kill deer wherever the two species occur together but this merely establishes the *fact*. The *effect* of this killing on deer numbers, the really meaningful and important aspect to consider, has scarcely been looked at in an objective way."

Others disagree, suggesting that lions have a serious impact in areas where their populations are high. Popular belief has it that a mature cougar kills about one deer per week, but some biologists put the figure at half that number. By translating that figure to actual cougar populations in important mule deer states, we can come up with interesting possibilities. In Arizona, for example, an estimated 2,500 cougars stalk the mountains and deserts. If *half* that number were mature cats capable of each killing 25 deer per year, the total kill would be 31,250 deer annually taken by lions. During the 1980 hunting season, less than 12,000 mule deer were killed by hunters. Remember that we're speculating about the proportion of the lion kill, but even if it was reasonably accurate, one would hardly suggest that cougars be eliminated to favor deer.

Lions have their own place in the scheme of things. As Dr. Hornocker said, "Mountain lions and mule deer evolved together in the West. Both have survived, often flourished. Their relationship is a simplified straight-line one: habitat equals mule deer equals lions. Mule deer depend on habitat, lions depend on mule deer. If we improve habitat, we can increase the numbers of deer in the long run; if we decrease lions only, with no habitat change, the results won't be the same."

Coyotes are far more controversial than cougars, no doubt because livestock interests, particularly sheepmen, have long raised havoc over

This little buck leaps along with great strides. Mule deer can really pour on the coal when they want to clear out in a hurry.

the destructive nature of the animal. Much of the stockmen's bitterness is justified, because the coyote is an efficient killing machine that opportunistically preys on anything it can overcome and eat. Wildlife biologists throughout the West are painfully aware of the inroads made on deer herds by coyotes.

Coyotes can and do kill mule deer. It happens every day, as naturally as an infant drinks milk, and the killing will continue as long as there are coyotes and deer. The important question, of course, is the overall impact by coyotes on deer populations, and their long-term effects on deer over broad regions instead of isolated localities.

In some states, biologists are convinced that coyotes need to be reduced in order to protect deer herds, particularly on winter ranges when deer are weakened and concentrated. In Oregon's Steens Mountains, state wildlife officials conducted an aerial control program to kill coyotes on selected winter ranges. Elsewhere, states are spending much money to determine the effects of coyote predation on mule deer. Though there is much disagreement on coyotes and their impact on deer, most biologists concede that predation becomes an important mortality factor when deer populations are down. Healthy herds of deer do not suffer as much as depressed herds.

In February 1972, President Richard Nixon banned the use of coyote poisons on federal lands. Many toxins such as 1080, cyanide, strychnine, thallium, and others, were outlawed indefinitely. Predictably, stockmen were outraged, but their petitions met with little approval in Washington. For the most part, poisons are still banned.

It might have been coincidental, but mule deer populations began crashing in the West in the early 1970's. With coyotes on the increase due to the termination of poisoning, and mule deer on a severe decrease for unknown reasons, many observers were quick to point the finger of blame at the coyote. As a former wildlife biologist in prime mule deer country, I'm convinced that coyotes indeed take a big toll of mule deer herds in *some* areas, but I can't confirm or document widespread losses throughout the West.

Today we enjoy hunting mule deer in every Western state, and hunter success is excellent in the top states. But it wasn't always good. A bit of early history depicts another picture of mule deer.

In 1805, Captain Meriwether Lewis and Captain William Clark penetrated the innards of the Western wilderness during their famous trek up the Missouri River and down to the Pacific via the Snake and Columbia Rivers. One can only imagine the reactions of these explorers when they first saw a mule deer with its strange ears and large antlers.

Lewis and Clark are credited with writing the first detailed account of mule deer habitat requirements. Evidence suggests that Captain Lewis originated the name "mule deer" when he stated, "We have rarely found the mule deer in any except rough country. They prefer the open ground and are seldom found in woodlands or river bottoms."

Early explorers and trappers rarely mention mule deer in their journals. Relatively little is known about mule deer populations prior to the arrival of early pioneers. In the 1820 to 1834 period of extensive exploration and trapping, mountain men recorded only incidental mule deer in their diaries, although elk, antelope, bison, and beaver were regularly recorded. Explorers Peter Skene Ogden, John Kirk Townsend, and Alexander Ross recorded the scarcity of deer in comparison to other wildlife.

The mule deer has a thin, white, rope-like tail tipped with black.

Father Escalante, a missionary who led a journey into the Western territories in 1776, made no mention of deer, though he traveled through some of the finest mule deer range according to present standards. At times the party killed their horses for food, traded with Indians for bighorn sheep meat, but did not describe the presence of deer.

Why weren't mule deer numerous in the pre-settlement days? One can only speculate, but a prime reason was no doubt the abundance of large predators that kept deer herds in check. Grizzlies and wolves ranged throughout the West, and cougars were plentiful everywhere in mule deer country. Indians harvested deer regularly as well.

As the West was settled, the white man brought his livestock and began dividing and working the land. Cows and sheep took the place of deer, bison, and elk, and big game was hunted indiscriminately for food or because it was competing with livestock or feeding on crops. Forests were cut for timber, land was burned and plowed, and fences divided big game ranges. Great herds of livestock plundered vast areas of the West as their nomadic owners maneuvered them randomly according to the abundance of water and feed, and seasonal weather changes.

Big game was driven into the backcountry, and thousands of herds were eradicated. Bison, buffalo, deer, and elk were driven to the point of near extinction.

Apparently, mule deer were not scarce in all the West during the periods of settlement, because history indicates instances where individuals or parties killed huge numbers of animals in a few days or hours. Obviously, some regions had large herds, but these were quickly wiped out. Ernest Thompson Seton, one of America's most famous naturalists, estimated that about 10 million mule deer and more than 40 million white-tailed deer occupied their original range. Many observers strongly dispute these estimates, including me. I take all early estimates of wildlife with a grain of salt. How could anyone determine animal populations accurately? By what census methods? Wildlife management did not come into being as a recognized profession until the 1930's, so early inventory techniques had to be very rough guesses. Where and how did naturalists get their information? Did they have so-called experts in each region count animals? Even today, with the use of aircraft, remote sensing and other sophisticated methods, biologists often cannot count big game accurately. The state of Montana, for example, steadfastly refuses to give population figures on big game, admitting they don't know how many

animals they have. Thus, for Seton to say that there were 10 million mule
deer suggests he was making a wild guess. Though I admire the man, I
believe his estimates, and those of other early naturalists, are far off base.

Seton stated the entire U.S. deer population hit an all-time low at the
turn of the century, numbering only 500,000 in 1908. Again, this figure is
suspect, but he was right about populations being extremely low. Most
biologists believe the populations were at rock bottom during the 40-year
period from 1875 to 1915.

My father-in-law, DeMarr Dudley, was born in 1901 near the Utah-
Colorado border. He recounts times in his boyhood when it was a thrill
to see a deer track, let alone a deer. His grandfather settled in Utah during the mid-1800's with early pioneers, and along with other settlers, used
mule deer extensively for food. DeMarr's father made trips into western
Colorado with several other men each fall to obtain their winter meat
supply. They took horse-drawn wagons into the country near Meeker

Notice the difference in the
rangeland on each side of this
fence. Livestock overgrazing
can have adverse impacts on
deer range.

and filled them with mule deer. Each man took six or eight deer to keep his family in meat. Since it was in the late 1800's, no seasons and laws protected deer. It was necessary—and honorable—to kill game for the table in those days.

As livestock developed into a thriving industry, large predators were killed indiscriminately. Grizzlies and wolves were driven out quickly, with most gone by the early 1900's. Cougars were hunted relentlessly, but they maintained populations in every Western state.

The famous Kaibab incident illustrates what can happen to a mule deer herd if hunting is stopped and predators killed off. The Kaibab Plateau in northern Arizona was an isolated area with productive mule deer range. It was the favored hunting ground of Navajos and Paiutes who harvested most of their winter meat from healthy herds that roamed throughout. A thriving cougar population kept deer herds thinned to optimum levels.

White men saw the Kaibab as a perfect place for livestock. In 1885, 2,000 cattle were turned loose on the rich rangeland. By 1913, there were 15,000 cattle and 5,000 sheep.

On November 28, 1906, President Theodore Roosevelt created the Grand Canyon National Game Preserve. Hunting was stopped, but predator killing continued at a rapid pace. Government hunters and trappers in the area reportedly killed 781 cougars, 30 wolves, 4,889 coyotes, 554 bobcats, and many eagles.

Predictably, deer herds on the Kaibab flourished with the absence of predators and termination of hunting. The deer population at the time the preserve was established numbered about 4,000 animals. By 1924, the herd was estimated to be an incredible 100,000. The Kaibab rangeland was a shambles from overgrazing by deer and livestock alike. In an effort to provide some relief for the area, in 1924 a large group of sportsmen attempted to drive deer out of the Kaibab across the Grand Canyon into other parts of Arizona where herds were depleted. George McCormick, leader of the drive, made a deal to deliver between 3,000 and 8,000 deer to the South Rim of the Grand Canyon where he would be paid $2.50 for each deer delivered. The plan was to drive the deer from South Canyon to Saddle Canyon, down into Nankoweep Canyon in the Grand Canyon, across the Colorado River, and up the Tanner Trail to the South Rim.

On December 16, 1924, 125 drivers took their positions. Carrying tin cans, cowbells, and other noisemakers, they formed a line on foot and horseback. As they moved forward, the line became irregular, and a bad storm made it all but impossible to see. Many lost their way in the blizzard, and fell out of ranks to find a familiar landmark. Others realized the futility of the drive and turned back. Finally, when the remaining drivers reached Saddle Canyon, they discovered thousands of deer behind them but none in front. At that point the great drive was abandoned.

That winter was the final chapter for thousands of deer. They died horrible deaths of starvation when snow covered what little food was left. One account states, "Those deer that lived ate every leaf and twig till the whole country looked as though a swarm of locusts had swept through it, leaving the range torn, gray, stripped, and dying."

Deer losses continued the next three years on the beaten-down rangeland. In 1928, government hunters were hired to execute as many deer as possible to allow the range a rest. On December 15, 1928, the government hunters set out on their grisly task. Each was supplied with a horse and team, and each was responsible for dressing and moving carcasses where they could be picked up by buckboard. The result of the carnage was 1,124 deer. The hunt aroused public controversy, and the state of Arizona sued the United States of America. The U.S. District Court handed

Proud hunters with big bucks they killed on the Kaibab Forest in Arizona in 1931 after the preserve was opened to hunting. *(Photo courtesy of the U.S. Forest Service.)*

down a decision in favor of the state, but the Supreme Court later upheld the U.S. Government's authority to kill deer on the Kaibab by federal hunters.

Deer hunting by sportsmen was allowed on the Kaibab afterward, but the effort was too little and too late. The habitat had suffered long-lasting scars, and deer continued to die every winter. By 1930, an estimated 20,000 deer remained, and by 1940 the number was down to 10,000. Wolves were forever eliminated from the great game range, and only a few cougars remained.

In reference to predator control, Ben H. Thompason wrote: "It was done then with the idea that proper wilderness utilization would consist of killing the bloodthirsty animals so that people could enjoy the gentle ones. But we have seen what happened to the deer of the Kaibab and Grand Canyon. Unfortunately, the Kaibab was only the type case; the same thing happened in many places throughout the West in both National Parks and National Forests where deer and elk have been protected and their enemies destroyed. The whole difficulty arises because we have learned to appreciate only a few wilderness aspects."

Settlers simply could not exist with predators that ravaged their livestock and placed fear in their hearts. The mentality of the era was not one of respect and admiration of predators, but one of disdain and hatred. In fact, the earliest "wildlife" programs of the infant Forest Service were aimed at destroying predators. In 1909, Gifford Pinchot stated that in that year alone, 51 rangers spent 107 working days killing 108 bears, 96 mountain lions, 144 wolves, 62 wolf pups, 3,295 coyotes, 571 wildcats, and 81 lynx.

An important lesson can be learned from the Kaibab and other areas like it, one that wildlife biologists recognize as being essential to sound wildlife management: permanent stockpiling of big game animals is impossible. Sooner or later, the carrying capacity of the range no longer supports the demands placed on it. People have largely replaced predators; people must maintain healthy wildlife populations, or nature will do it for us as she did on the Kaibab.

In the early 1900's, most states formed wildlife agencies to deal with fish, birds, and animals. In Utah, for example, a hunting and fishing license was required in 1907 for all sportsmen over the age of 14. For $1, a hunter could kill all the deer he wanted, but only in a specified 6-month season. Herds were so depleted from the last several decades of exploitation, however, that the season was closed from 1908 through 1912. In 1913, hunting was allowed again, but only for 15 days and for bucks with antlers at least 5 inches long. Hunters killed 600 bucks that season.

With regulations limiting deer take, populations grew throughout the West and peaked in the late 1950's. Practically every Western state reported the same trend: mule deer were almost nonexistent in the early 1900's, then herds built gradually to all-time highs in the 1950's and 1960's. Because of peak populations, game managers in most states began a program to reduce deer. Special doe permits were offered, buck-only hunts were changed to either-sex hunting, and pre- and post-season hunts were

This buck displays typical breeding behavior during the rut. He's testing the air, seeking the scent of females in heat.

held. In Colorado, for example, does and fawns were authorized as legal game in 1940, but not until 1948 did harvests of them become relatively significant. During that year, 25,000 were harvested, and from then on, harvest figures climbed steadily higher. In 1957, antlerless deer killed were in excess of 50,000. In 1963, some 81,000 does and fawns were taken. Added to the buck harvest, Colorado hunters killed more than 100,000 mule deer each season between the years 1959 and 1965. The biggest take ever, in 1963, amounted to 147,322 deer.

Utah showed similar trends. The first doe season was held in 1934, but 1951 was the year that the extensive antlerless hunts were held. In that year, 34,308 does and fawns were harvested. For the next 20 years the antlerless take exceeded 30,000 with a high in 1962 of 55,092. By combining the buck take, Utah hunters killed more than 100,000 deer each year from 1954 to 1964, with an all-time high harvest of 132,278 deer in 1961.

But suddenly, in the early 1970's, the bottom dropped out. Mule deer skidded into a frightful decline in many leading states, and no obvious reasons could be pinpointed. In April 1976, wildlife managers from around the West gathered for a symposium at Utah State University titled "Mule Deer Decline In the West". All mortality factors were detailed and explored, but no specific causes were isolated. If anything, attendees were more confused after the symposium than before. Papers presented dealt with nutritional problems, winter range inadequacies, predation by lions and coyotes, diseases, and a number of other factors.

Because of low deer populations, many states terminated the antlerless harvest in all but special problem areas. In some hunting units, deer hunting was closed completely or restricted to four-point or better bucks to protect young bucks and does and to attract fewer hunters.

For whatever reasons, deer herds began a slow but gradual increase in the late 1970's. The severe, history-making winter of 1978-79 caused a setback in some regions, but deer numbers now seem to be on the upswing in states where they had declined badly. The Appendix in this book details the current status of mule deer in each state.

Mule deer management is a complex issue. The decline clearly illustrated that wildlife managers didn't have all the answers. Nonetheless, muleys are comfortably entrenched in every Western state, and should continue to be the favorite big game animal west of the Mississippi.

The Blacktail Deer

I've seen some dense living quarters for deer, but nothing quite matches the coastal environment of the blacktail. Some forests are so thick it's impossible to see a companion 5 yards away, much less a deer.

As mentioned in the previous chapter, blacktails are close relatives of mule deer. In fact, they *are* mule deer, but are considered a separate subspecies. Two subspecies of blacktail are recognized, the Columbian subspecies that lives along the West Coast from California to British Columbia, and the Sitka subspecies that dwells in coastal forests in B.C. and Alaska. Both are much smaller than the Rocky Mountain mule deer, and Sitka deer are normally smaller than Columbian blacktails. Antler development is the same as with mule deer, but much smaller. These subspecies were named because of their tails, which are black toward the tip, brownish at the base, and white beneath. Ears of the blacktail are smaller than those of mule deer, but larger than whitetails. Population estimates for Columbian and Sitka blacktails are a total of about 1½ million.

Now back to their dense habitat. Actually, these deer are not exclusively denizens of impenetrable rain-forest tangles. Blacktails are just as comfortable in brushy country, oak forests, in and around farmland, and high in the Sierras where snows linger until late summer. Some of the finest hunting is in semi-open woodland where oak trees and low brush provide essential forest and cover.

But dense forest is what we think of as blacktail habitat. Dripping, mossy forests overgrown with horrid growths of salal, thorny berry bushes, Devil's Club, and other plants that rip, tear, and bloody your body from head to toe should you foolishly try to penetrate it. Damp places where ferns grow luxuriously thick and trees grow so big you can't see their tops from the ground. This is the home of the blacktail. If the ocean is nearby, foggy mists shroud the forest, and the smell of salt touches the air. A spooky place indeed, but tailor-made for the deer of our West Coast forests.

I became most intimate with this unique world while working as a timber cruiser in Oregon's coastal forests during my college years. Working with a crew of other would-be foresters during the summer, our job was to inventory timber by sampling predetermined tracts of land. We took dozens of measurements on each sample plot, and spent much time walking

A lovely black-tailed buck estimated to weigh about 280 pounds. *(Photo courtesy of Dick Bolding, Washington Game Department.)*

on slippery logs, crawling through dank tunnels made by bears and deer through the thickets, and otherwise having a terribly tough time squeezing our bodies through the incredibly thick rain forest. No Carolina swamp or Maine alder thicket came close to comparing to that jungle nightmare. It wasn't really a bad place to work. It was just difficult. In a way, the forest had a special enchantment, one that couldn't be found anywhere else. The thick West Coast forest begins in California and extends to Alaska, where Sitka blacktails dwell. Rain is a fact of life, especially in the winter and spring months.

Blacktails differ from muleys in that they seldom travel far in their daily behavior patterns. Whereas muleys may travel miles each night to find food and water, the blacktail finds all the essentials of life in a small area. This habit creates a special hunting challenge, because animals don't move about much and are less likely to be seen. The hunter must go to them, and seek them in their forested world.

Old forests along the West Coast often yield little feed. Because the rays of the sun cannot strike the ground due to heavy foliage, the lush undergrowth needed for food is lacking. Animals tend to select areas with available food.

Before settlement, blacktail deer were attracted to areas burned over by natural fires. As the land recovered, leafy undergrowth appeared and blanketed the fire-scarred landscape. Most of those plants were preferred by deer. As settlers homesteaded the forests, they cleared the land and planted crops. Logging became an important industry, and the large Douglas fir forests of the Northwest were opened to extensive logging. Tree cutting had the same effect as fires. With the old-growth timber removed, clear-cut areas quickly grew lush. Blacktails moved in and stayed as long as food remained. When the forests grew and closed out the sunlight — and subsequently the brush — deer moved on elsewhere.

Hunters who know blacktail habits hunt clear-cuts regularly. Many national forests allow public access, and several private timber companies own huge tracts of land. Each has its own policy toward hunting.

There are many access roads into blacktail country, especially in national forests. Some roads are closed to vehicular traffic, particularly those constructed to allow logging access into remote areas. After logging, the Forest Service often closes roads to allow them to reseed and grow in with vegetation, thus preventing erosion. In areas with active logging, be cautious about driving the logging roads. Big log-hauling trucks take more of the road than your vehicle, and the results could be bad should you meet one unexpectedly.

The dense cover in blacktail country lends itself well to deer drives, but vantage points that offer a good view might be hard to find. A large boulder or fallen log on the side of a canyon is a good choice if the vista includes a look at the far sidehill and the canyon bottom as well. Blacktails don't run uphill to escape hunters as much as mule deer, and often head down to creek bottoms where they can seek shelter in red alder thickets and other tangles that infest canyon bottoms.

Because blacktails are creatures of forest cover in much of their range, they stay in such cover as much as possible. Like whitetails, they shun openings, and commonly go out of their way to remain in timber rather than cross a meadow. This isn't always true, however, particularly during dim light times of early morning and late afternoon.

One of the best ways to waylay a blacktail is to take a stand early in the morning where you can glass a clearcut or old burn. Since undergrowth in the feeding area might be high, an elevated stand where you can look

Carrying a daypack, Rich La-Rocco looks over California blacktail country while bow-hunting. (Photo courtesy of Rich LaRocco.)

Northern California's blacktail country is steep. Here, outdoor writer Dwight Schuh climbs a slope while bowhunting for blacktails. *(Photo courtesy of Rich LaRocco.)*

down into the brush is preferred. If you're hunting in a place fairly close to an urban area, you might be sharing your spot with other hunters. You might want to take a walk and find a clearcut over the next ridge where there are no hunters.

Blacktails are masters at hiding, and have no problem sitting tight while a hunter fights through the brush. More than once I almost stumbled on a bedded deer in thick timber.

In open, brushy country where you can see long distances, binoculars are important for early morning and late afternoon glassing. Like all other deer species, blacktails move little in broad daylight, and are often bedded when the sun climbs high. During much of the season, however, particularly in Oregon and Washington, rain is common and days are cloudy. Deer may wander about feeding, paying little attention to precipitation. Rain is a way of life for blacktails; they don't mind getting wet.

In California, blacktail hunters have the option of hunting in the summer when daytime temperatures reach extreme highs. It's not uncommon for the air temperature to reach the high 90's or even 100's during the early hunt. Bowhunters can hunt Zone A in California during mid-July, and riflemen are allowed afield in early August.

Deer are active mostly in the cooler hours of evening when daytime temperatures are high and the sun shines brightly. Successful hunters must be in good deer country, glassing thoroughly, or waiting quietly on stand during the first and last minutes of shooting light.

Hunting clothes during early season should be loose-fitting and light-weight. A pair of low-cut hiking boots are fine, but tennis shoes should be avoided. Brush and rocks are hard on unprotected feet.

Obviously, a deer killed in summer's heat must be field-dressed immediately and placed in the shade to cool. As soon as possible, the carcass should be quartered and iced down. Beware of flies, since it takes only minutes for them to discover and deposit eggs on a fresh carcass.

Andy Lightbody is all smiles with his northern California blacktail. (Photo courtesy of Ray E. Lightbody.)

In the rainy season, blacktail hunters wear wool because of its superiority when wet. An uncomfortable hunter is usually a poor hunter, so take all necessary steps to stay dry and warm.

Rain is rough on rifles as well; not only the rust problem, but it also fouls scopes. If you use a scope, make sure it's waterproof. You should also protect the lenses with caps.

Blacktail country is often big and seemingly endless. Many drainages have no road access, and mountains are steep and as wild as anyplace in America. It's easy to get turned around, especially when the sun is hidden by storm clouds. A compass is a must, and a map is a big advantage. It's easy to walk into an unfamiliar drainage and become completely bewildered without the aid of a compass. Many hunters learned the hard way that the coastal forests are to be trekked carefully, always with an eye on the direction you're heading, and the direction you want to take out.

When I was cruising timber in Oregon's rain forests, it was nothing to walk 7 or 8 miles to locate our sample plot. Often we crossed three or four drainages to get to where we needed to be. We used base maps and compasses extensively, and whenever possible, followed creek courses. Most creek bottoms, however, were so jammed with tangles of fallen logs and thick brush that it was practically impossible to get through.

Hunters would do well to stay high on ridgetops or sidehills. Game trails are often defined well enough that they can be seen easily below and followed. National forests have regularly maintained hiking trails which provide excellent access for hunters.

There is much debate in blacktail country over the best choice of firearms. In the more open areas of the California oak-brush country, deer are often killed at long ranges. Shots of 200 to 300 yards are not uncommon, and hunters like flat-shooting rifles. In the dense forests, however, there is a definite loyalty to "brush guns"—calibers effective only at short range with bullets that drop quickly beyond 100 yards. The old .30/30 is seen frequently, as well as other favorites.

Some hunters prefer using an autoloader in heavy forests because they can take a bead on a deer running through brush and keep firing without losing sight of it. This group of hunters feels that working a bolt or lever between shots is a distraction that can allow the deer to be lost momentarily from sight and made difficult to locate quickly.

Ed Park, my good friend from Bend, Oregon, uses a bolt-action Remington 721 .30/06 for his big game hunting, including blacktails. Ed feels as

I do: It's much more important to be familiar with a gun and know how to handle it in all situations than to use a different rifle and caliber with each change in situation. Ed makes the first shot count, and doesn't worry about follow-ups.

Although blacktails are generally smaller than mule deer of the Rockies, some bucks grow to large sizes, especially in Oregon and Washington. Deer that dress out better than 150 pounds are fairly common. Hunters should use calibers capable of handling animals that weigh 200

Getting to a blacktail can be tough!

pounds on the hoof. The chapter on firearms details popular rifles for Western deer.

Although blacktails are plentiful in the Western forests, they take a back seat to the bigger, more handsome, Rocky Mountain mule deer. Each fall, long lines of vehicles head eastward from Seattle, Portland, and other Northwest cities to hunt the Rocky Mountain bucks that live in the mountains east of the Cascade range. Californians pour out of Los Angeles, San Francisco, and elsewhere to hunt the big muleys of Utah, Colorado, Wyoming, Idaho, Montana, and other Western states.

Because hunters prefer big bucks and open country, blacktails are underhunted in many parts of their range. In remote areas, deer seldom see humans, and grow big with relatively large antlers.

Of all the big game in the West, blacktails are perhaps the most under-utilized in many regions. But plenty of savvied blacktail hunters wouldn't have it any other way. When the majority of outdoorsmen head east, the serious blacktail hunter smiles and heads for the steep, heavily timbered drainages to outwit a buck in its brushy domain. With the energy crunch upon us, more and more West Coast hunters are discovering that the blacktail is a worthy quarry. Not only are they fine eating, but plentiful and challenging as well.

This young blacktail buck was light enough to be carried out.

The Trophy Buck

Much is written about trophy mule deer, but the subject is fraught with riddles. First off, what is a trophy buck? How is it defined? Is it a buck whose antlers score high enough to make the record books, or a buck that has a certain spread or number of points? Or is it simply a buck that satisfies the hunter who shot it, regardless of the deer's physical assets?

Indeed, a trophy, like beauty, is in the eyes of the beholder. My wife's first mule deer, for example, was a modest forked-horn buck, but it represents a great accomplishment. The little buck is a beloved trophy to her, and though my wife may bag bigger bucks, the first one will always be cherished.

To many people, a trophy is not an expression of antler measurements or body size, but represents an emotional moment in the outdoors. A deer that required a grueling stalk for the killing shot might be more esteemed than a larger buck shot from the side of the road. A deer killed by an arrow or musket ball often commands more respect than the one downed with a swift, sleek, bullet.

For the purposes of this chapter, however, we will concentrate our attention on truly big bucks—those with massive antlers that quicken the heartbeat of all hunters, young or old, rookies or veterans. The kind of buck that immobilizes you out of sheer shock, rendering you a slavering idiot if you miss or fail to get a shot. And if you get him? Sit down on a log and get control of yourself. Unless you have emotions of steel, you will be overwhelmed.

The most popular of the mule deer subspecies, the Rocky Mountain mule deer, routinely possesses enormous antlers *if* his environment and hereditary factors are favorable. The antlers usually fork off a main beam, and are high, wide, massive, and yes, handsome as well.

Murry Burnham with an unusually symmetrical six-point buck from Colorado, an exceptional trophy. *(Photo courtesy of Murry Burnham.)*

When a really big buck lopes along through the forest, sagebrush, or whatever, he is a sight to behold. The big body seems to churn along smoothly and fluidly. Powerful muscles carry him across rocky hillsides, through heavy brush, and thick forests. As he runs, he carries his head forward and slightly lowered, swaying his glistening rack back and forth to avoid obstructions in his path.

Some writers say mule deer jump on all fours as though on a pogo stick. True, but does, fawns, and small bucks are usually the only ones that bounce along in this fashion. A trophy buck sails along like a race-horse, especially if he wants to put some space between himself and something he doesn't like.

The first big buck I ever saw was one I'll never forget. I was hunting with my fiancée, Lois Dudley, and several members of her family. Lois's dad, DeMarr, was our guide. I had arrived at camp the evening before opening morning, and had never seen the hunting area in daylight.

We left the huge wall tent well before dawn, with uncles, cousins, and nephews all going to favorite spots. DeMarr scraped a hole in the frosted windshield, started the old '53 Ford, and coaxed the sputtering pickup in-to the night. We drove for miles, and finally he pulled off the rutted road, leaned back on the emergency brake, and ordered us to our stand. With-out a flashlight he made his way across the sage, and told us to sit quietly in the canyon until he came by for us later in the morning. If a buck showed, he said, it would be in the very bottom of the canyon, about a 100-yard shot.

DeMarr left Lois and me, and I began to have misgivings about our hunting area.

"I didn't see any trees while we drove out here," I said to Lois. "Nothing but sagebrush. How can there be deer where there are no trees?"

"Hush," Lois whispered. "It's getting light. We might spook deer if any are nearby. And yes, there are no trees."

I shivered in the darkness, pulled my collar a bit tighter, and watched as the grayness unveiled the landscape before us. No trees. Just sagebrush as far as one could see.

We sat there for an hour and a half seeing no more than a squawking magpie. I fiddled with the old British Enfield .303 cradled in my arms, wondering if I'd get a chance to use it. I had borrowed it from a buddy, be-cause I had traded my Model 94 Winchester .30/30 to a fraternity brother for ready cash. College living was expensive.

Suddenly an animal appeared below us like an apparition. It was an enormous buck, with four or five points on each antler. I lowered the .303, trained it on the buck, and followed him as he walked down the canyon bottom. I was obviously mesmerized by his rugged appearance, and continued to track him with the sights lined up on his chest.

"Shoot!" Lois hissed, "or I will."

The trance broken, I squeezed the trigger and saw the buck lurch at the shot. He bolted and started bounding up the sidehill of the canyon, directly away from us. I chambered another cartridge, lined up on his heaving body, and touched off another round. The bullet struck high, just over his back. My third shot anchored him in mid-stride, and he collapsed in a sagebrush bush.

DeMarr appeared suddenly and beat us to the buck.

"Gracious sakes," he said as he approached the deer, "what a buck!"

"Good one, huh?" I replied happily.

"A *very* good one," DeMarr responded. "Dandy antlers, and look at the size of him. He'll go well over 200 dressed."

We packed the deer out on a horse, but not before having a little rodeo of our own in the canyon bottom. The horse was unhappy with the sight and smell of the buck, but DeMarr and his brother, Lynne, quickly made a believer out of the balky horse. In no time we had the buck back to camp, and the following day weighed it on accurate grain scales on DeMarr's farm. The buck registered 232 pounds. To this day I haven't killed a buck that outweighed my first; some with bigger antlers, but not heavier in body. My dad has that buck mounted in his cottage in New York's Adirondack Mountains. Whenever I go back for a visit, I relive that wonderful morning in Utah more than 20 years ago. I shall never forget the sight of those antlers as the buck walked down the canyon.

It's interesting that many hunters, perhaps the majority, come completely unglued when they're treated to the sight of a grand buck. Seasoned outdoorsmen quickly overcome their excitement and usually react with a well-placed shot, but many bucks go on living because a hunter simply couldn't settle down and make a deliberate aim. If big antlers make you nervous you can do little other than continually remind yourself that you are going to be absolutely cool and calm when a big buck shows. Maybe you will and maybe you won't. Your brain will act accordingly when the time comes.

There are scoring systems that quantify the physical dimensions of antlers, but a curious standard exists that sets nice antlers apart from "trophy antlers." Somehow, a buck with a 30-inch outside spread has become the standard, the trophy to strive for. More than one hunter has looked at bucks on my wall and said, "Are they 30-inchers?" For some obscure reason, 30 inches is a magic number among some hunters. Each year, I receive letters from hunters, especially East Coast sportsmen, wanting to know where they can kill a 30-inch mule deer.

Actually, a 30-inch buck is a *big* buck, and the standard is much too high in most of the West. It is applicable in states where giant mule deer are not uncommon, because 30-inch bucks are taken, though not with consistent frequency. But in many states, a 27- or 28-inch buck is tops, and only a rare specimen breaks 30.

Some outfitters in top hunting areas advertise how many 30-inch bucks their clients have taken over the years. Without question, the 30-inch standard is becoming more popular each hunting season.

I too have fallen victim to the magic 30-inch stigma. During a recent

Utah hunter, James Dan Perkins, shows a lovely symmetrical buck that ranks high in the Boone and Crockett record book.

autumn, for example, I hunted mule deer in four top Rocky Mountain states – Montana, Colorado, Wyoming, and Utah. I hunted areas in each state that historically produce big bucks with the intention of killing a 30-incher. As it turned out, I took nice bucks in Colorado, Utah, and Montana, but didn't hit the 30-inch mark with any. They ranged from 26 to 28. Respectable bucks all, but not in the magic circle.

I came closest to the dream buck in Wyoming. I was hunting the fabulous Grey's River country with outfitter Grant Barrus and saw three bucks that easily topped the 30 mark. Two were monsters that escaped by clambering over rimrock along a high-country glacial cirque where we couldn't follow because of treacherous terrain. A shot wasn't possible because they spooked when we were 600 yards away. During that hunt, I passed up shots at no less than 15 four-point bucks and ended up shooting none. That hunt was perhaps the finest of them all that season though I never fired a shot. My good buddy, Tom Opre, outdoor editor for the Detroit Free Press, killed a magnificent 30-plus-inch buck in the same general area in Grey's River that year. Unfortunately, Tom doesn't let me forget it.

While the 30-inch standard applies unofficially, the Boone and Crockett trophy scoring system is the gospel to North American big game hunters. It is the official list of record-class animals. To make the Boone and Crockett (referred to as B&C) is to make the big time.

The B&C scoring system had its beginnings in 1932 when the first records book was published by the late Prentiss N. Gray. Only 500 copies of the book *Records of North American Big Game* were published, making it a treasured collector's item. Mr. Gray made only a single measurement on trophies, and recognized his system had shortcomings. He wrote in his book, "There is always the question of which measurements or combination of measurements should be regarded as constituting the record. We have not attempted to answer the question in this edition... We recognize fully that no one dimension is the controlling factor, and we hope that eventually some fair method of scoring a head may be devised which is acceptable."

In 1939, the second edition was published, and though it contained interesting information on big game, it still did not incorporate an improved scoring system. Finally, in 1952, the third edition was published, this time with a scoring system that was fair and all-inclusive. It is the same scoring system used today, and is a tribute to the gentlemen who put so much time and effort into designing it. Four more editions have since appeared, making a total of seven.

Through the years, the only changes in the B&C system have been the upgrading of minimum scores, or, in the case of some species, the lowering of minimum scores.

The minimum score is a set standard which must be met or exceeded to qualify a head for the book. For example, the minimum score for mule deer in the typical category is 195. To be eligible for the record book a head must score at least 195.

The B&C book lists two categories for mule deer—typical and nontypical. The typical category recognizes symmetry and antler mass as the important factors. In 1950, the minimum mule deer score was 165. It was upgraded to 170 in 1953, 175 in 1961, 185 in 1963, and finally to 195 in 1968, where it remains today.

Symmetry, or balance, is exceedingly important when measuring a typical mule deer buck for the record book. Abnormal points or differences between the measurements of each antler are penalized and subtracted from the total score. Once I was invited to see a set of typical antlers now listed in the book. I was astounded to see the rack, since it was not as enormous as I had expected. But it was practically perfect, with four tines on each antler almost exactly matched.

Nontypical mule deer started off with a minimum score of 195 in 1950. They were revised to 200 in 1953, 225 in 1963, and 240 in 1968. Currently they remain at 240.

Many hunters aren't aware that nontypical racks are also penalized for differences between antlers. However, abnormal points are measured and *added* to the score, rather than *subtracted* as they are in the typical category. The current 1977 edition lists 293 typical mule deer and 240 nontypicals.

Black-tail deer, officially called *Columbia Blacktail Deer* in the record book, have only the typical category. Racks are measured precisely the same as typical mule deer. Because blacktails are smaller than mule deer, their minimum qualifying score is much lower—130 as opposed to 195 for mule deer. Interestingly enough, the minimum blacktail score was 135 in 1950, dropped to 100 in 1951, raised to 110 in 1963, and up to 130 in 1968. There are 290 heads listed in the 1977 record book edition.

How do you determine if one of your trophies makes the record book? At the end of this chapter are charts with measuring instructions. Follow the directions, using a flexible steel tape if possible, and write your measurements in the chart. If the rack exceeds the minimum qualifying score, allow it to dry under natural atmospheric conditions for at least 60 days before having it measured officially. If you don't know an official measurer, contact your local game department or write to Boone and Crockett for a list of measurers.

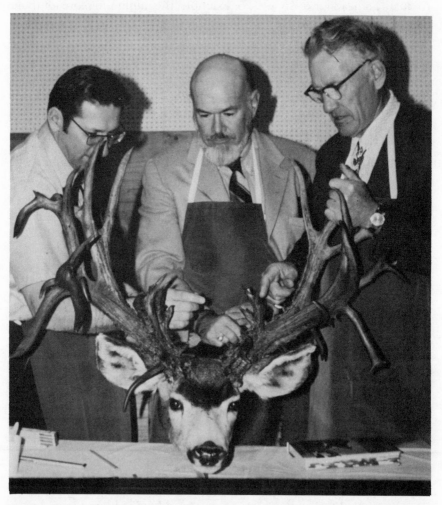

Boone and Crockett Club judges discuss the proper measurement technique for Harold Laird's non-typical mule deer. *(Photo by William H. Nesbitt, courtesy of Boone and Crockett Club.)*

Since official measurers are volunteers, it's up to you to make an appointment at their convenience and to transport the antlers to and from the place you've agreed to have them measured. If your trophy exceeds the minimum qualifying score, the official measurer will inform you as to the next procedure.

Trophies killed with bow and arrow are subject to the same scoring system, but are listed by the Pope and Young Club, which is the official records-keeping organization for bowhunters.

If you have a trophy that qualifies for either record book, or you *think* it might qualify, treat it with tender, loving care. If a point breaks off, for example, it cannot be reaffixed to the rack and can cause a costly penalty during measuring. If either antler is loose for any reason, the rack is immediately disqualified.

Store antlers in a cool place with plenty of circulation, but be careful they can't fall to the ground or be carried off by neighborhood dogs.

Both Boone and Crockett and Pope and Young record books make for interesting reading. Serious trophy hunters would do well to obtain a copy. Besides record listings, there are many informative chapters on big game hunting and other matters dealing with record animals.

If you're a bowhunter, your chances of making the record book are greater because the minimum qualifying scores for Pope and Young are much lower than B&C. Typical mule deer minimum score is 145; nontypical is 160. The blacktail minimum is 90.

Of course, it's much more difficult to take a big buck with an arrow, but the fact remains that many more record bucks are available to bowhunters. To illustrate, let's say that on a mountain range are 100 bucks that score more than 145 points in the typical category, but only 10 of those 100 score higher than 195. A bowhunter turned loose on that mountain could make the record book by killing any of those 100 bucks, but a rifle hunter would have to take one of the 10 to make the book. Obviously, the hunter who uses a firearm has fewer record animals to choose from.

It's one thing to measure a trophy rack with a steel tape, but quite another to judge a live buck in the woods, especially since big bucks seldom stay put long enough for the hunter to evaluate antlers carefully. Let's say, however, that you find a big buck within range of your rifle, bow, or muzzleloader. How do you tell if the deer is truly of trophy proportions? Experience is the best teacher. If you've seen lots of big bucks in your day, you'll probably be able to make a snap judgment. But if you're a neophyte and haven't been treated to the sight of a big deer, you'll undoubtedly want to shoot at the first mature buck that waltzes by.

Skilled trophy hunters often judge the width of a buck's antlers by comparing the spread of the rack to the ends of the ears. If the antlers are equal to the out-side ear tips, they say, then the buck has a 20-inch spread. Sounds easy, but not all bucks have a 20-inch ear span. Many do, but I've measured them at from 18 to 23 inches. Apparently older bucks have larger heads and bigger ears, because most of the 2½- to 3½-year-old bucks I've measured have had 18- to 20-inch spreads, while older bucks had slightly wider distances between their ears. All this means little since a trophy hunter isn't normally splitting hairs when he's sizing up a buck, but the ear width indeed offers a basis with which to compare antlers.

If a buck has antlers that extend 4 or 5 inches past his ears, he is about 30 inches. An inherent danger in using the ear comparison is the possibility of seeing the buck's rack at a slight angle and being fooled into thinking he's much bigger than he really is.

I mention this with authority, because I was fooled by a Colorado buck several years ago. The deer was in an open stand of quaking aspen and was feeding lightly as he walked. I held my shot, wanting a better look at his antlers. I intended to take nothing but a 30-inch buck since I already had an elk and an antelope in the freezer. The deer snapped his head up and looked in my direction. A quick glance convinced me that his antlers were at least 6 inches beyond his ears, but I failed to note that his head was canted a bit.

I killed the buck and put the tape to his antlers. He measured 27 inches. Though not the 30-incher I had hoped for, he was a dandy buck and quite welcome. I learned a lesson, and promised myself that if I used the ear factor again, it would be only when a buck was looking *directly* at me.

The length of a mature buck's ear is about 9 to 10 inches. By comparing the length of the ear to a part of the antler, you can come up with a relative measurement, such as the length of a tine.

If you're looking for a record book buck, you must consider symmetry as the all-important element. A huge buck with extremely thick, long tined antlers might not make the book if he has too many abnormal points or unequal antlers.

The trophy hunter who lives in the East or South and has never seen a mule deer has his work cut out to kill a record buck, or even a large animal. The best way to start the educational process is to closely examine mounted deer. A friendly taxidermist is a good start, since many have mule deer on display in their trophy rooms. Sporting goods stores in the West are prime places to look at mule deer heads, as are game department offices, museums, and natural history exhibits.

One of the greatest difficulties facing the trophy hunter is passing up mediocre, average, or even above-average bucks. Watching a nice buck disappear over a hill or become swallowed up in brush when you had him dead to rights isn't easy, but this is precisely what a trophy hunter must do if he seriously wants a record-class animal. Many purists pass up shots rather than kill a lesser buck. On the other hand, some trophy hunters will wait until the final hours of the hunt, then take a "meat" buck for the freezer.

A common joke among hunters is to set high standards for the first couple days of the hunt, then progressively lower them until a "one-horned" spike shows up. The gang I hunt with displays this mentality. For the opening weekend, only four-point bucks are worthy quarry; for the next couple days a medium three-point gets the nod; and on the final day, anything with antlers had better watch its backtrail.

While wide racks are desirable among many hunters, excessive width can actually *decrease* the score. If this seems confusing, check the B&C charts for typical and nontypical categories. Item D states "IF inside Spread of Main Beams exceeds longer antler length, enter difference." Note that all measurements in the "difference" listing of Column 4 are *subtracted* from the total score. Thus, if you're shooting for a B&C trophy rather than something to simply grace your wall, memorize the scoring chart. Look for bucks with symmetry, as well as thick and high antlers. Height signifies length, and the longer the tines, the better.

If you're a dedicated trophy hunter, or even a casual one, prepare yourself for an onslaught of intimidating remarks from non-hunting acquaintances. In some social groups, it's chic to accuse trophy hunters of "killing off the superior animals, thus leaving the inferior individuals to breed." Don't fall for that rationale, because trophy hunting has no such effect on the mule deer population.

The statement might be true if *all* outstanding bucks were systematically executed, one by one. That scenario is clearly impossible, yet some people sincerely believe it occurs.

In order to be a trophy animal, a buck must live at least four years, preferably five or six. Obviously, he becomes wise to the ways of hunters and learns to avoid them. A big buck is foxy, and relatively few are killed from a herd each season. Many are left to breed.

Furthermore, and perhaps more importantly, by the time a buck reaches record-class status, he has already sired countless other bucks, all of which possess his superior genes. Mule deer bucks are polygamous, breeding several females. It doesn't take many generations for a trophy buck to infuse his superior characteristics into the herd.

Another fact never mentioned is the genetic makeup of does. Female deer also contribute to the physical assets of mule deer populations, yet few critics recognize that does are equally important in the production of superior animals.

Besides the genetic factor, trophy deer must have good habitat to have quality antlers. Adequate food containing necessary minerals and elements is essential, as is proper winter range. Finally, plenty of escape cover is required to allow the buck to grow antlers you dream about.

During the rut, bucks aren't as wary and are often easier to stalk.

Now that we've discussed what makes a trophy buck and why we can hunt them in good conscience, the next obvious question is *where* can we find one?

The first place to look is the record book, since it tells where each trophy buck was killed. A quick glance at the listings won't do, however. For a complete picture, let's look at the record animals and determine where most have come from.

In the typical category for mule deer, Colorado wins hands down. No other state comes close. Of 293 record animals in the latest edition, 123 were killed in Colorado. The rest are as follows in order of most records killed[1]:

New Mexico	37
Idaho	33
Utah	27
Wyoming	20
Arizona	15
Montana	9
Oregon	8
Washington	5
Nevada	4
British Columbia	4
Saskatchewan	3
Mexico	2
Unknown	2
Alberta	1

Since a disproportionately large number of bucks were killed during the "banner" years of the 1960's (discussed later in this book), a logical step would be to determine where recent entries have been killed. Since 1970, here is the breakdown according to the current edition[2]:

---

[1] *North American Big Game*, 7th edition. Published by the Boone and Crockett Club and the National Rifle Association.
[2] *Ibid.*

Colorado 22
Idaho........................... 14
New Mexico 5
Utah 5
Arizona......................... 3
Wyoming 3
Montana 2
Washington 2
Oregon 1

Colorado still leads, but Idaho is surprisingly close. Considering all the entries as well as the most recent ones, Colorado, Idaho, New Mexico, and Utah offer the best odds, with Arizona and Wyoming good secondary choices. Statistics can be misleading, however, because some states no longer produce as many record-class bucks as they used to. Many of New Mexico's bucks, for example, were taken from the Jicarilla Indian Reservation when it first opened in the 1960's. Few bucks on the reservation are of trophy stature now. Likewise, a number of Arizona's trophys came from the Kaibab Region, but this area seldom produces the bucks it once did. A complete breakdown in the Appendix details the best places in each state to hunt mule deer.

The top states for blacktail deer according to record listings are California 125, Oregon 85, Washington 68, British Columbia 11, and unknown 1. Since 1970, the breakdown is as follows: California 22, Oregon 18, Washington 11, and British Columbia 1.

The best blacktail hunting areas will likewise be detailed in a separate chapter in the Appendix.

Knowing where big bucks have come from in past years won't guarantee you'll meet one face to face. You must seek them where they live, and that is what separates the hunter from the trophy hunter. A big buck has plenty of age on him, and he gets that age by avoiding hunters over the course of several years. Gene Decker, a wildlife professor at Colorado State University, says that Colorado bucks grow big for a number of reasons, a primary one being the abundance of escape cover.

The successful trophy hunter must penetrate that escape cover and challenge the buck in his hiding places. Here is a basic difference between hunting for trophy whitetails and trophy mule deer. A big crafty whitetail buck can live a long life on a back 40 or in a brushy woodlot. He challenges the mental skills of the hunter. However, many huge whitetails have been killed from tree stands just 100 yards or so from a road. A whitetail can be taken by outsmarting him on his own turf with a minimum of legwork.

A record-class mule deer, on the other hand, almost always requires physical outlays. Because of the open nature of the West, a big buck often pulls back into a remote spot that few hunters invade. Places such as rug-

Doug Burris's world record typical mule deer that was killed in southwest Colorado in 1972. This buck scored 225⁶⁄₈ in the Boone and Crockett Club record book. (Photo courtesy of the Boone and Crockett Club.)

ged rimrock ledges, dense evergreen stands, oak brush thickets, and remote canyons are favorite havens for wise bucks. Getting to those areas takes some doing, and only hunters willing to work hard consistently get anywhere near trophy mule deer. This is not to say that big bucks don't frequent areas close to urban regions as do whitetails. One of the loveliest muley bucks I've ever seen lived in a farming community where he was seen often by passersby. But *most* truly big bucks are in a godforsaken place where they won't be disturbed by humans.

All this means that you must seek remote hiding places when you're trying for a trophy. Use your skills to their full potential. Scout incessantly, always peek over the next ridge, and don't ever stop being curious. Your dream buck might just be in that next patch of mountain mahogany.

Some states offer specially designated "trophy areas." The number of permits for those areas may or may not be limited, depending on the management plan for the unit. Most trophy areas have a "four-point" specification, meaning only bucks with four or more points on one antler are legal quarry. The four-point rule attracts trophy hunters but discourages hunters who are simply out for a buck. Consequently, pressure is usually lower, and more big bucks are available since young bucks are allowed to grow into four-pointers.

A few years back I hunted a four-point trophy area in Wyoming with my son, Danny, who was 10 years old at the time. I had spotted some big bucks while hunting sage grouse in the area a month before deer season, and intended to ambush a deer handily. Soon after opening light, three dandy bucks appeared and began feeding in our direction. Danny and I were lying in a patch of serviceberry, well-concealed from the deer.

Try as I might, I couldn't find a buck with four points. Incredibly, all three were three-pointers, and big ones at that. One particular buck was most interesting, with high, thick, antlers and at least a 28-inch spread.

The deer fed within 80 yards of us for 20 minutes and bedded down nearby. I was amazed that not one of them had an extra point. Wyoming law said only one antler needed four points, so it appeared the bucks would live to an older age.

We left the deer, but not before spooking them from their beds and taking one last look. No use. All were illegal.

Later, while we ate lunch, a game warden drove by and inquired about our luck.

"No good," I exclaimed. "We got into three big three-pointers, but nothing legal."

The warden looked up quizzically. "You mean none of those bucks had brow tines?"

"Yes they did," I answered. "In fact, all of them had brow tines."

"Better read up on the Wyoming laws," the warden said. "We count *any* point legal if it's longer than one inch, *including* brow tines."

And that was that. A stupid mistake which could have been easily avoided had I read the regulations. I simply assumed that a four-point buck was a typical deer with double forks, never once considering brow tines as legal points. In Utah, where I live, brow tines were not legal points in trophy four-point areas, so I assumed Wyoming laws were similar.

As an old college professor used to say, "A word to the wise is sufficient." If you're going to hunt for a trophy, be familiar with the regulations of the area you're hunting.

During the remainder of that Wyoming trophy season, I passed up 17 legal four-points and never fired a shot. I never saw a buck as big as the so-called three-point I thought was illegal.

We've already determined that finding a record-class buck in his bailiwick takes some doing, but how about the best times to seek him? Three basic choices exist: during a special early hunt, during the regular general season, and during a late season. Each period has its advocates, and I'd like to draw upon some outstanding mule deer hunters to shed light on their reasoning.

Grant Barrus is a skillful outfitter. He hunts the marvelous deer and elk country of Grey's River, Wyoming, and more often than not, his hunters kill big bucks. Grant likes to hunt the early season designed for four-point bucks. In Wyoming, opening day for the special hunt is around the second week of September.

Since trophy bucks are in the high country that time of year, Grant hunts exclusively from horseback. He rides high to windswept passes, to rimrock ledges where big bucks remain in seclusion. One of his pet methods is to post hunters on the tops of ridges; then he rides in a big circle, driving deer to the standers. Because Grant is so familiar with his hunting area, he is uncanny about predicting where big bucks will run when spooked. Countless huge bucks have been taken by clients who were in the right spot at the right time.

There are a number of reasons why trophy hunters would do well to try for a big buck during the early season. First, since few hunters bother to pursue deer in the high country, the quarry is relatively comfortable and not disturbed. Wary bucks won't have retreated to backcountry areas and remote hideouts. They do so, however, when general season opens and hunters scour the hills. Another reason to hunt early is the possibility of running into big bucks almost exclusively. For the most part, the deer you see in the rimrock are the Roman-nosed, mossy-horned busters that you dream about in your wildest fantasies.

Kirt Darner with one of his seven mule deer bucks that has scored in the Boone and Crockett Club record book.

During general-season hunting, Kirt Darner is one of the best. In fact, Kirt has achieved an incredible accomplishment. He has *seven* mule deer bucks in the record book, a feat not duplicated or bettered by any other hunter.

How has one man been able to take so many record-class bucks? For openers, Kirt hunts Colorado and New Mexico, two top states for trophy bucks. Furthermore, he's a forester and spends much time outdoors, looking constantly for signs of big deer.

Of course, not many of us can take the time to seek trophy bucks as Kirt does, but his scouting and hunting techniques are just as important as finding areas that support big deer. Kirt spends the entire season hunting, and passes up lesser deer while holding out for a trophy. He uses a horse to get into the backcountry, and when he knows a huge buck is in the vicinity, he stays in that general area as long as necessary.

When he finds big buck sign or catches a glimpse of one, he hunts slowly—sometimes walking less than one-quarter mile each day. He still-hunts and sneaks quietly in the area he likes best, the 8,500-foot elevation zone that often marks the transition area from oak brush to quaking aspen.

If scouting for a trophy buck, he walks 8 to 10 miles each day, looking for huge tracks and rubbed trees that signify buck activity. One of his favorite tricks is to query sheepherders as to the whereabouts of big bucks. If anyone knows what's happening in a chunk of wild land, sheepherders do. These nomads are valuable sources of information, and few hunters take advantage of that fact.

Kirt has proven time and time again that record-class bucks can be taken during regular season hunts when the woods are full of sportsmen, and most of his trophies have been killed on public land. He follows the rules of all serious trophy hunters: spend as much time as possible in the woods each season; hunt big buck country and stay with an area if a trophy is suspected to be about; pass up bucks—even big ones—to have an opportunity at a trophy; and hunt skillfully, using every trick you know.

Late-season hunting is often considered to be the best time for record-class bucks because they're not as wary as usual. This is the time for breeding, when deer go into the so-called rut. The necks of bucks swell considerably, and much of their attention is focused on does. Love-starved muleys are vulnerable, and knowledgeable trophy hunters are keenly aware of this opportunity.

James Dan Perkins of southern Utah has three Boone and Crockett bucks to his credit because he capitalized on late-season behavior. Dan hunts intensively when bucks are courting does, even though the late season often means bitter cold and deep snow. Dan's three trophy bucks were killed in the 1960's when Utah offered late season hunts, but the state has since discontinued the post-seasons. Nonetheless, other states offer late hunts, and big bucks are often the reward for hunters who take the trouble to pursue deer during the rutting period. In most mule deer country, late November and early December is breeding season.

Whenever you decide to hunt trophy mule deer, remember that you're after one of the smartest big game animals in North America. Not long ago muleys were called "stupid" and "dumb," but those days are gone forever. The big bucks that roam the West, the ones that carry magnificent antlers, are just as savvy as their whitetail counterparts. If you don't believe it, come see for yourself. There's lots of room under the big Western sky.

It's breeding season. The buck tests the doe to determine if she's ready to mate.

OFFICIAL SCORING SYSTEM FOR NORTH AMERICAN BIG GAME TROPHIES

Records of North American
Big Game

BOONE AND CROCKETT CLUB

205 South Patrick Street
Alexandria, Virginia 22314

Minimum Score:
  mule   195
  blacktail 130

TYPICAL
MULE AND BLACKTAIL DEER

Kind of Deer _____

DETAIL OF POINT
MEASUREMENT

Abnormal Points	
Right	Left
Total to E	

SEE OTHER SIDE FOR INSTRUCTIONS			Column 1	Column 2	Column 3	Column 4
			Spread Credit	Right Antler	Left Antler	Difference
A. Number of points on Each Antler	R.	L.				
B. Tip to Tip Spread						
C. Greatest Spread						
D. Inside Spread of Main Beams	Credit may equal but not exceed length of longer antler					
IF Spread exceeds longer antler, enter difference						
E. Total of Lengths of Abnormal Points						
F. Length of Main Beam						
G-1. Length of First Point, if present						
G-2. Length of Second Point						
G-3. Length of Third Point, if present						
G-4. Length of Fourth Point, if present						
H-1. Circumference at Smallest Place Between Burr and First Point						
H-2. Circumference at Smallest Place Between First and Second Points						
H-3. Circumference at Smallest Place Between Main Beam and Third Point						
H-4. Circumference at Smallest Place Between Second and Fourth Points						
TOTALS						

ADD	Column 1		Exact locality where killed
	Column 2		Date killed By whom killed
	Column 3		Present owner
TOTAL			Address
SUBTRACT Column 4			Guide's Name and Address
FINAL SCORE			Remarks: (Mention any abnormalities or unique qualities)

I certify that I have measured the above trophy on _____ 19____
at (address) _____ City _____ State _____
and that these measurements and data are, to the best of my knowledge and belief, made in accordance
with the instructions given.

Witness: _____ Signature: _____

OFFICIAL MEASURER [ ][ ][ ][ ]

INSTRUCTIONS FOR MEASURING MULE AND BLACKTAIL DEER

All measurements must be made with a ¼-inch flexible steel tape to the nearest one-eighth of an inch.
Wherever it is necessary to change direction of measurement, mark a control point and swing tape at
this point. Enter fractional figures in eighths, without reduction. Official measurements cannot
be taken for at least sixty days after the animal was killed.

A. Number of Points on Each Antler. To be counted a point, a projection must be at least one inch
long and its length must exceed the width of its base. All points are measured from tip of point to
nearest edge of beam as illustrated. Beam tip is counted as a point but not measured as a point.

B. Tip to Tip Spread is measured between tips of main beams.

C. Greatest Spread is measured between perpendiculars at a right angle to the center line of the
skull at widest part whether across main beams or points.

D. Inside Spread of Main Beams is measured at a right angle to the center line of the skull at widest point between main beams. Enter this measurement in Spread Credit column if it is less
than or equal to the length of longer antler; if longer, enter longer antler length for Spread Credit.

E. Total Lengths of all Abnormal Points. Abnormal points are those nontypical in location such as
points originating from a point (exception: G-3 originates from G-2 in perfectly normal fashion) or
from sides or bottom of main beam or any points beyond the normal pattern of five (including beam
tip) per antler. Measure each abnormal point in usual manner and enter in appropriate blanks.

F. Length of Main Beam is measured from lowest outside edge of burr over outer curve to the tip of
the main beam. The point of beginning is that point on the burr where the center line along the
outer curve of the beam intersects the burr, then following generally the line of the illustration.

G-1-2-3-4. Length of Normal Points. Normal points are the brow and the upper and lower forks as
shown in the illustration. They are measured from nearest edge of beam over outer curve to tip.
Lay the tape along the outer curve of the beam so that the top edge of the tape coincides with the
top edge of the beam on both sides of the point to determine baseline for point measurement. Record
point lengths in appropriate blanks.

H-1-2-3-4. Circumferences are taken as detailed for each measurement. If brow point is missing,
take H-1 and H-2 at smallest place between burr and G-2. If G-3 is missing, take H-3 halfway between
the base and tip of second point. If G-4 is missing, take H-4 halfway between the second point and
tip of main beam.   * * * * * * * * * * *

FAIR CHASE STATEMENT FOR ALL HUNTER-TAKEN TROPHIES

To make use of the following methods shall be deemed as UNFAIR CHASE and unsportsmanlike, and any
trophy obtained by use of such means is disqualified from entry for Awards.
   I.   Spotting or herding game from the air, followed by landing in its vicinity
        for pursuit;
   II. Herding or pursuing game with motor-powered vehicles;
   III. Use of electronic communications for attracting, locating or observing
        game, or guiding the hunter to such game;
   IV. Hunting game confined by artificial barriers, including escape-proof fencing;
        or hunting game transplanted solely for the purpose of commercial shooting.
        ****

I certify that the trophy scored on this chart was not taken in UNFAIR CHASE as defined above by the
Boone and Crockett Club. I further certify that it was taken in full compliance with local game laws
of the state, province, or territory.

Date_____ Signature of Hunter_____
(Have signature notarized by a Notary Public)

OFFICIAL SCORING SYSTEM FOR NORTH AMERICAN BIG GAME TROPHIES

Records of North American
Big Game

BOONE AND CROCKETT CLUB

205 South Patrick Street
Alexandria, Virginia 22314

Minimum Score: 240

NON-TYPICAL
MULE DEER

Abnormal Points	
Right	Left

DETAIL OF POINT MEASUREMENT

Total to E

SEE OTHER SIDE FOR INSTRUCTIONS			Column 1	Column 2	Column 3	Column 4
A. Number of Points on Each Antler	R.	L.	Spread Credit	Right Antler	Left Antler	Difference
B. Tip to Tip Spread						
C. Greatest Spread						
D. Inside Spread of Main Beams	Credit may equal but not exceed length of longer antler					
IF Spread exceeds longer antler, enter difference						
E. Total of Lengths of Abnormal Points						
F. Length of Main Beams						
G-1. Length of First Point, if present						
G-2. Length of Second Point						
G-3. Length of Third Point, if present						
G-4. Length of Fourth Point, if present						
H-1. Circumference at Smallest Place Between Burr and First Point						
H-2. Circumference at Smallest Place Between First and Second Points						
H-3. Circumference at Smallest Place Between Main Beam and Third Point						
H-4. Circumference at Smallest Place Between Second and Fourth Points						
TOTALS						

ADD	Column 1		Exact locality where killed
	Column 2		Date killed By whom killed
	Column 3		Present Owner
	TOTAL		Address
SUBTRACT	Column 4		
	Result		Guide's Name and Address
Add Line E Total			Remarks: (Mention any abnormalities or unique qualities)
FINAL SCORE			

I certify that I have measured the above trophy on _____ 19___
at (address) _____ City _____ State _____
and that these measurements and data are, to the best of my knowledge and belief, made in accordance
with the instructions given.

Witness: _____ Signature: _____

OFFICIAL MEASURER ☐ ☐ ☐ ☐

INSTRUCTIONS FOR MEASURING NON-TYPICAL MULE DEER

All measurements must be made with a ¼-inch flexible steel tape to the nearest one-eighth of an inch.
Wherever it is necessary to change direction of measurement, mark a control point and swing tape at
this point. Enter fractional figures in eighths, without reduction. Official measurements cannot
be taken for at least sixty days after the animal was killed.

A. Number of Points on Each Antler. To be counted a point, a projection must be at least one inch
long and its length must exceed the width of its base. All points are measured from tip of point to
nearest edge of beam as illustrated. Beam tip is counted as a point but not measured as a point.

B. Tip to Tip Spread is measured between tips of main beams.

C. Greatest Spread is measured between perpendiculars at a right angle to the center line of the
skull at widest part whether across main beams or points.

D. Inside Spread of Main Beams is measured at a right angle to the center line of the skull at widest point between main beams. Enter this measurement again in Spread Credit column if it is less
than or equal to the length of longer antler; if longer, enter longer antler length for Spread Credit.

E. Total of Lengths of all Abnormal Points. Abnormal points are those nontypical in location or
points beyond the normal pattern of five (including beam tip) per antler. Mark the points that are
normal, as defined below. All other points are considered abnormal and are entered in appropriate
blanks, after measurement in usual manner.

F. Length of Main Beam is measured from lowest outside edge of burr over outer curve to the tip of
the main beam. The point of beginning is that point on the burr where the center line along the outer
curve of the beam intersects the burr, then following generally the line of the illustration.

G-1-2-3-4. Length of Normal Points. Normal points are the brow and the upper and lower forks, as
shown in the illustration. They are measured from nearest edge of beam over outer curve to tip. Lay
the tape along the outer curve of the beam so that the top edge of the tape coincides with the top
edge of the beam on both sides of the point to determine baseline for point measurement. Record
point lengths in appropriate blanks.

H-1-2-3-4. Circumferences are taken as detailed for each measurement. If brow point is missing,
take H-1 and H-2 at smallest place between burr and G-2. If G-3 is missing, take H-3 halfway between
the base and tip of second point. If G-4 is missing, take H-4 halfway between the second point and
tip of main beam.   * * * * * * * * * * *

FAIR CHASE STATEMENT FOR ALL HUNTER-TAKEN TROPHIES

To make use of the following methods shall be deemed as UNFAIR CHASE and unsportsmanlike and any
trophy obtained by use of such means is disqualified from entry for Awards.
     I.   Spotting or herding game from the air, followed by landing in its vicinity
         for pursuit;
    II.   Herding or pursuing game with motor-powered vehicles;
   III.   Use of electronic communications for attracting, locating or observing
         game, or guiding the hunter to such game;
    IV.   Hunting game confined by artificial barriers, including escape-proof fencing;
         or hunting game transplanted solely for the purpose of commercial shooting.
    ****

I certify that the trophy scored on this chart was not taken in UNFAIR CHASE as defined above by the
Boone and Crockett Club. I further certify that it was taken in full compliance with local game laws
of the state, province, or territory.

Date _____ Signature of Hunter _____
(Have signature notarized by a Notary Public)

Basic Hunting Techniques

The rules that apply to whitetail hunting in America are equally effective in mule deer country; in fact, more so. There are many more ways to hunt mule deer than whitetails because the West is a mosaic of varying environments. Take your pick from lowland deserts to timberline, from cornfields to brushy thickets. The hunter who says mule deer are exclusively deer of the open country has never known the ins and outs of the West. Maybe he once killed a buck in a sagebrush flat and figured that was all there was to it. Indeed, there is a lot more to it.

This book has nine special chapters that tell how to hunt each of the different environments of mule deer and blacktails. But first let's look at basic hunting methods that work well everywhere, regardless of terrain or vegetation. This chapter links techniques and mule deer behavior patterns; what to expect from muleys—why, when, and where.

Six basic techniques can be used to hunt deer: stand shooting, still hunting, driving, tracking, stalking, and jumpshooting. All are very well suited to mule deer hunting.

Stand Hunting. This method is defined as taking a stationary position and waiting for a deer to show. In whitetail country, stand hunters often wait for a deer to approach on a trail, but in the West the stand hunter often surveys a vast chunk of real estate that offers many more opportunities to see deer.

While some hunters are scornful of the stand method, it is a deadly way to hunt mule deer if properly executed. The secret is knowing *where* to select your vantage point. And once there, *staying* at that spot without yielding to the temptation to move on, thinking you're missing out on something over the ridge.

Because the West offers such a diversity of cover, an eager hunter is often tempted to see as much country as possible. Some feel that they are obligated to walk so many miles each day, and to do anything less isn't hunting. If deer aren't on one ridge, the eager hunter tries another and another. Or if they aren't in the quaking aspens, maybe the bucks are in the oak brush. In their view, the stand hunter is a lazy sort who doesn't put out enough effort to deserve a good buck.

Certainly a hunter walking in reasonably good country may see a lot of deer, but unless he's hunting slowly and using all his skills, he might not get a decent shot. The stand hunter, on the other hand, holds the trump card when it comes to having odds in his favor. If he picks a good place to watch from and is well concealed, he can make the first move when the quarry is sighted.

Although tree stands are common elsewhere in the country, they're seldom used in the West. Because the terrain is mountainous, a good vantage point is as close as the nearest ridge or hillside. Western bowmen use tree stands much more than rifle hunters because of their need to get closer to deer. Some types of vegetation, notably high brush, offer enough screening cover for deer that an elevated vantage point is often a must for a clear shot.

Lois Zumbo waits quietly on a stand overlooking a brushy basin where deer feed. Note how she breaks up her outline by standing near a tree.

In the event you find a worthy tree that offers the potential of spotting deer in "jungles," and you decide to go through the trouble of building a stand, be sure to construct it well before the season opens so the deer become well conditioned to the presence of your brainchild. When choosing a stand location, consider wind direction. In mountain country, breezes blow downhill at night and uphill in the daytime because of air temperature differences. This does not refer to prevailing winds, but light surface air movement. If you figure on occupying the stand in early morning, you can expect downhill breezes until the sun warms the air, then the wind direction will shift back uphill. If you're worried about breezes, sprinkle a bit of deer scent on the floor of the stand and on the branches around you.

A stand does absolutely no good if you're seen, which brings up the next problem—concealment. Just being in a tree is not an advantage unless you blend in naturally with the landscape. This is doubly hard if hunting regulations require hunter-orange garments. Nonetheless, remember this all-important aspect of stand-hunting, or you might as well be back at camp in a warm sleeping bag.

Don't assume mule deer can't see you if you're elevated. You might have read that deer don't look up, a notion applied to whitetail hunting, but I'm convinced there isn't an ounce of truth in that statement. Mule deer live in steep mountain country much of the time and look up as much as they look down. Remember that.

The typical stand used by Westerners is not a fabricated blind or elevated platform, but a natural overlook that affords a wide view below or across a drainage or basin. There are jillions of places in the West where you can do this. You can park your vehicle (or "outfit," as Westerners call it) and walk a few hundred yards, or you can walk a mile or more, whatever your pleasure. Choosing the right place to sit and watch, however, is not a simple decision if you want to improve your odds of seeing deer at reasonable ranges within the limits of your firearm or bow.

Let's say you'd like to take a stand from a ledge with a good view. You don't have a particular place in mind, but will settle on any vantage point that "looks good." You walk to a drainage where you expect to sit until the sun is high. It's dark when you start out, so you dally along until you can see well enough to find a ledge.

Two things are wrong with this strategy. First, you shouldn't be moving during those precious early few minutes. That's the prime time to spot muleys. You need to be sitting quietly then, waiting patiently for enough light. And when the first fuzzy gray aura of dawn ascends, look intently for movement, even though it's too dark to see antlers, or even identify deer. This is the time of day that muleys are on the move—big bucks, little bucks, does and fawns. Even the next world record buck—wherever he is—moves about during those minutes.

As the light gradually increases, watch those moving forms until you can make them out clearly. If a big buck or whatever you're after is in range of your rifle, don't chalk it all up to luck. Some of it was, but skill played an important part, too. But if you're not quiet during those golden minutes, you risk spoiling a grand opportunity, for though it looks gray and shadowy out there to you, mule deer can see you. What you don't want to hear is the *thump thump* of spooked deer, and that's precisely what you'll hear if you're spotted first.

Earlier I described my very first mule deer hunt. I killed a nice buck while on stand in a canyon. When my wife and I walked in to that stand with her dad, we spooked a deer close by, but it was pitch dark and we couldn't see it. I'm convinced the buck I killed was the same deer we scared off, but because it was night, the animal didn't spook badly. Had we been a half hour later walking to the stand and the deer seen us, it probably would have high-tailed it for rougher country.

I glass for deer early in the morning. If a buck is spotted, a careful stalk is required to close the distance.

The second thing wrong with randomly selecting a stand is not paying attention to where the sun rises. This has much bearing on your choice of vantage points. In the mountains, slopes facing east light up first. That being the case, you want to watch *shaded* slopes and mountainsides as long as possible. This may be contrary to a lot of things you've read about mule deer. I don't know how many times I've heard someone say, "Look at the sunny hillsides first because deer go there to get warm." Nonsense. Just because you're cold doesn't mean deer are. Remember, deer have warm, furry coats. They don't need to seek sunshine. Furthermore, by looking into shaded areas you're more likely to find feeding deer. They are much harder to see in the shade, so you need to pay special attention. If anything, deer stay and feed in the *shade* as long as possible, longer than on sunny slopes, despite the air temperature.

Once you're on stand, use your binoculars constantly. We'll talk more about this in the chapter on optics, but *always* carry binoculars. *Never* use your rifle scope to spot deer. It's unwieldy, ineffective, and is dangerous should you want to identify a far-off hunter.

When I'm scanning for game, I first let my eyes wander, looking briefly for obvious signs of deer such as white rumps and gray forms close to the ground. If I don't see anything, then I use my binoculars to search for details. If I see some deer far off and feel like I'm seeing only part of a herd, I might change positions to get a better look. If I see a buck a long way away that I want to know better, I begin plans for a stalk. Many times I've spotted a buck a half mile away or more. My decision to stalk or not depends on how big the buck is and what he's doing. If he's a good one and I like him but he's walking steadily along a ridge or down a draw, I'll let him go and figure a place to ambush him the next morning—unless I'm reasonably sure I can cut him off by being in position when he shows up. If he's feeding in a small area and isn't moving much, I'll leave my stand and try to get up on him.

If you're blessed with snow, visibility is increased manyfold. Deer show up easily against the white background, but don't be too confident in your ability to see all the deer around you just because the ground is white. Many deer will be out of sight in little pockets of brush or timber stands. Snow is a great ally, but don't outsmart yourself by moving around in it carelessly. Deer can see you a lot better in the snow, too. Stay in that stand if your scouting efforts have shown that many deer are using the area you're watching.

Stand hunting in the morning enables you to see deer moving from feeding areas to bedding grounds. Interestingly enough, some hunters think bedding places are mysterious haunts located in deep, dark canyons, and high, lonely ridges. Not so. A big buck is liable to bed right before your eyes. I've seen it a number of times. For that reason, watch a deer carefully if the sun is rising high, because your quarry could quickly bed down and disappear from sight, leaving you wondering where in the world it went. Before a mule deer beds down it doesn't go through a long routine. It simply walks up to a piece of ground it likes, paws the earth with a front foot, and lies down. If you've missed it, you might leave the area, thinking the deer gave you the slip when actually it's right under your nose.

Once I was hunting elk in Colorado and watched a huge buck feeding in a mix of sagebrush and mahogany. I was amazed when the old boy plopped down in the brush. I expected him to bed somewhere off in a thicket, but he apparently decided the sage was a fine place to snooze for the rest of the day.

If you're hunting from a stand in late afternoon, any deer you see is moving from bedding back to feeding areas. This is the time to concentrate your efforts in feeding areas. If fresh sign is present, deer will show up sooner or later.

In the mid-1960's, when the West was enjoying the banner era of high mule deer populations, many states offered multi-permits and late season hunts. I was in Utah's famed Dolores Triangle in late November, looking for a buck for the freezer. I was a young forester with a wife and two infants, and deer meat was a staple food in our household. The eating quality of mature bucks in the rut was questionable, so I was searching for a tasty little guy. I had only one day to hunt, and try as I might, I couldn't find a buck I wanted. Night was coming, so I took a stand on a ledge overlooking a big snow-covered sagebrush flat tracked heavily by deer. Shooting light was almost gone when five deer stepped onto the far side of the sage flat. My binoculars showed a fat forked-horn, precisely what I was looking for. I found a steady rest and my bullet claimed the buck. I simply capitalized on the knowledge that deer were going to walk onto that flat, and I had enough confidence to wait until the last possible moment.

How long should you remain in your stand? If you're on watch in the morning, wait until deer have quit moving. Mule deer bed at odd hours in the morning, depending on a variety of conditions, such as hunter pressure, availability of food, and weather. Many hunters say a full moon is bad for hunting because deer will feed all night and bed early. Though I'd like to speak with authority on the subject, I'm afraid I can't because every time I think the moon has an effect, the deer do something contrary. In my experience as a wildlife biologist, I've seen deer feeding on the blackest, foggiest nights. I've also seen deer bedded under a bright, full moon, so I won't draw any conclusions. I hunt the same way regardless of the moon, and don't let its phases interfere with my plans.

If plenty of hunters are about, deer most definitely seek shelter early and bed down in a hiding place. If food is sparse, or deep snow covers much of the forage, deer may feed an hour or two longer to fill their bellies. If the weather is miserable, deer may seek shelter early if a stiff wind is blowing, or may even feed longer if the day is gloomy and overcast. I believe deer dislike a strong wind, and get away from it whenever they can by dropping into the leeward side of a ridge or heading into a protected canyon. I also feel that big bucks aren't fond of full sunlight. They bed early on balmy, bright days and late when it's cloudy and dark. Perhaps their instincts tell them to head for shelter when the sun shines brightly.

Generally speaking, most deer are bedded by 9 a.m., but there are plenty of exceptions. I've seen a number of big bucks feeding and walking after that time, but again, most have bedded. If I had to pick the prime time that mule deer bed down on a bright day, I'd say between 7:30 and 8:30 a.m.

In the afternoon, deer move according to local conditions, just as they do in the morning. Hunter activity and weather are important factors. If hunters are plentiful, deer hang back in timber and brush, or simply stay in their beds longer. Once darkness falls, deer show up as if by magic. If deer are undisturbed, they begin moving about 3 p.m. Do not look for a big old buck during that early hour however. He'll stay bedded much longer than does, fawns, and younger bucks.

Hunters often make a mistake by leaving their stands too early, either because they don't want to walk out of the woods in the dark or they simply figure no deer are nearby. That is a profound error in judgment. Unless you can't stand walking in the outdoors at night, carry a flashlight and plan on remaining at the stand until the very last minute. The buck of your dreams could be lingering in cover until shooting hours are practically over. When he steps out, you want to have your scope's crosshairs on his mighty chest rather than be walking back to camp.

When selecting your stand, get as comfortable as possible. Watch for cactus before you sit, and wiggle into a position that won't leave you sore and put your feet and legs to sleep. Make sure you can maneuver your rifle or bow into position with a minimum of movement. Do it all right and old mossy-horns might be yours.

Still Hunting. This technique is confusing, because it infers that the hunter is still, or immovable. Not so. The still-hunter is a sneaker, a slow-moving, ever-watching, intensely concentrating hunter who slips furtively through deer cover, looking for the slightest trace of anything that spells deer. Because deer have all the advantages on their own turf, the still-hunter must be skillful enough to overcome those odds. Of all the methods to hunt mule deer, I rate still-hunting as the toughest in terms of pitting the human brain against that of the creature being hunted.

This technique can be used all day long, but the hunter must vary his approach with the time of day. In early morning, deer finish feeding and work slowly to bedding areas. During the heat of the day, deer bed and remain in them much of the daytime. Late afternoon is the time of renewed feeding and movement from bedding to forage areas.

By still-hunting slowly in the oak brush, Murry Burnham killed this buck in the early morning while it was feeding. *(Photo courtesy of Murry Burnham.)*

If a hunter is familiar with an area, he has some idea where these spots are and can hunt them accordingly. If he doesn't know the country, he can quickly size up an area by using good judgment. In either case, the still-hunter looks for recent deer sign such as tracks and droppings. Rubs won't be any help because all they indicate is that bucks were in the area at one time, and not necessarily in the last day or so. But rubs have a value in that they excite you to renew your concentration, which is exactly what this method requires.

Concentration. The nature of the human being is such that the brain refuses to remain focused on a subject unless it's forced to. How many times have you fallen asleep in a lecture? How many times have you been conversing with someone or a group of people and never heard a word? How often do you remain absolutely alert when driving down a highway? If you're typical, you often drive in "auto-pilot." You're maneuvering the car, but you can't remember a thing about the last 10 or 20 miles. Your mind was busily engaged in thoughts that took all your attention.

To be distracted and inattentive in the woods is just as easy, if not more so. As you walk, different objects come into view. You see a gnarled juniper here, a cone-laden pinyon there, a rock with attractive lichens catches your eye, a cottontail dashes out of its hiding place and runs for cover — all these things and others momentarily distract you. Your mind begins to wander as you think about lichens or cottontails and you've lost it. No way will you see the veiled clues that scream *deer*. Your reward for not paying attention will be a glimpse of swift movement through cover, or hearing the telltale thumping of a running deer. Of course, seeing a concealed deer is often impossible, but that's no excuse for not paying attention.

The still-hunter has three basic shots at deer: one that is bedded, one that is running, or one that is standing or moving slowly. Of the three, the standing or feeding deer is easiest to hit because it's off the ground and more or less outlined. A steady rest and a bullet into a vital will put it down. A bedded deer is almost always in some kind of cover, requiring you to figure where you can thread the bullet without it glancing off a branch or thudding into a tree. A running deer is toughest for obvious reasons. You must find an opening to shoot into at the same time the deer reaches it, and your lead must be accurate.

I had an experience during the 1980 Colorado deer hunt that was most unnerving. I was hunting on a ranch as a guest of the American

Sportsman's Club. On this particular day, Bob Good, ASC's Chairman of the Board, Harry Straight, and I were driving back to camp when Good made a remarkable observation. Using binoculars, he had spotted a dandy buck at least 800 yards away. We had been stopping the vehicle every now and then to look into brushy draws and pockets, but this buck was bedded under a clump of serviceberry bushes. How Bob spotted him I'll never know, but there he was, big as life. Good and Straight had already filled their tags, so I was elected to take the deer. No question arose as to whether I wanted him or not. His antlers were very nice.

I made a big circle around the deer to come up on the back side of the draw he was in. My route covered a half mile, and it took some time to slip quietly through the brush and keep checking the wind. I was afraid of spooking other unseen deer that might alert the buck and send him running before I got there.

This was a simple stalk strategy, but it quickly became complicated. I didn't know it, but the buck moved from his bed, walked 30 yards and re-

An alert buck. Look at his ears. You need to be skillful to get within shooting range of this old boy.

bedded. Bob Good watched the performance from the road, but couldn't relay the information. Meanwhile, I approached the crest of the knoll and slithered along, taking cover behind a bush. I eased up, peeked over, but the buck wasn't in the precise spot I had committed to memory from the road. With binoculars I scrutinized every bush before me. No buck. I circled around 10 yards to get a different vantage point, crawled back up to the crest, glassed again, but still no buck. Again I circled, this time 20 yards, and when I edged over the top I saw my prize. He was standing, looking directly at me, ears alert, and every muscle of his body poised for a break. The deer stood in a pocket of brush; all I could see was his head and part of his neck. I made a quick decision to take him in the chest. I mentally outlined the buck and decided which way he was standing. By tracing what I thought was his body behind the screening brush, I made out a patch of fur precisely where his lungs should be. My bullet was to slip through an opening the size of a grapefruit, and I was thinking dead deer when the .30/06 roared. To my utter astonishment, the buck took a mighty leap forward and crashed through the brush, angling off to my left. Instantly I knew I had missed him cleanly. He hadn't been standing broadside at all, but directly facing me. The patch of fur I imagined was just that—imagination. The bullet went where I sent it, but the deer wasn't there. I chambered a round quickly and fired as the buck stormed past an opening in the brush. The lead was too long; the bullet thumped into the ground in front of him. I bolted another cartridge home, took careful aim and let another bullet go. This time the buck stumbled, but maintained his footing and continued on his way with 15-foot bounds. I had time for one more shot, and fired again before he disappeared over the hill.

I was dumbfounded, but I had no time to cuss or think about anything more than to run to the top of the hill and hope for another shot as he crossed a big sage flat below. I knew the third shot hit him, but I had no idea how badly he was hit. As I ran, I heard loud thrashing in the brush just over the ridge. I recognized the noise, realizing the buck was down, and walked slowly over the crest where I knew he was lying. He had dropped in a clump of brush, completely supported above the ground by a stout bush. Apparently he died in the middle of a leap and crashed down into a bush. My bullet tore out the top of his heart.

Had I not known the deer was in the little draw, I might never have spotted him first. Though I *knew* he was somewhere in the area, it took me three tries to find him.

Unfortunately, the still-hunter never knows exactly when he is approaching a deer, but an astute outdoorsman can often predict the types of cover deer will be in and hunt them carefully. I am intimately familiar with a lovely ridge in Colorado where I can predict, nine out of 10 times, where deer will be bedded. Huge thickets of serviceberry in the midst of low sagebrush and sparse quaking aspens are too good for deer to pass up. Before I enter the thicket, I tell myself, "Zumbo, deer are all around you. Concentrate. Look. Listen. Penetrate." I take a single step, and use my eyes so hard they water. If I see nothing, I take another step, resuming the whole process. Besides using my eyes, I listen. Too many hunters don't use their ears as they should.

Deer are not silent when they feed or sneak. Branches and leaves rattle and rustle as deer move about, nuzzling vegetation in search of twigs, stems, and other parts of plants they like. Deer also make noise as they walk, despite what you might have read about the incredible stealth and silence they employ when moving around. It's true that they walk very quietly, but a trained ear can pick up the foot-falls. No deer can walk very far without brushing against a branch or stepping on a leaf. Their furry coats make little noise against vegetation, but unless they're in sand or short grass, they must sooner or later make noise. Snow, unless it's very fresh and powdery, is not conducive to quiet walking either. Still, those tiny sounds are there. The still-hunter must know what to listen for, and react accordingly when he connects those sounds to deer.

If I'm still-hunting early in the morning or late in the afternoon when the sun is low, I try to hunt so I'm not heading toward the sun. With the sun at my back, I can see ahead clearly. A buck in the brush ahead of me might be betrayed by the sun's rays glinting off an antler tine.

Before worrying about the sun, however, I check the wind, which is the single-most important factor in still-hunting. I suspect many more deer in brushy cover are spooked by scenting hunters rather than seeing them. It's logical that deer are alerted to the presence of humans by either seeing, hearing, or smelling them. If a deer hears a foreign sound, it perks up its ears and focuses its attention in the direction of the sound. There are many natural sounds in the woods, so a deer normally doesn't crash off frantically if it hears a twig snap. But, by hearing the twig, it comes to life and "tunes" in. If a deer sees you, it may stand quietly, provided you aren't traveling directly toward it. By knowing exactly where you are, a deer might not move at all, but let you pass by. But I've never, ever, seen a deer hang around when the wind was at my back, pushing my scent forward. One whiff and every deer within breathing space is off and running. Some still-hunters claim the deer scents manufactured these days mask human odor effectively. Bob Good swears deer actually walked up to him when he was wearing Skunk Skreen scent, but he was after Texas whitetails at the time. I haven't experimented much with scents, but other mule deer hunters tell me they work with varying degrees of success.

When deer are bedded, they don't sleep soundly. They doze lightly, but the slightest noise puts them at instant alert. Proper clothing helps the hunter minimize noise, because the sound of garments brushing against branches is the worst offender. Woolens are the best choice for quiet walking, and cottons are also good. Nylon and artificial materials are horrid. Many mule deer states require hunter-orange garments, and most are made of cheap material that rasp and scrape loudly every time a twig brushes against them. I wear a lightweight zippered cotton sweater in hunter-orange that gets me by in most places, though it isn't as good as wool. If you have them, buckskins are ideal for slipping along quietly in the brush. Denims or blue jeans make a terrible noise, but perhaps 90 percent of the resident hunters wear them (including me). Jeans have been such a way of life in the West for so many years, hunters simply wear them out of habit.

As I just mentioned, deer make little noises as they move about, and *big* noises when they're scrambling away from a hunter. Surpringly few hunters can recognize the sound of a spooked deer, running for all he's worth across the great outdoors. A deer doesn't make a "clippity clop" sound like a shoed horse, but it makes "thumping" noises that are quite frequently muffled. If a deer breaks cover 100 yards away and isn't busting branches as he runs, the noises he makes are distinct but still need to be interpreted. Many times I've walked with one or more hunters and heard the unmistakable thumping of a flushed deer. "Hear that?" I'll whisper. "Hear what?" says the non-listener. A frustrating experience, but it happens all the time.

If you're still-hunting and hear a deer bound off, the last thing you should do is tear off running as fast as you can to get a look, *unless* you know the terrain and are certain the running deer will break cover and run into the open. Otherwise, stop walking and do nothing but stay still for several minutes. Walking to where the deer flushed is useless because it will be watching that spot—and you—if it's still in the vicinity. Instead, *turn around* and make a wide circle, trying to approach the deer from the direction he might be heading.

When you're still-hunting, always remember that you're the stranger in the deer's little world. He knows every trail and thicket, but you don't. Try to remember the slogan that applies to approaching railroad crossings: *Stop, Look, and Listen.* I'll add one more: *Concentrate,* as hard as you can.

Deer Drives. Some hunters, and outdoor writers, think the art of driving deer is exclusively a whitetail technique. Westerners have been driving mule deer as long as Easterners have been driving whitetails. Because of terrain and the variety of vegetation, some basic differences exist.

Driving can be defined as the method whereby one or more hunters walks through cover to flush and force deer to other waiting hunters called standers. The standers take a position with a good view.

Deer drives seldom fail provided deer are in the area. Let me qualify that statement. The drivers usually do what they are trying to—jump deer and make them move. That's not tough to do. What *is* tough is to get the deer to show up where they can be seen and shot at by the standers or

An enormous buck, completely unaware of the photographer. Few hunters see a buck of this size in his bed. Careful stalking or still-hunting is required to pull this off.

The Zumbo clan waits for something to show.

drivers. In that regard, drives are often not successful. Deer may circle the drivers and remain in the brush, they may slip out unseen by the standers, or they might run out too far away for a shot.

When planning a drive, all sorts of variables must be considered before laying out a strategy, including the type of cover, steepness of terrain, probable escape routes for spooked deer, the number of drivers, and the number of standers.

Flushed mule deer almost always run uphill during their initial flight. Once they've gained a ridge-top, they might keep on going for higher ground or wander down into a thicket or timber stand where they can hide. There are exceptions to this uphill movement, however, particularly if an area below them is thicker and more secluded than the upper ridges. But I'd estimate 90 percent of spooked deer run uphill.

Before deciding how to split up the party into standers and drivers, a good rule of thumb is to have more standers than drivers. If drivers are thorough and take adequate time, they put most deer in an area on their feet. The trick is to *see* those deer. In most places, the standers at good vantage points have a better chance of seeing them than the drivers.

Mule deer are seldom guided in a certain direction, no matter how skillful the driver is. They are much too unpredictable, and don't follow patterns as whitetails do. When I lived in upstate New York, I was taught much about whitetail hunting by a woodsman who had an uncanny way of predicting where a spooked buck would run. On our first hunt together we made a simple drive, he the driver and I the stander. He told me to sit on a certain rock that he called "rocking chair rock" because of it's similarity to a rocking chair, and pointed out a trail that he judged the deer would run out on. Sure enough, a half hour later I killed a four-point buck running precisely where my mentor said it would. The following year I sat on the rock and killed an eight-point buck in the same place, and the next fall I took a six-pointer there.

Mule deer aren't that cooperative because they aren't as trail-oriented as whitetails. You need to deploy as many standers as possible to cover all the possible places deer can run through.

Because muleys like to run uphill, that's the obvious place to put most of the standers. And if there's a saddle on the ridge, by all means put a hunter where he can watch it. You should also put standers along either flank of the area being driven, and if there's an extra man, put him *behind* the drivers. If you know a particular area is often more productive than others, put two standers together. If two bucks come out, you have a chance to get both.

Drivers can either make loud noises while they're moving in cover, or remain silent. I've seen both work well, but tend to favor the quiet drive since deer can't pinpoint the location of drivers as well if drivers are making noise. If a silent drive doesn't work and you're sure deer are still in the cover, then a noisy effort might get them moving. You don't need any elaborate contraptions to make noise on a drive. Some hunters bang away on a pot or pan with a stick, rattle stones in a can, bark like a dog, or do all sorts of silly things to scare deer. Forget these, and use what you were born with — your voice. The human voice turns a deer inside out quicker than anything else you can contrive. My favorite trick is to sing as loudly as I can. Any buck (or person) within earshot is foolish to hang around very long, because my singing is definitely not of Neil Diamond quality. If it were, I'd be in Hollywood making money rather than writing books and magazine articles. (As far as choice of songs go, I believe deer are a bit more fond of "I've Been Working On The Railroad" than "Yankee Doodle," so I sing the latter.)

To drive correctly, you must do more than simply walk from point A directly to point B. Wander about in a zig-zag fashion, and walk as close as possible to any blowdowns, thickets, or extra-thick clumps of brush. Do *not* assume that every deer around will automatically flush. Many stay in their beds, eyeing you carefully, or get to their feet and stand motionless. Another trick is to stop often and remain very silent. If a deer loses track of you, he may finally crack and head for safer parts. The whole idea in driving is to get the deer nervous and fearful so it runs.

By making a silent drive, drivers have an excellent chance of getting a shot at deer that try to slip back through the ranks or get to their feet and show themselves quietly. You might also get a jump-shot. Remember, however, that other drivers and standers are around you, so be careful if you shoot.

Some drivers like to signal to standers that deer are on the move by whistling sharply, shouting, or barking. Occasionally I signal a stander by cawing like a crow, but usually I let the stander take matters in his own hands.

When selecting a stand, take pains to find a place where you're concealed. Do not make the mistake of thinking that just because drivers are pushing deer that all their attention is directed to drivers. A spooked deer is totally alert. All his senses are revved up, and he's looking everywhere as he sneaks, trots, or runs from the drivers. What you don't want him to do is spot you and quickly slip back into cover.

Long drives for mule deer are useless, since pushed muleys seldom stay in front of you. A quarter mile is maximum, unless you have a small army and can effectively cover a big area with lots of standers.

I once took part in a drive with 23 hunters. We marched across an entire mountainside and put deer out everywhere. Ten of us drove and 13 watched. When the smoke and dust cleared, eight bucks were killed, three by drivers, five from standers. The deer ranged from spikes to large five-pointers.

Big drives work well in large draws and basins where you can effectively walk the entire area and cover up the best escape routes with standers. Drives don't work very well on tops of mesas where deer can scatter to the four winds, or in heavy cover such as pinyon-juniper or evergreen timber where visibility is limited.

A nice drive is to walk a bunch of drivers through a slope blanketed by evergreens. In many areas, evergreens grow on slopes with a northerly exposure, while the south-facing slopes are more open. The standers take positions on the south slope and watch for deer as they drain out of the timber and up into the open areas. This could backfire easily, because some deer run up through the timber unseen. You can foil them by putting a stander or two atop a ridge near the evergreens.

My favorite drive of all is to watch a big aspen-covered slope when the leaves are off the trees. From a high vantage point, the entire scenario unfolds before you. To see 20 or 30 deer routed by drivers is not uncommon.

Ever try a one-man drive? Sounds ridiculous, but I've done it successfully. To do it, you need a steady breeze blowing, and you need to be in an area with rocky outcroppings or ledges where you can quickly jump up on a high perch and see into the cover you're driving. Start the drive by walking into the brush with the wind at your back. Move quickly, and don't worry about making noise. Once you've traveled through the cover for 200 or 300 yards, back off and *trot* back the way you came, making a wide circle around the brush. If you've done the first part right, your scent has blown into the area and alerted deer, getting them up on their feet. As you circle, get up high and look. Deer will be directing their attention to the place you've vacated, and may be moving enough for you to see them. If no deer show, drop back into the brush and move a little farther. Again fall back, circle, and take another look. Keep this up until you've worked the cover out. By darting in and out with the wind blowing into cover, you thoroughly confuse the deer. Many of them may run out of the area completely during your first efforts, but one or two might hang in, figuring to take their chances. And you only need one to fill your tag.

Grant Barrus, one of my favorite Wyoming outfitters, makes deer drives from horseback, and usually produces granddaddy bucks for his clients. I had an experience with Grant that illustrates how unpredictable mule deer can be. We were riding along a ridgetop just after daybreak, heading for rimrock country where big bucks lived. On the way, we spotted a buck bedded at the edge of a clump of firs. He was well-outlined in snow, but much too far for a shot. The deer apparently hadn't spotted us, so we circled and laid plans for a drive. We decided to place two standers on high ridgetops, while three of us rode toward the buck. One of the standers dismounted, tied his horse to a tree, and walked to the spot Grant had instructed him to. Because we were in a basin, the buck could not sneak away unseen. Someone was going to get a shot. While everyone made their way to vantage points, the three of us doing the driving circled, got off our horses, and had just tied them up when a big buck appeared, running pell-mell across the slope. We heard a rifle shot, and the buck cartwheeled completely and disappeared in some firs. The buck reappeared 50 yards away, looked toward us, and trotted off. Before disappearing, it looked at us once more and ran over the hill. It gave no sign of being hit.

We couldn't believe it. The buck looked like it was smacked hard, but it seemed healthy to us. Suddenly a much bigger buck appeared, and beat a path straight up the ridge. We waited for the unseen hunter to shoot, but no shot came. I had my scope hairs on the big deer, but held my fire, waiting for the other hunter to let loose. I was after a wall-hanger, and this one wasn't exactly what I had in mind. I judged his antlers to be about 26 inches wide. The buck disappeared unscathed.

We walked over to where the hunter had shot at the first buck, all the time Grant saying the deer had to be dead. I agreed, but we couldn't explain the deer's actions after the shot. It all made sense when we spotted the hunter bent over a very dead buck. The buck that we saw trotting off was a twin, which meant three bucks were bedded together. But the biggest surprise was yet to come. As we rode over to get the hunter's horse, we saw where the third buck had practically collided with the horse. The deer had to swerve and jump over a small fir to miss the bronc.

Grant makes many drives in the rimrock, because flushed bucks don't run uphill. They're already as high as they can get. So Grant often strings his standers down low in a draw, and moves the bucks from the rimrock into the canyons. A most effective way to ambush a big buck.

Driving mule deer doesn't require a great deal of skill, but a well-planned strategy often spells the difference between fresh liver and onions, or foodstuffs purchased from the grocery store.

Tracking. This is an exciting way to hunt mule deer, because you can "read" what the deer is doing by his tracks, even though you don't know when he'll show up. To track a deer successfully, you need snow, wet ground, or a soil surface that betrays a deer's presence. Snow is by far the best medium, because you can stay with the deer as long as you can hold out, or until nightfall, whichever comes first. Tracking without snow often becomes a guessing game, unless the prints are so vivid and distinctive you can follow them.

Fresh tracking snow excites me. I know how a hound dog feels when he's ready to go. Give me a daypack with a little grub and the steaming track of a big buck, and stay out of my way.

The best tracking snow is the kind that falls all night, blanketing the ground enough so it won't melt away if the day turns warm. If it stops snowing by the time you're ready to hunt, fine enough, but if snow is still falling, it's still O.K.

I want to be out of camp, heading for prime deer country where I know big bucks hang out well before shooting light. Ideally, I like to spot a big buck in the distance with binoculars, then cut his track and dog him until he's mine. Usually that doesn't happen, so I walk ridges and draws, looking for a big track to follow.

Tracking is a one-on-one proposition — just you and the deer. Whether you catch up and get a killing shot depends on your skills. A small blunder ruins your efforts, so you've got to be on your toes constantly, always watching ahead, anticipating the quarry just around the bend, over the knoll, or in the thicket.

The freshness of the track indicates how far you are behind the deer, as well as what it's been doing since it left the print. If the deer passed by 6 to 8 hours ago in the night and his track is lined out, you'll have a long day, and maybe nothing to show for it. However if the track is an hour or so old and the deer was wandering about feeding, you might be just a few minutes behind it. And, while you're tracking a deer, another one may pop up unexpectedly, or you might find an even better set of prints. Anything can happen, and usually does.

Tracking means more than watching the ground and following prints. You must always look ahead. At times, you might want to leave the track and climb a hill to look far ahead. You might make a big circle, hoping to ambush the deer as it ambles along.

If you've got a fresh track at the first hint of light, you stand a good chance of running into the deer as it feeds. If that's the case, a good plan is to keep the track in sight, if possible, and move a few yards uphill for a better position.

Should you follow the track until the sun is high, figure your deer is bedded and approach all likely thickets and timbered areas with caution. At that point, you become a still-hunter, but you've got a track to follow rather than hunting blind. Look for telltale clues of a bedded buck. In the snow, he'll be well outlined, more so than on dry ground.

While you're following, sooner or later you should run into droppings. If the tracks are fresh and the pellets warm (go ahead, take your glove off and feel them—they don't bite), you are just minutes behind the deer. Pellets don't remain warm in the snow for very long.

Falling snow is a wonderful assist in determining the freshness of a track. Obviously, if the print is clean and snow is falling rapidly, take no more steps. Put the rifle to your shoulder and be ready to snap off the safety. Your deer is just a few yards away.

If you track enough deer, you quickly learn that most are uncooperative. It hears, smells, or sees you, and the prints suddenly evolve into a much different pattern. Instead of predictable, regular tracks, they're groups of four prints with hooves splayed far apart. The jig is up. Your furry friend is off and running. You say something to yourself like, "Now what in hell did I do wrong?" But take comfort in the fact that mule deer grow big antlers because they outsmart lots of hunters like you (and me).

When your quarry is spooked, he'll likely bound full stride for 200 or 300 yards, then settle down into a fast trot, then a fast walk. But by the time he gets to a slow walk where you can catch up again, he might be a mile or two ahead. If you're down low in a draw and the buck circles, hotfoot it for a ridge and try to cut him off at a pass (if there is a pass, that is).

Not all deer run out of the country when spooked. It depends on how badly they're scared. Some settle down again, figuring they've given you the slip, and you might very likely get right up on them again. But don't be terribly confident about sneaking up on them a second time. They'll be edgy, nervous, and *constantly* watching behind. You're going to need a bit of luck this time.

Most big bucks that have been through this before simply make a beeline for the roughest, toughest, most miserable country around. He'll get up high where he can watch his backtrail, and will be off and away as soon as he sees or hears you. You'll likely not see him again that day.

If a lot of deer are about, it might be difficult to single out one and follow it. Following a herd of deer rather than one is a different game. True, you have a chance of seeing a deer because there are more of them, but, more importantly, they see you quicker because more eyes, ears, and noses are at work.

The chapter on scouting describes deer tracks, but you want to be sure you aren't following a big old doe if you have a buck tag in your pocket. Or a medium buck if you want a trophy for the office wall. If you're not sure what you're following, you have to take your chances and hope you can find out.

Tracking deer is satisfying. As you follow, you become intimate with the animal in front. You see where he puts his feet down, where he fed, where he voided himself, and he begins to become a challenge. You can't wait to catch up and see his head. Your imagination runs wild as you envision a grand buck earning you a spot in the record book. And sometimes, just when you figure the deer is around the corner, your heart sinks as you see yet another track—that of *Homo sapiens*. Another hunter has cut the track you're following and is ahead of you. But don't despair. More deer are out there, and all put their feet on the ground. Another track is waiting for you somewhere. Go find it.

Stalking. As I define it, stalking is working your way within shooting range of a particular deer once it's spotted. Because the deer is in sight, you must take advantage of available cover to get close. Since the area must be reasonably open to see a deer in the distance in the first place, you're using all your senses and skills to remain unseen.

The stalker operates up high so he can look down over vast areas. Some vantage points are always good to spot deer from, but long walks might be necessary to find what you're looking for.

Since deer must be up and about to be seen, early morning and late afternoon is the best time to stalk. You're taking chances in the afternoon,

A still-hunter must be sharp to spot this big buck standing in the brush. Look for his eye in the center of the picture.

because by the time you get up on the deer, shooting light might be gone.

Deer will likely be feeding as you stalk. If you know something about a foraging deer, you have a better chance of approaching it. First, a mule deer isn't as nervous as a whitetail. It won't fling its head up every few seconds, but grubs around a bit, casually looking around as it moves. Watch a deer closely to see how often it glances around. When you have an idea of the timing, make your move, and time your advance according to the deer's behavior. If necessary, get flat on the ground and crawl, commando style. Raise up every now and then to check the location of the deer, but do so only when you can peek *around* an object, such as a bush, rock, tree, or whatever. Never rise straight up and stick your head above cover.

Before making any stalk, always check the wind first. A cardinal sin is made if you even *attempt* a stalk with the breeze at your back. You'll get a little exercise, but that's about all.

When I'm stalking, I seldom head directly for the deer, but make my way to an object that I can put between him and me. A rock outcropping, blowdown, or even a bushy tree offers enough shield to get me where I want to go. At times, I make a mental note of a route I want to take. For example, maybe a big ponderosa pine screens me for 20 yards, then beyond that a fallen log for another 15 yards, then a boulder for 30 more, and so on.

During the fall of 1980, I was hunting in Montana with Kevin Rush, my guide. We rode horseback, and fresh tracks in the snow indicated several deer in the area. We topped a little rise and spotted several deer feeding. One was a nice buck. With the horses hidden in trees, I made a stalk while Kevin watched. The deer were about 600 yards away, and I wanted to halve that distance. The first 75 yards were easy, because I could use the trees for cover, but from there on was knee-high sagebrush. When I reached the edge of the trees, I lost sight of the deer. I was in a dip, and a semi-frozen creek had to be crossed. Stooping low, I gingerly tip-toed across the ice without breaking through. I crawled to the top of the knoll and spotted the buck again. Because of the terrain, I couldn't gain another foot. I had to wait for the deer to feed along until he dropped into a small draw. Ten minutes later I saw the top of his antlers disappear, and I made another move, this time gaining 100 yards. But the buck also gained another 100 yards by the time he dropped out of sight. I crossed two more rises and dips in the next 20 minutes, still playing cat and mouse. Finally, as I bellied up to the last knoll, I peeked over the top and looked face to face at a startled doe. She had me pegged, and stood there aghast. I made a final move by crawling another 3 feet, expecting a running shot at the buck. To my surprise, he was feeding, and I wasted no time finding a steady rest and sending a bullet on its way. The buck didn't know what hit him. I was mighty thankful the doe was a half-wit and stared at me as long as she did.

Many times when making a stalk, a deer sees part of you and comes to attention. If the wind is right, and you've been caught in the open, stop instantly and stare back. All you can do is hope the deer decides you're part of the local flora and resumes feeding. If you're caught in brush, slowly lower yourself to the ground and stay there. Often a deer sees the tip of your rifle or bow, or sees a branch or tree move, and is satisfied when all calms down.

If you stalk a herd that has a buck or two that look good, you must be much more cautious because you need to outwit many more eyes. Don't take it lightly if a doe or fawn spots you. You've probably had it. When one of the herd members goes at alert, they all do. And when one takes off, they all do, including the buck. Deer communicate by their reactions. You can put a herd of 40 or 50 deer to flight if just one fawn sees you and bolts away.

Bowmen and black powder hunters often rely on stalking to get close to their quarry. In most cases, "primitive" hunters are not required to wear hunter-orange clothing. This is a great advantage, because they can blend in easier with camo garments.

If you're trying to stalk deer and livestock are about, be extremely careful about spooking the cattle or sheep. Deer are just as apt to run if the stock is scared. More than once I've had a buck put to flight by a herd of frightened cows that I'd blundered into. I was paying so much attention to the buck I didn't give the cows much thought. When they crashed through the aspens in a thundering herd, the buck simply wheeled and ran off the mountain. That's happened three times.

Stalking a feeding deer is one thing, but stalking a bedded deer is a horse of a different color. The foraging animal is distracted. Its head is down much of the time finding food. A bedded deer, on the other hand, is lying silently. It might look like it's dozing, and it is very lightly, but its senses are fine-tuned.

I've killed three bucks that I knew beforehand were in their beds. Each was a major accomplishment. When making the stalks, I never knew my heart could beat so hard and so fast.

I watched one lie down from a distance of about 600 yards and made a one-hour stalk that involved wading a waist-deep river, crawling through a spruce blowdown, and gingerly picking my way over a talus slope. Because of the lay of the land, I traveled almost a mile to take advantage of cover. Sometimes I crawled, sometimes trotted, but always I selected little goals ahead. Once I made it to that objective, I carefully worked out the next. When the moment of truth arrived, I eased into shooting position, flipped off the safety, and put a bullet into the buck's neck at 90 yards.

Sneaky people aren't much appreciated in our society, but you must be a champion sneak to stalk successfully. The more you skulk, slink, sidle and pussyfoot, the better you'll be.

Jumpshooting. This technique sounds like something you might do when hunting mallards, but it applies to mule deer hunting when conditions are right. I define this method as a plan in which you walk along with the express purpose of flushing deer from their beds and shooting on the run. This isn't an exact definition, however, because many jumped deer simply get to their feet and stand motionless for a moment until they identify what disturbed them, or they might flush and run a bit, then walk slowly into cover, or they might dash away like a scalded demon.

My favorite jumpshooting spot is a sagebrush flat with clumps of high serviceberry bushes. The bushes are in small groups, so bedded deer must expose themselves by running into the sage when flushed. The area is on a mesa, and I have plenty of time for a shot before a deer moves out of range.

Obviously, this type of hunting works well in cover that affords some visibility, but open sage flats aren't necessarily the only places that jumpshooting can be done. Aspen stands with sporadic thickets lend themselves to jumpshooting if the aspens are relatively sparse. Jumped deer often run a ways and stop in the trees. A quick shot threaded through the tree trunks can make him yours—if you can thread straight. Ponderosa pine forests are favorite places to jump deer because of the openings between trees.

Deer can be jumped in other ways. Many hunters throw rocks into brushy draws or thickets on steep mountainsides. Some use slingshots to unnerve deer in a distant thicket. "Rocking" a timbered sidehill often produces startling results.

Some years ago, I was hunting along an old burn in Utah. Deer sign was plentiful, so I found a high spot and settled down to watch. Presently two hunters walked by. They were tossing boulders off a ledge, and before they moved out of sight, they'd thrown two dozen rocks over the sidehill. I stayed put, and watched them disappear, but I could hear the rocks clattering long after they were gone. Suddenly I heard a crashing noise just over the lip of the hill and saw two sets of antlers swiveling about just above the brush. I snapped my rifle to my shoulder, and was ready when the deer bounced over the top. They were running flat out when I toppled the biggest, a nice five-point. As I field-dressed him, I mentally thanked the hunters who had spooked the bucks from their hiding places.

Because a snap shot is often necessary when jumpshooting, debate often arises about the need for a scope. Personally, I wouldn't consider hunting without a scope. I can get on a running buck with crosshairs as quickly as I need to, and have never found the scope to be a disadvantage. Many times a bedded group of deer bounce out of sight into heavy brush and stop momentarily. That's a critical time, and I want to be able to see antlers instantly.

Since I want every second I can get, I move against the wind when I'm jumpshooting. The deer won't be able to scent me a long way off and run out unseen. They have to see or hear me. I've jumped deer within 10 yards and had plenty of time to settle down for a shot I had confidence in. When I'm shooting at a deer in headlong flight, I want my scope filled with fur, rather than a distant object bouncing along. Getting close is the best way to overcome the physics of striking a moving object with another moving object. I want all the help I can get.

The Do-it-Yourself Hunt

The West is big, a mighty vast region with lots of hunting land to make tracks on. But, if you're unfamiliar with mule deer country, you probably have some apprehensions about hunting it yourself. Maybe you and your pals are on a budget trip and want to economize as much as possible. Or maybe you just enjoy the challenge of hunting a new area. With a bit of planning, you can put together a trip yourself.

If you know much about the West, you're aware that unbelievable chunks of public land are open free to hunting to anyone. Hundreds of millions of acres that do not, *cannot*, have posted signs. Because most of it is federal land, it belongs to every American, whether he lives in Florida or Maine, or any other state in the Union.

We will explore these public lands in detail, but first let's discuss private Western lands. Excellent mule deer hunting can be had on private property. But getting on it may be tough, or downright impossible. Like everywhere else, private Western lands can be posted to the hilt.

The best way to get on private property is to know a landowner or be related to him. That's a good trick, but not impossible. The best way to get related to him is work it out so your son marries his daughter. If you have no son, you follow Plan B and get to know him. How? Park your rig in front of his house, knock on his front door, and politely ask permission to hunt on his property. Don't be surprised if he says yes, and don't be disappointed if he says no. More doors are down the road to knock on.

Of course, if you live on the East Coast, you can't very well plan a dream trip around the hopes of maybe finding a landowner who will let you hunt.

Ideally, you should have a place already in mind to hunt. Then, when you're on the hunt, scout around for places next year.

Some landowners charge trespass fees on a daily, weekly, or seasonal basis. Others take boarders and allow hunting on the property as well.

Local chambers of commerce often have lists of landowners who lease hunting rights or sell trespass permits. Leasing is big in some areas, especially in the mule deer country in Texas where public land is almost non-existent. Leases are often purchased by groups of hunters, and the best leases are tied up year after year. But some landowners lease on a daily or weekly basis to individuals on a first-come first-served basis.

In the East, sportsmen's clubs often lease parcels of land that are open only to members, but relatively fews clubs exist in the big public land states of the West. A notable exception is the American Sportsman's Club based in Denver. The club leases properties in seven states for 15,000 members. Each member pays annual dues and is entitled to hunt, on a reservation basis, properties leased by the club. In the Rockies, Colorado has the finest mule deer hunting for ASC members.

Heading for deer camp. I check the ropes to be sure extra gasoline is securely fastened before getting into the rough roads of the high country. *(Photo courtesy of Tim Irwin.)*

Private land is often hard to identify, since some states do not require landowners to post their lands. In Utah, landowners are allowed to merely paint the top of their fenceposts bright yellow—which automatically means keep off. Wyoming does not require landowners to post property. I well remember an incident that was embarrassing, but typical.

I was hunting in the Bighorn Mountains with a friend. Neither of us had been in the area before, but we were well-supplied with maps of Bureau of Land Management acreage. The unit we hunted was open only in "off-forest," which meant we could hunt only private or BLM land, but not in the Bighorn National Forest. We pulled into the general hunting area the day before the season opened and carefully looked over the possibilities. The first thing we wanted to do was park my camp trailer on BLM land reasonably close to the area we wanted to hunt. We talked to other hunters, looked for identifying landmarks, and concluded that a nice little flat surrounded by quaking aspens was public land. After parking the camper, we scouted the country and planned our morning hunt. We hunted the next day, and decided to pull camp onto another mountain that appeared more promising. When we arrived at the camper in the evening, a note on the door said we were parked on private land, but if we'd talk to the landowner at a livestock corral the next morning, he'd give us permission to camp. A nice enough note, but we had decided to move anyway. We talked to the rancher a couple days later, and he told us all he wanted was to know who was on his property. Some similar stories don't end as politely as ours. If in doubt, double-check and ask people in the area who know private land boundaries.

Many big ranches are in business to sell trespass permits. You can bring your own camp to some, or stay at lodges or boarding houses. Some offer trophy hunting and have excellent potential for big bucks. Details on the major ranches are spelled out in the state directory later in this book.

Indian reservations often offer superb mule deer hunting in many Western states. These tracts are often huge, incorporating hundreds of thousands, even millions of acres. Some of my fondest hunts have been on Indian lands. Nowadays most tribes sell limited permits and most have seasons that coincide with regular statewide seasons. More information on Indian reservations is in the state directory in the Appendix.

Some wildlife refuges administered by the U.S. Fish and Wildlife Service offer excellent mule deer hunting. The huge C. M. Russell Refuge in eastern Montana comes to mind as one of the best. Many more exist. Maps for these refuges are usually available at refuge headquarters.

In every state, the state wildlife agency has property available for hunting, including very good mule deer lands. Usually called Wildlife Management Areas or Game Management Areas, they are open to public hunting, although there might be restrictions as far as closed areas, special seasons, and other regulations. State wildlife departments can supply maps and information.

State forestry departments manage state forests, some of which are good for mule deer. Again, these agencies can furnish necessary information and maps. Because these tracts are administered for forest products, hunters might be limited to certain areas.

Each state has a land board which manages state lands, not to be confused with wildlife or forestry lands. Much of this acreage is used for livestock grazing, and states such as Montana allow stockmen who lease these public lands to close them to hunting. Much of this land is in a "checkerboard" pattern, with square mile sections in a quilted fashion. Some of this public land is also called "school" lands, sections that can be randomly scattered or uniformly divided in each township. Write to state land boards for information.

Now we come to the big land agencies, the Bureau of Land Management, referred to as the BLM, and the National Forests. Together they manage an incredible 630 million acres in the 11 Western states and Alaska. (At the time of this writing, about 100 million acres of BLM land in Alaska is scheduled to be transferred to other agencies.)

Let's look at the BLM land first. Acreages in the 11 Western states are as follows:

Nevada	48,400,000 acres
Utah	22,600,000 acres
Wyoming	17,400,000 acres
Oregon	15,700,000 acres
California	15,600,000 acres
New Mexico	13,000,000 acres
Arizona	12,600,000 acres
Idaho	12,000,000 acres
Colorado	8,400,000 acres
Montana	8,100,000 acres
Washington	300,000 acres

The BLM was created in 1946. It combined the General Land Office, originated in 1812 to dispose of public domain, and the Grazing Service, established in 1934 to administer the Taylor Grazing Act. BLM land is essentially "land that nobody wanted" when the West was first being homesteaded. In the beginning, livestock grazing was the primary BLM function, but as America began discovering the forgotten lands, the agency was directed to manage the public domain on a multiple-use basis. Wildlife, which had been ignored in favor of domestic sheep and cattle, suddenly became an important resource. In 1960, the BLM had one wildlife biologist. Now it has about 250.

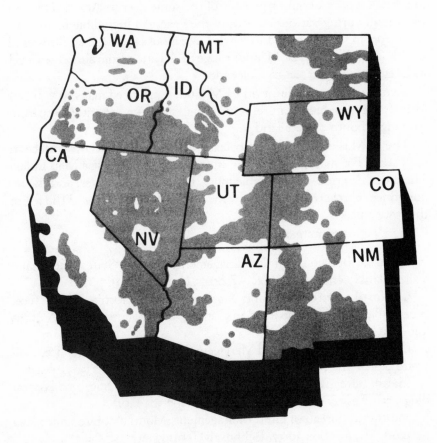

BLM lands in the western United States. (*Courtesy of the U.S. Dept. of the Interior, Bureau of Land Management.*)

Although BLM lands are open free to public hunting, many large tracts are unavailable to hunters because they're surrounded and blocked off by private lands. When Western lands were settled and homesteaded, pioneers obviously selected the rich, valley bottoms for their homestead, rather than the steep, timbered mountains or the vast, arid deserts. As a result, many ridges were unclaimed and remained in the public domain. Today, these isolated parcels are managed by the BLM, but many are totally inaccessible if there are no roads to them. Although the BLM has worked out easements with landowners on occasion, much public land continues to be used as a private hunting ground by adjacent landowners.

To a mule deer hunter, BLM lands are extremely valuable. According to a BLM report, about 65 percent of the mule deer in America live on BLM land during various seasons of the year. An incredible figure, but not surprising when you consider the enormous land mass administered by this federal agency. BLM lands range in elevation from almost sea level in Oregon to 13,000 feet in Colorado.

If you're planning a hunt on BLM land, you'll need maps so you can identify topographical features and, perhaps more importantly, keep from straying off onto private land.

The BLM is divided into districts which answer to a central office in each state. For maps, write to the state office and request a Map Index. The Index describes the available maps, the areas they cover, and the required fee. Circle the maps you want on the Index, and send the fee to the state office.

Here's a list of state offices:

Arizona. Bureau of Land Management, Arizona State Office, 2400 Valley Bank Center, Phoenix, AZ 85073 (602-261-3873).

California. Bureau of Land Management, California State Office, Federal Bldg., Room E-2841, 2800 Cottage Way, Sacramento, CA 95825 (916-484-4676).

Colorado. Bureau of Land Management, Colorado State Office, Colorado State Bank Bldg., 1600 Broadway, Denver, CO 80202 (303-837-4325).

Idaho. Bureau of Land Management, Idaho State Office, 398 Federal Bldg., 550 West Fort St., Boise, ID 83724 (208-384-1401).

Montana. Bureau of Land Management, Montana State Office, 222 N. 32nd. St., PO Box 30157, Billings, MT 59107 (406-657-6462).

Nevada. Bureau of Land Management, Nevada State Office, Federal Bldg., Rm. 3008, 300 Booth St., Reno, NV 89509 (702-784-5451).

New Mexico. Bureau of Land Management, Federal Bldg., South Federal Place, Santa Fe, NM 87501 (505-988-6217).

Oregon and Washington. Bureau of Land Management, 729 N.E. Oregon St., PO Box 2965, Portland, OR 97208 (503-234-4001).

Utah. Bureau of Land Management, Utah State Office, University Club Bldg., 136 South Temple, Salt Lake City, UT 84111 (801-524-5311).

Wyoming. Bureau of Land Management, Wyoming State Office, 2515 Warren Ave., PO Box 1828, Cheyenne, WY 82001 (307-778-2326).

Because very little BLM land has access signs, it is difficult to identify public tracts. A good map is essential.

In areas where access to BLM land is difficult because of private landowner patterns, excellent hunting is often available. These parcels can often be reached on foot or by horse. For example, let's say a 5,000-acre BLM tract is surrounded on three sides by posted private lands with no road access on the fourth side. By hiking across national forests or state sections, you might be able to legally gain access to the BLM block. One of my favorite hunting spots is a lovely timbered basin owned by the BLM. The only access is by way of a private road behind a locked gate, and the landowner gives permission to use the road only to relatives and close friends. The rancher owns only a few 40-acre blocks in the bottom of the basin, but this is enough to effectively close the area to most hunters. But, by climbing up the backside of the basin through steep slopes and thick timber, an enterprising hunter can practically have the basin to himself. I make that miserable trek every fall, and every fall I vow never to do it again, but I always return. Funny how you forget quickly the pain and suffering when you're sitting on a sofa planning the autumn hunt.

A common misconception among people unfamiliar with BLM acreage is that such lands are barren wastelands unfit for man or beast. Don't believe it. You find lush, aspen-blanketed valleys, timbered basins, and alpine tundra; practically every Western environment. The astute mule deer hunter does not overlook any of these habitats.

The U.S. Forest Service, which manages 188 million acres in the U.S., 160 million of which are in the 12 Western states, celebrated its 75th Anniversary in 1980. In the 12 Western states are 95 national forests administered by the U.S. Forest Service, most of which have excellent mule deer hunting. Forests offer everything from well-traveled access roads to expansive wilderness areas.

Managed by the U.S. Department of Agriculture, national forest land is public and use is free of charge. Most forests were originally established for their timber reserves, and logging is an important use of the land. Hunters may be restricted in the areas where active logging is underway, especially if temporary quarters and equipment are in the vicinity of lumbering operations.

Unlike BLM lands, national forests are much more intensively managed for recreation. Campgrounds and major access roads abound. Most major roads are passable by sedan, but four-wheel drive may be required for secondary and logging roads. Forest travel maps may show restricted areas. Many trails are off-limits to certain types of vehicles, and roads may be closed to all but foot traffic.

For maps and information, write to the appropriate regional office and indicate the forests you're interested in, or write directly to the forest. When you write, they will send you a free mini-map, if available, or they'll inform you of more detailed maps that are sold for a small fee. A visitor map costs 50¢, and shows general features such as forest boundaries, campgrounds, access roads, and others. Scale is ½ inch or less to the mile. A

A do-it-yourself camp in Colorado, set up by a party of hunters who camped on public land.

base map costs $1 to $3, and shows more detail. Scale is ½ inch to the mile or larger.

Here are the addresses for Forest Service Regions in mule deer country:

Region 1 (Northern Region). Includes northern Idaho and all of Montana. Write to Northern Region, U.S. Forest Service, Federal Bldg., Missoula, MT 59807 (406-329-3316). National forests in this region are:

Montana – Beaverhead, Bitterroot, Custer, Deerlodge, Flathead, Gallatin, Helena, Kootenai, Lewis and Clark, and Lolo.

Idaho – Clearwater, Idaho Panhandle (formerly consisted of Coeur d'Alene, Kaniksu, and St. Joe National Forests), and Nezperce.

Region 2 (Rocky Mountain Region). Includes Colorado and parts of Wyoming. Write to Rocky Mountain Region, U.S. Forest Service, 11177 W. 8th Ave., Box 25127, Lakewood, CO 80225 (303-234-3711). National forests in this region are:

Colorado – Arapaho, Grand Mesa-Uncompahgre, Gunnison, Pike, Rio Grande, Roosevelt, Routt, San Isabel, San Juan, and White River.

Wyoming – Bighorn, Medicine Bow, and Shoshone.

Region 3 (Southwestern Region). Includes Arizona and New Mexico. Write to Southwestern Region, U.S. Forest Service, Federal Bldg., 517 Gold Ave. S.W., Albuquerque, NM 87102 (505-766-2401). National forests in this region are:

Arizona – Apache, Coconino, Coronado, Kaibab, Prescott, Sitgreaves, and Tonto.

New Mexico – Carson, Cibola, Gila, Lincoln, and Santa Fe.

Region 4 (Intermountain Region). Includes Utah, Nevada, southern Idaho, western Wyoming, and part of California. Write to Intermountain Region, U.S. Forest Service, Federal Bldg., 324 25th St., Ogden, UT 84401 (801-626-3201). National forests in this region are:

Southern Idaho – Boise, Caribou, Challis, Payette, Salmon, Sawtooth, and Targhee.

Utah – Ashley, Dixie, Fishlake, Manti-LaSal, Uinta, and Wasatch.

Nevada – Humboldt, Toiyabe.

California – Toiyabe.

Wyoming – Bridger-Teton.

Region 5 (California). Write to California Region, U.S. Forest Service, 630 Sansome St., San Francisco, CA 94111 (415-556-4310). National forests in this region are:

California – Angeles, Cleveland, Eldorado, Inyo, Klamath, Lassen, Los Padres, Mendocino, Modoc, Plumas, San Bernardino, Sequoia, Shasta-Trinity, Sierra, Six Rivers, Stanislaus, and Tahoe.

Region 6 (Pacific Northwest). Includes Oregon and Washington. Write to Pacific Northwest Region, U.S. Forest Service, 319 S.W. Pine St., Box 3623, Portland, OR 97208 (503-221-3625). National forests in this region are:

Oregon – Deschutes, Fremont, Malheur, Mount Hood, Ochoco, Rogue River, Siskiyou, Siuslaw, Umatilla, Umpqua, Wallowa-Whitman, Willamette, and Winema.

Washington – Colville, Gifford Pinchot, Mount Baker-Snowqualmie, Okanogan, Olympic, and Wenatchee.

Besides Forest Service maps, you should obtain topo-maps of the area you intend to hunt. They show detailed features such as marshes, knolls, contours, tiny drainages, distinctive landmarks which are easily identified for orientation purposes, and other aspects. Write to the U.S. Geological Survey, Box 25286, Denver Federal Center, Denver, CO 80225, and ask for a free Map Index for the state you're interested in. Individual topographic maps cost $1.25 and $2, depending on the size you order.

On a do-it-yourself hunt, you won't have an outfitter to accommodate your needs. You're going to have to prepare yourself for the hunt.

Weather is an important factor when considering a mule deer hunt. Autumn is a fickle period in the West. Balmy, blue-sky days can immediately change to surly, overcast skies and plummeting temperatures. Be prepared for everything and expect the worst. I've been stranded in deep snows during deer season more times than I care to admit. But because I was ready, I weathered the storms and enjoyed excellent hunting afterwards. Snow is common after the first of October, and is no surprise during September at higher elevations. A blizzard can lay down a foot of snow or more overnight, turning a long-awaited hunt into a fiasco.

Pay attention to weather forecasts. If heavy snow warnings are broadcast, consider moving your camp closer to all-weather roads if you're in a high elevation far from major roads, particularly if it's late October or November. You might experience the first of the snows that linger the rest of the winter with no melting. Early snows often thaw in a day or two, but later storms might be the real thing. In the Rockies, you might not see the ground again until April or May, and later at very high elevations.

Scattered storms often bring snow to localized areas while the sun shines just a few miles away. These are not the storms to worry about. When the weatherman says travel advisories are out over several states, then be concerned and prepared.

Fog can be a problem in the fall, accounting for plenty of lost hunters, some being experienced woodsmen. Stay close to camp in a dense fog. Better yet, sit in camp and wait for it to lift.

Mountain roads are often treacherous during a rainstorm or just afterward. Clay soils turn into gooey muck similar to grease. Even chains won't get you moving when roads are at their worst. Unless you want to know what heart palpitations and shortness of breath feel like, never drive on sharp "dugways" or switchback roads carved into the sides of mountains when it's been raining or snowing. They're scary enough when they're dry, let alone greasy. If the storm is of short duration and high intensity, and the sun shines warmly after the clouds pass, wait for the road to "set" or firm up before driving on it.

Alan Massey cooks breakfast in the great outdoors. A small stove is all you need on a do-it-yourself trip.

Bring clothing that's comfortable in heat and cold. You need both. Temperatures can be near zero when you leave camp before dawn, but might climb to the 40's or 50's later on in the day. Use a day-pack to stash extra clothes as you shuck them.

If you have a tight budget, you can keep expenses trimmed and still enjoy a good mule deer hunt. Ideally, you can pool a trip with two or three friends and drive west in an economy vehicle. If the rig isn't meant for rugged roads, you can restrict your driving to paved highways or secondary roads. All kinds of places exist in the West where a hunter can head out from a paved highway or all-weather gravel road and find plenty of deer. If you want to get off the major roads, you might rent a four-wheel-drive vehicle. Of course, that ups the cost of your trip considerably, *if* you can find a 4WD to rent.

By staying at motels or boarding houses close to hunting areas, you can eliminate camping expenses. If you rent rooms with kitchenettes, you can cook your own meals and save money. Dude ranches and ski resorts welcome hunters, because most hunts are during off-season. You can rent a camp trailer, tent trailer, or pickup camper, but expect to pay premium rates.

When using a vehicle for transportation while hunting, be aware of its limitations. A small car might be delightfully fuel efficient, but woefully inadequate on back roads. Secondary roads might be impassable to vehicles with insufficient power or low clearance.

Most Western hunters drive a pick-up truck or four-wheel-drive rig. Despite the advantages of back-country vehicles, however, they get stuck just as miserably as a passenger car. The old saying that a 4WD gets you mired farther back in the boonies is often accurate. I shudder all over when I think of the places I've had my pick-up truck stuck. By rights it should still be in some of those "bottomless" pits and rocky escarpments.

Avoid problems by using your vehicle prudently, unless you want to spend precious hunting hours digging out. If the road looks bad, get out and look it over.

The most valuable asset of a 4WD is its ability to get you out of the mountains in bad weather. I can remember a hunt in Colorado's White River National Forest that was cut short by a bad storm. A long, winding road from hunting country down to major roads was in terrible shape from mud, ice, and snow. Hunters who should have known better jammed motorhomes and other fair-weather rigs into drifts and mudholes—a nightmare for dozens of hunters.

In some mountainous regions, you can't get to prime hunting country unless you have a 4WD. Climbing into upper elevations to find deer is often necessary. Competition being what it is, better-equipped hunters get to the best hunting area. For example, a forest road might start from a paved highway at 6,000 feet elevation, but you might need to drive 25 or 30 miles on steep, winding roads to get to good hunting country at 8,500 or 9,000 feet elevation. Of course, many other options are available, but your vehicle might limit your hunting opportunities. A bad spot in the road a dozen miles short of your destination could stymie your hunt.

Whenever you plan an extended trip in the mountains, bring extra gasoline—more than you think you'll need. Many hunters have a second tank installed in their hunting vehicle. A good rule of thumb is to have at least 50 gallons of fuel before heading for back roads. My truck has a 35-gallon tank, and I lash four 5-gallon Jerry cans full of gasoline to the luggage rack on top. The Book Cliffs, where I hunt often, is an 80-mile drive one way. In one area, I drive 25 miles from camp one way to a ridge where I leave the vehicle and hunt all day.

When you head for mule deer country, *always* take sturdy tire chains that you know fit your tires. A dependable jack and a shovel are also essential items. A flashlight, matches, and flares are also handy, as well as water for the radiator (and you) if you're in arid country with little water available. I carry sealed rations, a sleeping bag, first-aid kit, and a survival kit in my rig whenever I'm in the boonies. No telling when those items will be needed.

Certainly, putting together a do-it-yourself trip to the West is a major undertaking, but you can do it if you really want to. Life is a matter of priorities. If one of your fantasies is to kill a mule deer, do it while you can. You aren't getting any younger, and inflation makes it tougher every year.

Let's take an example and figure what it would cost you and two buddies to make a trip from Philadelphia to Colorado's west slope. Assume that you own all the camp gear you need, including a tent, and the three of you will share expenses equally.

We're going to be very frugal in our estimates, baring expenses to a minimum. Figures are 1981 prices:

Total miles (round trip): 4,000
Miles per gallon: 15
Price of gasoline: $1.40 per gallon
_____
Total cost for gasoline $372.00

If the trip takes about two days and you don't stop in motels (by switching drivers, you can make the trip in less than 50 hours), let's figure your only road expenses are tolls and food. If you limit your food stops to fast food restaurants, let's figure 6 meals per person at $5 per meal. That amounts to $30 per person one way, or $60 round trip: $180.00

By shopping wisely, you figure meals in camp to cost $20 per person, or $60 per day total. Assuming a five-day hunt, the cost would be: $300.00

Colorado nonresident deer license: $90 each $270.00

Miscellaneous expenses: tolls, oil for vehicle, ice, film, propane fuel, gifts for family, amount to $75 per person $225.00

Total:　$1347.00

Per person cost:　$449.00

Can't afford it? Try taking on part-time work and set up a special savings account for the three of you. I know a group of outdoorsmen who together paint three or four houses each summer to finance their trip. Like I said, it's a matter of priorities. If you really want a pretty muley buck on your wall, do it now.

Outfitters and Guides — Should You Hire One?

In much of the best mule deer country, outfitters are available to provide you with a hunt. Should you hire one? There are both advantages and disadvantages.

Outfitters in some areas must pass strict examinations and agree to a number of conditions before they receive a license to conduct a business. They must adhere to a variety of state and federal regulations, and they might also need to be accepted into the professional outfitter's association in their state.

Outfitters' expenses are enormous, and profits are slim. Insurance, guide salaries, horses, tack, tents, camp equipment, groceries, vehicles, gasoline, and a host of other expenses quickly eat into their pocketbook. Because of this outlay, hunting fees are set to defray costs, and ideally, to leave enough for the outfitter to live on.

Hunting fees vary, depending on the services the outfitter provides, such as use of horses, camp equipment required, number of hunters per guide, and other factors. Basically, fees run from $100 to $250 or more per day, with annual increases because of inflation.

Mule deer hunts normally last from 5 days to a week. This is usually enough time to take a buck, with a day or two extra in case the weather turns bad.

Should you go to the expense of paying an outfitter to take you hunting? First off, let's look at expenses if you *don't* hire an outfitter. You need to provide your own food, a place to stay, vehicle expenses getting to and from the area you're hunting, gasoline during the hunt, and perhaps trespass fees if you plan to hunt private land. Besides the monetary expense, you need to find a place that is reasonably good for hunting, and you need to get your game out by yourself after a kill. If you intend to camp, you need to provide a camp unit or a tent as well as countless other items.

If you're willing to do all these things and provide the needed equipment, then you can probably get along just fine without an outfitter. A big question, of course, is the probability of getting what you came for – a mule deer. If you've never been in the country you plan to hunt, will you be mobile enough and skillful enough to find what you're looking for? Having a companion along who already knows the country helps immensely. But if you can't, you should seriously consider what you're getting in to. In the long run, an outfitter might be the most economical way to go if you weigh the services provided *and* the odds of killing a deer.

Outfitter Larry Gurr (left) of Vernal, Utah, and client with a massive four-point buck taken in Utah.

The type of country you intend to hunt has a bearing on whether or not to hire an outfitter. If you plan to hunt vast expanses of public land that are reasonably easy to negotiate with plenty of access roads, you might do very well on your own. Of course, you must provide your own vehicle, and if you're driving from either coast, the Midwest, or the South to the Rockies, this could be a big disadvantage, even if you have a rig that will comfortably negotiate mountain country.

If time is a factor and you can't drive, your next obvious option is to fly. Unless you have a friend in mule deer country who will pick you up at an airport and take you hunting, you might have no choice but to settle on an outfitter.

Finally, if you want a trophy buck, you must hunt with someone who can at least put you in big buck country. Outfitters are the obvious choice.

Once you've decided that you want to hire an outfitter, your next step is to find one who offers the type of hunt you're looking for. The task isn't easy, because you'll be paying a total stranger to take you hunting. All your trust and hopes are in his hands.

Word-of-mouth is a good way to select an outfitter. If a friend hunted with an outfitter and brought back a favorable report, that's the place to begin. Ask your friend the details of his hunt, and be sure the outfitter offers the services you expect.

It's important to be selective, because the outfitting profession has its bad eggs just as any other. Most outfitters are honest and provide everything they advertise, but some are cheats out for a fast buck (not the four-legged kind, either).

Where do you look if you don't know anyone who has hunted with an outfitter? One way is to write to an outfitter's association and ask for their listing of members. Some associations publish newsletters, and some have attractive booklets, such as the Montana Outfitter's Association.

State wildlife agencies may have lists of outfitters, and chambers of commerce may be able to tell you who is outfitting in their area.

The National Rifle Association has a "Denali" listing of outfitters. It is a state-by-state compilation of outfitters who have been judged by the NRA to be reputable based on questionnaires filled out by hunters who have knowledge of outfitters' operations. Write to the NRA for information on the Denali Registry.

Numerous ads in the back pages of outdoor magazines are paid for by outfitters, but it's difficult to make a judgment based on an ad. Write to several outfitters in the area you want to hunt and make your decision after weighing the possibilities.

Another way is to book a hunt with an outfitter's consultant who teams you up with an outfitter offering the kind of hunt you want. Jack Atcheson of Butte, Montana, comes to mind as a reputable consultant. He handles bookings and deposits, and arranges trips. Because his reputation is at stake, Atcheson books only for outfitters who are tops in the trade.

Taxidermists are often good sources for finding outfitters, since they constantly work with hunters and hear frequently about hunting trips. Some may even book hunts for outfitters, and like consultants, generally deal only with honest outfitters in good game country.

Tom Opre (right), a Michigan outdoor journalist, smiles proudly with an enormous buck from Wyoming's Greys River country as guide Bob Carter, looks on. *(Photo courtesy of Tom Opre.)*

When querying outfitters about the hunt they offer, be sure to get details. Find out exactly how many days you will hunt, what size mule deer you might expect to find, how much walking is involved, if horses will be used, the type of camp or ranch you'll be based at, how to get your meat out, and any hidden costs that might not be included in the fee. In most cases, outfitters provide guides, transportation to and from hunting camp, food, sleeping quarters, and care of meat until it reaches your vehicle.

Be sure to determine at the outset the number of hunters for each guide. If an outfitter promises one guide for every two hunters, he should live up to that rule. This information should all be perfectly clear before signing to hunt.

Ask for references before you decide on an outfitter. Instead of writing to other hunters for their opinions and experiences, call on the telephone. You receive a more informal reply and can get much more information on the phone. Be sure to ask the outfitter for names of people who have hunted with him in the last year or two, rather than several years ago.

Most outfitters ask you to sign a contract or agreement when you book a hunt. This is a good practice, because it spells out details between hunter and client. If all the particulars aren't in the contract, get them in writing before you book.

Don't wait too long to select an outfitter. Many are booked full early in the year, so make your reservations as soon as you can. In states where lottery drawings are required for mule deer, such as Wyoming, you might have to wait until summer to learn if you were successful in drawing a permit. Outfitters in some states can pick up your license for you from license vendors or state wildlife offices.

Outfitters generally request a deposit when a hunt is booked. The standard procedure is to make a deposit of 25 to 50 percent, with the balance payable on your arrival.

Be wary of outfitters offering "guaranteed" hunts. Though some outfitters are in excellent deer country, they should not offer a successful hunt to every client. If a guarantee is offered, find out exactly what it means. Does it mean you get all or part of your money back if you fail to kill a deer, or get a shot, or *see* a shootable buck and not fire at it? If in doubt, don't book with outfitters who must lure customers with guarantees.

Once you've signed with an outfitter, what should you expect when

you get to the hunting area? Of course, the outfitter must provide everything the contract specifies, but he should do everything in his power to
see that your hunt is successful and comfortable.

You'll know when an outfitter is really trying hard for you, doing everything to get you within shooting range of a muley. And you'll know if he's
doing the minimum, letting the time pass until your hunt runs out.

Before you start hunting, the outfitter should know about any physical limitations you have. Some outfitters want a report of your physical
condition before you sign a contract. If you have a bad heart, a respiratory
problem or some other ailment that affects your ability to hunt, by all
means let the outfitter know. Don't be a "macho" type who is worried about
what the other hunters or guides might think. The last thing you want is
to get hurt or suffer a serious malady out in the hills.

Make sure the guide you're paired with is aware of your hunting preferences. You don't want the guide telling you that you must walk 4 or 5 miles a
day if you planned on hunting from horseback or at a more leisurely walk.

I recall a group of hunters who assumed they'd be driving logging roads
all day looking for game. When they found out they had to ride horses,

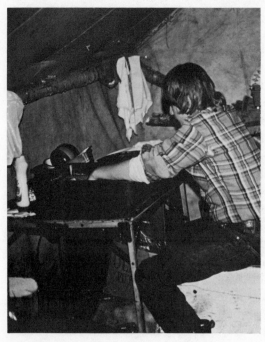

Another advantage of having
an outfitter—you don't need to
wash dishes!

the hunters promptly packed up and left for home. This was an unfortunate misunderstanding and shouldn't have happened.

If your guide is young and rugged, as most of them are, tell him to slow down a bit so you can keep up if you're having trouble. If he persists in leaving you behind, and your hunt is obviously suffering because of your inability to see game at the same time the guide does, speak to the outfitter and ask for another guide.

In the event your guide insists on taking his rifle along, be sure both of you understand who gets the first shot. This might seem academic, but some guides see nothing wrong with shooting an animal for themselves while a paying client is along. Nearly all outfitters forbid this, but it happens occasionally. If a guide says he wants to shoot "a small deer that you pass up," don't fall for that either, because you'll spend precious time field-dressing and transporting his deer.

Make sure the guide knows exactly what kind of a deer you're looking for, and don't allow him to talk you into something you don't want. If you simply want a meat buck or a doe, fine, but if you want an average buck or even a trophy buck, let the guide know. Better yet, be sure the outfitter knows too, so he can send you off in the country most apt to produce what you're after.

Some guides take advantage of their clients, especially if they're inexperienced. Because you must often rely on your guide's judgment, be sure he isn't going to urge a shot at a buck that doesn't meet the standards you already discussed. At the same time, instruct the guide to absolutely let you know when a deer you're getting ready to shoot is too small. Sometimes mule deer antlers, even average ones, cause novice hunters to come unglued and want to shoot quickly. Your guide should be able to evaluate a deer and tell you whether it's up to your expectations or not.

If you're a serious trophy hunter and know what you're looking for, tell the outfitter you want an experienced guide. If you *don't* know what you're looking for and want a trophy, be sure to ask for a guide with some years under his belt. A young guide might point out a lesser buck and tell you to shoot, and be perfectly innocent in his ignorance.

Besides outfitters who specialize in guided hunts, you can hire on with a rancher or farmer for extended or daily hunts. He may or may not provide room or board. You might be expected to stay in a nearby hotel, motel, or boarding house, depending on the arrangement. If you're on a hunt where you pay by the day, be leery of a person who may string you along for several days so he can collect as long as possible. Of course, it may be difficult to tell if this is so, but human weakness being what it is and grocery bills being what they are, the good old boy might be just looking for a few extra dollars from the city dude, all the while having intentions of showing the hunter a good muley on the final day.

Beware of the friendly chap in the small-town saloon who offers to take you hunting for a fee. He might take you all right, but not hunting. More than one frustrated hunter has sat in a bar, only to be propositioned by a local who will do little more than show the sport some country.

Some outfitters take hunters to drop camps, which means you are transported to an already established camp, dropped off, and picked up at a

Chow time at Grant Barrus' camp in Wyoming's Greys River country. Good hunting and good food here!

Guides cut wood with a "misery whip" crosscut saw in a Montana wilderness area. Wood stoves keep clients toasty warm in tents.

predetermined time. There are a number of advantages to drop-camping, and some disadvantages as well.

Cost is much less than a fully guided hunt. Budget-minded outdoorsmen find this a noteworthy advantage. Since you are on your own in a drop camp, you can come and go as you please, hunting at your own pace, and looking the country over as you wish. Some hunters like to do their own cooking and camp chores, and like the idea of being independent.

One disadvantage is being tied to a particular place for a length of time, with no means of moving to new country if the area isn't productive. Most drop camps are too far into backcountry for you to easily make your own way out. If you've been transported in by horse or airplane, you have no choice but to wait for the outfitter.

Another minus is having to pack your game from point of kill to camp. I don't know of any outfitter who leaves horses or mules with drop-camp hunters because the outfitter can't be sure the animals will be cared for properly, or kept from being hurt or lost somewhere in the backcountry.

Many outfitters are strongly opposed to drop-camping because the margin of profit is slim, and more importantly, some hunters learn the country and come back the next year by themselves without hiring the outfitter. This is true only on public land with access. When that happens, the outfitter is faced with competition in his drop-camp area, something that he'd just as soon do without.

In many guided camps, women are hired to do the cooking. It goes without saying, but I'll say it anyway, that hunters must respect a woman's presence by avoiding foul language and actions. Outfitters and guides take a dim view of unruly hunters who are offensive and obnoxious.

Which brings us to the point of alcohol in an outfitter's camp. Before booking a hunt, you should check to be sure alcohol is allowed—if it's important to you to have it along. Some very reputable outfitters forbid any alcohol in camp, not for religious and health reasons, but because they want their guides *and* hunters to be in top physical condition every morning. As one outfitter told me, "I'm not running a social club up here in the woods. If the hunters want to party, let 'em do it in town, not in my hunting camp."

By and large, the majority of outfitters allow hunters to bring liquor and beer, but the guides are usually not allowed to imbibe. Work begins

Outfitter Grant Barrus leads hunting party down to camp after a successful outing.

early in camp, with most guides and camp workers at their chores by 4 a.m. Outfitters want them to be bright-eyed and bushy-tailed each morning. As for yourself, you should be even more careful about staying in top physical shape, because the guides will no doubt have a head start on you. Few hunters out-walk their guides.

If you kill your deer early in the hunt, you'll have plenty of time to sit around if you elect to stay. Many hunters want to go out and see their pal score, and may want to help in a drive. This is usually O.K. as far as the outfitter is concerned, provided you don't get in the way and botch up a hunt. Most hunters enjoy helping the guides by splitting some firewood, leading the horses to water, or other little jobs that need doing.

All in all, guided camps are fun places to be, with plenty of camaraderie and jokes. You'll no doubt be apprehensive and a bit formal when you arrive, but the stiffness wears off when you've been around a day or two. To help things along, try to remember the names of the guides and camp workers, and just be yourself. Remember that the outfitter and guides are sizing you up, just as you're sizing them up.

Don't be surprised if you become close friends with a guide or outfitter. The closeness of the camp and the emotions and nostalgic remembrances of the hunt often cement lasting friendships. There are many happy reunions in mule deer country each fall when hunters and guides renew old fellowships. In some cases, hunters who fail to draw permits leave their rifles at home and bring their cameras—just to spend time with an outfitter or guide because they enjoy each other's company.

But besides that, the immediate reason for hiring an outfitter has four legs and big antlers. That's all the motivation you need to book a hunt.

The Hunting Gun

Some folks believe that mule deer hunters view rifles with the idea that any old one will do. But to others, a rifle must meet rigid requirements before gracing a gun case.

It's great fun to sit around a campfire at deer camp and discuss the merits of various rifles and loads. Do not, however, make the idiotic mistake of suggesting that your rifle is perfect mule deer medicine. Chances are excellent no one will agree with you. If perchance someone likes the caliber you do, he will invariably prefer another bullet type, or rifle action, or a myriad of other possibilities. Whether or not the debate ends on a peaceful note depends on the sobriety and good nature of the participants.

Quite often the outspoken people around the campfire usually have the least hunting experience. They might be able to spout all kinds of data on bullet velocities, energies, and ballistic coefficients, but don't expect much of an answer if you ask them how many dead deer they've bent over. More often than not, the quiet guy sitting off to the side with a battered, scratched, poor excuse for a firearm is the one who has pulled the innards out of more deer than anyone else in camp. And he probably does it with factory loads he buys on sale.

If the truth were known, the great majority of hunters become enchanted with a particular caliber not because they've made exhaustive tests on every comparable caliber, but for a variety of other reasons. When you buy a new car, do you road test a half-dozen models before making a decision? If you're typical, you buy what strikes your fancy, and depend on the car's reputation from conversation with friends.

So it is with firearms. Perhaps your dad or favorite uncle told you X caliber was best, or maybe you read several articles about it, or possibly the nice guy in the sporting goods store said it was wonderful. And, by golly, if you take the gun on a mule deer hunt and knock head-over-tail the first buck you see with it, you will be a devoted fan until you hunt enough years to realize that maybe you should consider something else. Or maybe the gun lives up to your expectations over the years and you're satisfied.

At this point I must mention my own preference, not because I believe my rifle is infallible, but because it's been good to me for almost 20 years.

Back in 1956 when I turned 16 I made two big purchases—a car and a deer rifle. New York State, where I grew up, allowed residents to drive and hunt big game when they reached that magic age. My dad was a car

In open country, don't count on getting close to a wise buck. You need a flat-shooting rifle capable of delivering adequate energy at big yardages.

salesman, so no problem on that item. For a rifle I went to Carpenter's Gun Shop owned by Russ Carpenter, a very well-known gun expert and one of the country's top gun writers.

It didn't take me long to make a decision, although I admit I delayed so I could have an excuse to hang around Russ's gun shop. Located only a dozen miles from my house, the shop was in a rustic wooden building with a set of moose antlers nailed over the front door. When customers weren't in the store, Russ was invariably in the back room, eyeglasses low on the tip of his nose, as he worked on a problem gun or a far-out wildcat just for his own pleasure.

Since I was going to live in the Adirondacks for two years while studying forestry in college, I chose a Winchester Model 94 .30/30 carbine. Most shots in those timbered mountains would be less than 75 yards, so I was happy with my choice.

The little carbine performed well on whitetails in the brush, but I made plans to continue studying forestry and wildlife at Utah State University after graduating from Paul Smith's College in New York. I carried the carbine with me, but never had a chance to use it. College attitudes being what they were, I sold the rifle to take a pretty lady to a Sweetheart Ball. I wasn't terribly disappointed in seeing the carbine go, because the deer country in Utah was a whole lot different than that of the Eastern mountains. Sooner or later, I would own something that could reach out and kill a deer at long ranges. My first mule deer fell to a .303 Enfield that I borrowed from a college classmate. Then, when I realized that I had miraculously managed to fulfill the requirements for a Bachelor's Degree, my future father-in-law DeMarr Dudley announced that I could go to the local sporting goods store in Vernal and pick out any rifle in stock as a graduation present.

I went to Basin Sportsman and, like a kid in a candy shop, looked over the possibilities. I must admit that I was a rabid Jack O'Connor fan, and nothing other than a .270 would do. But the store was out of .270's at the moment, primarily because it was 1963 and the new Model 70 Winchesters were just coming on the market. The old 70's in .270 caliber were sold out. I spied a .30/06 Winchester Model 70 in pre-1964 version, and looked it over carefully. It was a lovely gun, a featherweight model topped with a Weaver 4X scope. It was exactly like the firearm DeMarr owned; the only

My deer rifle, a pre-64 Model 70 Winchester Featherweight in .30/06, and a Colorado muley killed in an aspen forest.

difference being a higher serial number. DeMarr chuckled when I told the clerk to wrap it up.

I named the rifle Big Bertha, which was not very original. The Germans used a gigantic artillery piece named Big Bertha against the Allied Forces, but I was nonetheless satisfied with this name.

My affair with Big Bertha still continues. It is my favorite deer rifle, though my gun cabinet is jammed with assorted firearms.

Millions of words have been written about deer rifles. Each author expresses his own opinions, and readers may or may not agree. Some writers extoll the virtues of big bores; others like the lightweights. Some are middle-of-the-roaders and make no commitment.

Now then, since this is a mule deer book, I'm supposed to say (as do many writers) that mule deer are bigger than whitetails and because they live in open country you need a flat-shootin', hard-hittin' son-of-a-gun to kill them. Right?

Almost, which goes to show I'm not going to make a commitment. I hope you aren't expecting me to evaluate mule deer rifles and pronounce one of them "the best." No way. I won't do it because there is no "best" for everyone. I have a "the best" in my gun closet, and you may have one in yours, and we can argue until we're blue in the face, but it won't make any difference. Trouble is, we'll both be right. As long as we each have confidence in a rifle and it has the capability to do what it needs to do, that's it. End of discussion.

The perfect rifle is one you can handle comfortably and that places bullets where needed. Not only must it be matched to the quarry, but to the terrain and range as well. If you hunt the spruce-fir thickets of the high country and your .30/30 carbine knocks down all the deer you shoot at, have at it. If you like seeing muleys at 400 yards in the sage and your 7mm Magnum is just the ticket, wonderful.

But if you are unsure about the performance of your present rifle, or if you've never been mule deer hunting and intend to go, several factors should be considered before making a decision on a new rifle.

Let's start by looking at the physical make-up of a mule deer to see what's needed to put him to the ground quickly and humanely. The first thing I'm obliged to do is dispel the notion that mule deer are always bigger than whitetails. I think the scribes who write that sort of thing have seen few big whitetails. A well-fed Michigan whitetail buck might make an average three-year-old mule deer look small. Conversely, an average Montana mule deer towers over a full-grown South Carolina whitetail. Mule deer get big only if they grow old, and some never get big because of food supply and genetic makep-up. The same is true with whitetails. In this case, a big mule deer means 175 pounds and larger dressed. Most mule deer shot these days are less than three years old, and are no bigger than a comparably aged northern whitetail on good feed.

If you're thinking about those buster muleys you've read about that go 200 to 300 pounds, you still aren't fooling with impressive figures when comparing them to whitetails. If you think so, pull up a bar stool and let me tell you about the huge 250-pound-plus whitetails I've seen killed in New York's Adirondacks, the Maine woods, and New Brunswick.

It all boils down to the deer hunting exposure you've had with both species, and then judging muleys and whitetails accordingly. If you've been shooting 80-pound Alabama bucks all your life and are going to hunt a trophy muley that may weigh 200 pounds, then you must consider a larger caliber if you've been shooting lightweight bullets. But if you've been chasing 200-pound whitetails around Nebraska cornfields, you're all set for mule deer.

A muley isn't any tougher to kill than a whitetail, but he might be a heck of a lot harder to find if he's wounded because of the rugged nature of the country he lives in. But I've had whitetails give me a run for my money in pretty hairy places, too.

I haven't seen any figures on the matter, but I'd guess that eight out of 10 mule deer hunters use bolt-action rifles. The rest are carbines, and a few are semi-automatics. I'll be frank about semi-automatics. I don't think much of them because most hunters tend to shoot too quickly, knowing that plenty of back-up shots are on tap in case of a miss. If a deer is hit and wounded, chances are the remaining ammo won't finish the job anyway. Another problem with autoloaders is that the action is more likely to jam at a crucial time.

What do you do in this situation? The buck has you spotted, and you can't get a clear shot. Would a "brushbuster" do the job here?

You can't win 'em all. Lois Zumbo points to a bullet hole made by her .243. A nice buck stood behind the branch, but the bullet hit the branch and failed to penetrate.

The .30/30 has been popularly credited with having killed more deer than any other firearm. That *might* have been true, but no longer. Too many deer have been killed with other calibers, especially in the 1950's and 1960's, a banner era for mule deer. The .30/30 has also been credited with having wounded more deer than any other firearm. That also might have been true, because the bullet quickly loses velocity and falls out rapidly beyond 150 yards.

Many hunters favor the .30/30 in heavy brush, but gun experts are questioning the ability of the so-called "brush-busters" to rip and chew through branches and foliage to find a deer's vitals. Other calibers thought to do well on brush, such as the .45-70, .35 Remington, and .444 Marlin are equally suspect. The biggest factor is the hunter's attitude. If he figures his bullet will eat up plenty of brush, he might try a shot at a deer that shouldn't be made. Instead of waiting for the animal to move into a better position, the hunter squeezes the trigger and hopes for the best. In order for a bullet to get through brush, it must penetrate all the intervening matter, it must not be deflected off course, and it must not fragment. That's asking a lot, and the success of a bullet flying true depends on its configuration, weight, and make-up, as well as the brush.

All things considered, I wouldn't buy a firearm of the "brush-buster" variety if I wanted a gun for all-purpose mule deer hunting. If I was hunting exclusively in dense coastal forests for blacktails or Sitka deer, I'd give a brush gun some serious thought. In those heavy forests, I would discount altogether a fast-shooting rifle with lightweight bullets.

If we can agree that killing a mule deer doesn't require super-magnum hotshot rifles, then our next consideration is trajectory. But there's a catch. At the killing end of that trajectory must be enough foot-pounds of energy, which immediately discounts a number of calibers.

I'm going to crawl out on a skinny, rotten limb at this point and say that the minimum caliber for open-country, typical mule deer hunting should produce about 1,200 foot pounds of energy at 200 yards. My ballistics tables indicate the .243 is the smallest caliber for mule deer, and 100-grain bullets should be used rather than lighter ones.

I'm sure that devoted fans of the .220 Swift, .22/250, .222 and other lightweight calibers will scream in protest, but I've seen too many unfortunate woundings with these speedy bullets. Though the velocity is high, the bullets don't have the required knock-down power. Many explode on a shoulder or the hide and fail to penetrate to a vital area. And worse, light bullets are next to useless if they touch foliage on the way to the quarry. Deflection is a problem, and is always a consideration in mule deer country.

Some hunters claim a .243 is too light for muleys, but in the hands of a skilled shooter, it's an acceptable caliber. A good friend of mine has made one-shot kills on three *mature* bull elk with a .243, and has no problem with mule deer. As every gun writer has told you, proper placement is what it's all about.

Because mule deer are not always easy targets, proper placement is not that easy. That's when I want a rifle that performs. I want to know my bullet can penetrate the vital chest area from practically any angle. Big Bertha is my answer. I have shot mule deer from almost every conceivable angle, and have never had cause to blame the rifle or a bullet for a bad hit.

Some hunters think a bigger caliber anchors a deer regardless of where he's hit, but a .338 in the paunch has no more stopping power than a .243. A deer with a leg clipped off with a .375 H & H Magnum goes just as far as an animal made three-legged with a .22/250.

One of the dangers of shooting a big bore such as a .338 or .340 Weatherby Magnum is the fear of recoil, which in turn causes poor shooting. If you're afraid of the rifle you're shooting or are the least bit uncomfortable with it, put it in the gun cabinet and shoot something you can handle.

Another good reason to leave these big bores at home when you're hunting mule deer is the loss of meat. If you want to see wasted meat, take a look at a deer's front shoulders after being busted with a .340 Weatherby Magnum. Most of it is left behind to feed the coyotes. The .340 has a place in hunting, and packs a mighty wallop when you need it, but it's a bit much for muleys, at least in my opinion.

Last minute sighting-in is a good idea if you have time before heading into deer hunting country.

The 7mm Magnum is coming on so strong that it may be the most popular caliber these days. Ballistics on the 7mm Mag are marvelous, and are no doubt the reason for so many converts. Besides high velocity, the caliber spews plenty of energy and has a flat trajectory. This is a good long-range rifle, one that reaches out and packs plenty of power on the way.

The .270 is still the darling of the West to countless hunters. At 200 yards, a 150-grain bullet zings along at about 2,380 feet per second with an energy of about 1,890 foot pounds. Double the distance to 400 yards, and the bullet is traveling a respectable 1,920 feet per second with 1,225 foot pounds of energy. The .270 will long remain a favorite in mule deer country. Its devoted followers will not let it fade away. Interestingly enough, .270 buffs are almost violently faithful. I've never seen such enthusiasm for other calibers.

Other calibers of favored mule deer rifles, are the .300 Savage, .308 Winchester, .300 Magnums .25/06, .257 Roberts, 6mm Remington, to name a few. All have their place when handled by competent hunters.

The old stand-by .30/06 is no doubt the workhorse firearm most commonly seen in Western homes. Often called the "aught-six," this rifle is ubiquitous; you can't easily find a deer camp without one. For this reason, it's almost always possible to beg or borrow shells. The .30/06 has very nice ballistics as well. My favorite bullet, the 165-grain, moves along at 2,280 feet per second at 200 yards with a knockout punch of 1,910 foot pounds. At 400 yards, it's still zipping respectably with a velocity of 1,825 and energy of 1,220.

Simply said, the best deer rifle for you is the one you get along with best. Billy Stockton, one of my favorite Montana outfitters, has a saying I adore. "It don't matter what you're shootin', as long as you can shoot it." I don't know any better way to describe this all-important aspect of mule deer hunting.

If you don't know your rifle as intimately as you'd like to, do something about it. If you live in the East, practice on woodchucks or punch holes in paper. If you're a Westerner, plenty of rock chucks, prairie dogs, and jack-rabbits are nearby to test your firearm on.

I've been around a lot of skilled shooters, but my friend Herb Troester must rank at the top. Herb is a gun nut who could no doubt write an encyclopedia on firearms without referring to a scrap of research. He simply knows most of what there is to know about guns.

Herb showed me his expertise while on a mule deer hunting trip in

Wyoming's Bighorn Mountains. He was shooting a .257 Roberts Ackley-Improved rifle, one of his many well-cared-for and highly accurate guns. We were walking across a sage knoll when a buck jumped up and trotted off. Herb calmly walked to a boulder, laid his jacket on it, and took a prone position with his rifle snugged on the jacket. The buck stopped at a distance I judged to be 400 yards. Herb casually stated he was going to take the buck squarely in the anus because the deer was looking back at us over its rump.

When the rifle cracked, the buck collapsed instantly, dead before it hit the ground. The shot was perfect, precisely where Herb called it. It was the first time I had seen that particular part of the anatomy hit with a bullet, although I knew it was one of the deadliest, most humane shots that can be made. We paced the distance to the deer; it was 410 yards. Because Herb had chronographed hundreds of loads and a variety of bullets for that rifle, he was confident with the gun at any reasonable range. I don't know how high he had to hold at that range, but the ballistics tables say my .30/06, when zeroed at 200 yards, would have to be held 26 inches above the desired point of impact at 400 yards.

Very few hunters have Herb's shooting skills. A shot should be passed up unless the shooter can honestly say he can hit what he's shooting at. Too often I've seen hunters emptying their rifles at deer far across a canyon. Some shooters think they're operating an artillery piece and must get "zeroed" in on an unfortunate deer. One of the most appalling sights is a hunter who shoots at a bounding deer 500 or 600 yards away. I wouldn't even guess what the lead and elevation would be, but some keep right on plugging away. Now and then these few make a miracle shot and connect, but most of the time the deer is either unscathed or wounded.

One can hardly discuss rifles for mule deer without mentioning bullets and loads. The finest rifle in the world is only as good as the bullet it shoots.

As with rifles, the subject of bullets can be debated endlessly. If your mind is made up and you favor a certain bullet, no amount of logical discussion will change your mind.

To kill a deer, a bullet must penetrate into a vital area and destroy an organ which sustains life, or cause enough hemorrhaging to allow extensive blood loss. A bullet's tremendous speed and energy delivers a hard-hitting shock when it strikes flesh. Depending on the type of bullet and the velocity it's traveling, it may explode immediately on impact, it may penetrate several inches and then expand, or it may penetrate completely through the animal with little or no expansion. Hunters who pursue dangerous, thick-muscled game such as elephants and Cape buffalo often use a "solid" bullet which penetrates deeply to a vital, killing instantly. Mule deer hunters want a projectile that will not deflect or disintegrate on the front shoulder, but will pierce it and find the lungs or heart. If the front shoulder is missed, the bullet should expand inside the chest area and cause enough damage to kill the animal quickly.

For years I used 150-grain Remington Core-Lokts and Winchester Silver Tips, and was satisfied with their performance. Recently, my hunting buddy Parker Davies, Jr. talked me into trying the 165-grain pointed Nosler partition bullet in front of 57 grains of 4350 powder. I was about to embark on a desert bighorn sheep hunt, and could expect to get but one shot. Parker is a physician, and does his handloading as precisely as his surgical

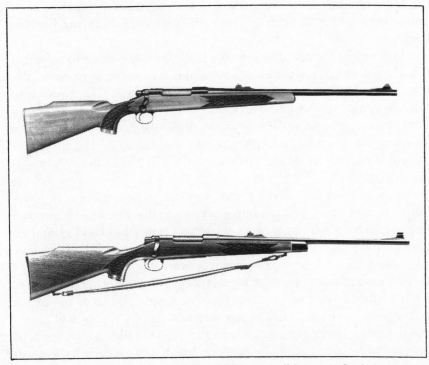

The Remington Model 700 in ADL and BDL are well-known rifles for mule deer. Various calibers accommodate every hunter. (*Courtesy of Remington Arms Co.*).

work. He had become enamored with the Nosler, and was eager for me to try it. Because of a complicated series of circumstances during the sheep hunt, which resulted in a pick-up truck burning to the ground in the desert, I wasn't able to try the Nosler on bighorns. But during the last 3 years I have killed eight buck mule deer with it in several states under varying conditions and ranges. None of the bucks required a second killing shot, although I missed some deer and needed other bullets to find the target.

Generally speaking, most modern factory cartridges are adequate for mule deer. You need not be a reloading bench wizard to build bullets and loads that kill muleys. Don't worry about the bullet. Instead, fret about putting the bullet where it needs to go. As I already said, varmint hunting and target shooting help you learn your gun's capabilities.

If you shoot extensively, that's still no reason to have confidence in your rifle *if* you have any reason to believe the firearm has been jolted badly while traveling to the hunting area. You must be sure all is in working order. In much of the West, you drive through miles of lowlands, often public land, where you can test your rifle before climbing into hunting country.

Don't be the last-minute type who rushes out to a range to sight-in a rifle. You should have plenty of ammo and time when sighting in. I've seen hurried hunters make a quick three-shot group, then rush off to hunting camp, memorizing where the bullets hit. Some of those groups were barely on the paper. The problem with a rifle that's off is that, when a buck appears, you might forget that your rifle is shooting 11 inches to the left and 6 inches high at 100 yards, or was it 6 inches to the right and 11 inches high?

To make the most accurate shot you can, *always* use a rest. *Never* shoot offhand unless it's absolutely necessary. Elsewhere in this book I described a hunt where I shot a buck in oak brush and had to stand on tip-toes to see his chest. That was one of the few offhand shots I've ever taken, and I don't intend to try many more.

There are all sorts of rests. If a tree, rock, branch, or other solid object is not available, you can quickly drape your hunting jacket or vest over a bush and use it for a rest. Even a standing 2-inch-thick sapling will do in a pinch. Once I was hunting in a blizzard and spotted a buck feeding about 250 yards out. I was in high serviceberry brush and needed all the elevation I could get, so I sneaked up to a thick vertical stem that was no more than 1 inch in diameter. I pressed the rifle stock against it with my left hand, and made the shot nicely. The branch was just stout enough to steady the rifle.

If you can shoot from a low position without brush obscuring your view, get down in a sitting stance and use your knees to support your elbows. I don't like this position, but have used it when necessary. Prone position is excellent, but I prefer to rest my rifle on a stationary object rather than on my left hand and elbow. For me, the best rest of all is the crotch of a tree where I can slide the stock forward to "lock" the rifle tightly against the tree. When I can do that, the rifle is as close to absolute still as it ever gets, and a deer in range is in trouble.

My Winchester Model 70 has a sling, which I consider to be necessary for carrying the rifle over my shoulder on long walks and to help hold the gun steadily while drawing a bead.

Handguns for hunting are becoming more and more popular as state wildlife agencies recognize their potency and recreational value. This is not as popular a sport as muzzleloading and bowhunting, and it probably will never be, but dedicated handgunners throughout the West shoot with nothing else. In most states where handgunning for deer is allowed, hunters must compete with riflemen, although a few states offer special units and seasons for handgun hunters.

Deer hunters who use handguns suffer a handicap because of the need to get close to the quarry. Most handgunners won't try a shot much over 75 yards, with 100 yards absolute limit. Handgun hunters need a dead rest, a stationary target, a lot of confidence, and plenty of ability.

Herb Troester bore-sights a rifle in the field to check the scope.

Practice means everything in this sport, just as with every other type of firearm used in hunting. But because the handgun has a short trajectory and must be mastered at various ranges, the deer hunter needs plenty of hours punching holes in paper targets. Experienced handgunners sight-in their guns at 50 yards, but also practice at 25, 75, and 100. It's important to know exactly where the gun is hitting at every practical range. Knowing your handgun's trajectory is one thing, but holding it steadily is another. This is the big trick in shooting a handgun, because it lacks the stock of a rifle and must be held in an extended position away from the body. The best way to steady the gun, of course, is to use a rest. When practicing on

Bob Good, Chairman of the Board for the American Sportsman's Club, poses with a 30-inch Colorado mule deer that dressed out better than 230 pounds. Bob killed the huge buck with a .357 Colt Python after making a two-hour stalk. (Photo courtesy of Bob Good.)

the range, try shooting from different positions. As you become proficient, take the gun into the woods and plink at safe targets. Use trees, branches, rocks—anything you can find, to rest the gun on. If no rest is available, the sitting position in which you draw your knees up, place your elbows on your knees, and place the palm of your free hand under your shooting hand is a common stance.

A number of handgun calibers are popular for mule deer, and each has its own group of followers. The .357 Magnum is well-known, and the .41 and .44 Magnums also have advocates. It's important to use a handgun with adequate punch, and it's better to be a bit overgunned than under-gunned, provided you can handle the firearm. There are a dozen or more popular calibers, and all work effectively if you can hit the target area at a reasonable range.

An advantage of handgun hunting is the ease with which you can move about. Because the gun is holstered, your hands are free to help you climb and dodge brush, and you don't need to haul an 8- to 12-pound rifle around the hills.

Handgunning isn't for everyone, but it's a fine way to hunt a mule deer. According to statistics, it's being discovered a bit more each year by hunters who are searching for a different dimension to deer hunting.

Whether you use a rifle, handgun, muzzleloader, or bow and arrow, the bottom line is your ability to hit what you aim at. I'll repeat the sage advice of Billy Stockton. "It don't matter what you're shootin', as long as you can shoot it."

Optics

A good binocular is as important to a mule deer hunter as any other item he carries, with the exception of his rifle. Muleys often live in open country, and locating them typically requires extensive glassing. Binoculars are the best way to fulfill that requirement.

In the case of long-range glassing, a spotting scope is ideal for picking out specks in the distance and transforming them into living, breathing deer. Far too few mule deer hunters use a spotting scope.

Binoculars, scopes, and spotting scopes are all designed to do one thing: magnify your view so you can locate animals and see details. The degree of magnification depends on the hunter's preferences and the type of country he's hunting.

Anti-hunters have said that hunting is too modernized and that sophisticated gear puts animals at a disadvantage. Rifle scopes have been particularly criticized. People who have never fired a rifle think the scope is a guaranteed assist in killing, that all one needs to do is place the crosshairs on the target and the animal is had. Such critics aren't aware that it's easier to miss the target with a scope than with iron sights. Because a scope magnifies, it's much more difficult to draw a steady bead. The higher the magnification, the more difficult it is to hold the rifle steady on target.

Optical equipment is an essential part of every serious hunter's list of needs. Without good binoculars and a reliable scope, he is handicapped. When hunting mule deer country, much more game is out of sight or partially obscured than in view. It's the partially obscured and distant animals that are made recognizable with optical systems. Some animals cannot be seen with the unaided eye, try as you might. There simply is no reason to hunt without binoculars.

Binoculars come in a wide variety of models, sizes, and capabilities. It's easy to be confused over the type that best fits your needs because of the assortment made available by a number of manufacturers, both domestic and abroad.

When selecting binoculars, do not let low prices be your guide. As in every other aspect of the business world, you get what you pay for. Buy the best glasses you can afford, and buy only from reputable firms that have been manufacturing binoculars for years. Stay away from discount models offered by mail-order houses or wholesalers. If you want to buy a low-priced binocular, try it first. Ask permission to take it outside where you can test it at various distances. If possible, test it in the late afternoon when light is low to simulate actual hunting conditions. Look for good resolution, ease of focus, and light-gathering capabilities. Never buy a cheap binocular from a mail-order catalog; you won't be able to test it and you might be hassled about getting your money back.

Binoculars are a "must" item for serious deer hunters.

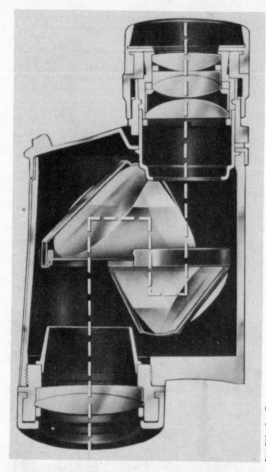

Cutaway view shows inside workings of typical binocular Porro prism. (*Photo courtesy of Bushnell Optical Co.*)

Binoculars can make or break your hunt, so pay attention to them. You don't want to be on a dream hunt and have it spoiled because your binoculars were inadequate.

The basic binocular has two prismatic-erecting telescopes that appear as one when placed to the eyes. Prisms rather than erector lenses are used to place the image into normal viewing position. Porro prisms are most common in binoculars and account for the offset profile of many binocular systems. The roof prism has been used rather than Porro in newer models to eliminate the offset housing, which decreases bulk and weight in the binocular, and also creates a new design.

The twin binocular tubes are connected by a hinge so they can be adjusted to fit different eyes. Some binoculars are focused by turning the eye-pieces on each cylinder separately, or by a single wheel between the two barrels. Bushnell introduced the Insta-Focus system a couple of years back, which gets my vote as being the most practical design for hunting. By pressing a flat lever between the tubes, you can adjust the focus instantly. This is superb for cold-weather hunting since you can focus while wearing heavy gloves or mittens, and only one hand is necessary to make the adjustment.

Most binoculars have some sort of eyepiece device to allow viewers with eyeglasses to be able to look squarely into the tubes. The best design is a simple rubber ring that can be rolled in or out depending on the need.

Binoculars are classified by two sets of figures, as in 7×35, 6×30, etc. The first figure means magnifying power, the second refers to diameter of the objective lens in millimeters. The objective lens is the one farthest from the eye, in front of the barrel. The rear lens closest to the eye is the ocular lens.

"Relative brightness," which is important to the hunter, is the relationship of power to the diameter of the objective lens, and is figured this way: Divide the diameter of the objective lens by the power, square the result, and you have relative brightness. For example, a 7×35 would have a relative brightness of 25. You get this by dividing 7 into 35, which equals 5, and 5 squared is 25. You have the same relative brightness with 6×30's and 8×40's, since all come to 5 when divided, with a result of 25 when squared. A 7×50, for example, would divide out to 7.1 and have a relative brightness of 50.4 Obviously, this binocular has much better light-gathering power in poor light, but this advantage is offset by excessive weight and bulk.

Are you thoroughly confused? Don't worry about technicalities when buying binoculars. If you're typical, you'll select the popular 7×35, which seems to be the front-runner. If you're doing a lot of very long-range glassing, you might move up to 8-, 9-, or 10-power glasses. These are being seen with more frequency in the West.

I use Bushnell Compact 7×26's when I'm in for a long hike. These little binoculars are of excellent resolution, bulk, and weight. I'm amazed at the number of hunters using these binoculars. Once, five of us gathered to talk, including two strangers. All five of us had Compacts hanging around our necks.

For more power, I use Bushnell's Explorer 10×50. I like it when on short walks or riding horseback. In my opinion, it compares well with much higher priced European-made binoculars.

If you can afford them, German-made binoculars are beautifully made instruments, and well worth the cost. Japan also produces excellent glasses, and in fact manufactures most popular brands.

You'll notice that the higher the magnification in the binoculars you're using, the more the view wavers. The binocular isn't causing the waver, it just details the object more clearly and you see the movement better. To eliminate long-range distortion when you're trying to get as much detail as possible, rest the binoculars on something solid, such as a fence post, rock, tree limb, or anything else that's stationary. If nothing is close by, sit down, draw your knees up to your chest, and rest your elbows on your knees.

Many mule deer hunters use binoculars incorrectly. Countless animals are overlooked each year because the person doing the glassing didn't know what he was looking for, or if he did, he didn't know where or how to look.

From a distance, the mule deer's white rump is the most obvious thing to look for. If snow covers the ground, brown or gray shapes are clues to deer. When glassing a distant area, don't let your eyes wander across the field of view randomly. Force yourself to focus on every square yard of country. Don't look for a full body if there is brush. Look for a *part* of the body, a horizontal form that doesn't fit. If something seems to move, hold your focus on that spot to identify what caused the movement. If brushy

Bushnell Compact binoculars— one of the most popular models in mule deer country. They're light, fit in a pocket, and have good resolution. (*Photo courtesy of Bushnell Optical Co.*)

draws or sparse timber are in sight, penetrate into the vegetation and look for deer in, alongside, and behind bushes and trees. You must look *into* the brush. Remember, the world is multi-dimensional, not a flat movie screen. Visually penetrate into every square foot of cover that might hold a deer, every little suspicious nook and cranny.

One of the most sensational "finds" I ever witnessed with binoculars occurred during a 1980 mule deer hunt in Colorado. I was riding in a vehicle with Bob Good, chairman of the board for the American Sportsman's Club, when Bob made a startling announcement after glassing a brushy basin with his binoculars. We had been stopping every half mile, passing time while heading back to camp after the morning hunt.

"I see a big buck," Bob exclaimed.

"Bull!" I countered.

"No, buck," was Bob's answer. "No kidding. He's a dandy."

I got out of the truck, glassed the spot that Bob pointed out, and was astonished to see a nice buck bedded in a clump of brush. Just enough sunlight was reflecting off his antlers to give him away. I conservatively estimated the buck to be 800 yards away, and I wouldn't be surprised if it had been 1,000. Even more amazing is that Bob glassed the buck through a semi-clean windshield. I made a stalk and killed the buck, all because of superb glassing by a person who obviously knew how to use binoculars.

I can't recall how many times binoculars have helped me spot deer that would have otherwise gone unseen. The most memorable incident occurred, of all places, along a busy Utah highway during deer season. I was driving in a line of traffic and saw a little draw off the highway with a strand of quaking aspen in full leaf. Most aspens had dropped their leaves, but this group of trees had lovely golden-orange foliage. I pulled off the road to take a picture of the pretty autumn scene.

After exposing a few frames of film, I walked back to the car, but something told me to look the area over closely. It was just "right" for mule deer, having all the ingredients of good deer cover. With binoculars I glassed the draw and slopes around it, and suddenly spotted a deer in a small clump of mountain maple. It was bedded, and my 10×50's showed it to be a nice buck. The deer was oblivious to traffic, and appeared to be watching the cars go by. The buck looked at me, but wasn't alarmed because of the busy world around me. I got back in my car, drove a full mile up the road before finding another pull-off, and made a stalk behind the buck. An hour later, I jumped the deer from his bed and killed him with my first shot.

Rifle scopes came into being in the 1930's but it took several years before they were accepted by the hunting public. Many sportsmen were distrustful of them, and many claimed you couldn't find a deer quickly enough if he was running or in timber. Others just didn't think it was "right" to hunt with them. I was a member of all those groups, and settled on a Winchester Model .30/30 carbine for my first deer rifle. In the circle of people I hunted with, it was unacceptable to use a scope-sighted rifle.

I'm happy to say those days are gone forever. Scopes are here to stay, and I read somewhere that 95 percent of Western hunters use scope-sighted firearms.

The basic rifle scope consists of an objective lens system in the front end of the tube, an ocular lens system at the rear, and an erecting lens in between the two. The objective lens gathers an upside-down image, the erecting lens returns the image to normal, and the ocular lens magnifies it. A reticule, whether it is a crosshair, dot, post, or whatever, is constructed

Bushnell ScopeChief. Riflescopes			
ScopeChief VI with Bullet Drop Compensator (BDC) and Multi-X® (MX) Reticle	MODEL #	Magnification	Reticle
	70-3002	3x-9x 40mm	MX/BDC
	70-2002		Multi-X only
	70-3580	2.5x-8x 32mm	MX/BDC
	70-2580		Multi-X only
	70-3545	1.5x-4.5x 20mm	MX/BDC
	70-2545		Multi-X only
	70-3001	4x 32mm	MX/BDC
	70-2001		Multi-X only

A variety of rifle scopes. *(Photo courtesy of Bushnell Optical Co.)*

in the tube so it can be adjusted to the desires of the shooter. A screw on top of the tube controls elevation, while one on the side adjusts windage.

Scopes are classified by "power," which is usually from 2× up to 20× or more. The smaller magnifications of 2× and 3× are generally used for .22's and handguns, while 4× up to 12× are common for deer. The higher magnifications are used for precision bench-rest shooting and by varmint hunters. Variable scopes that zoom from a low magnification to a higher one are very popular these days, allowing the hunter several options. The Leupold Vari-X 3×-9× and Bushnell Scopechief 3×-9× IV are good examples. Some scopes have an extra-wide field of view, such as Redfield's Widefield models.

Like binoculars, scopes with higher magnifications tend to waver more, but it's only because the view is enlarged and movement of the scope makes the object seem to wiggle around more. Shooters who use variable scopes normally look for detail on the quarry with higher magnifications and shoot with lower power.

I use a Weaver 4× scope with a 2-minute dot exclusively. Because the magnification is low, I have a wider field of view, which is precisely what I want when I'm hunting in quaking aspens, oak brush, or evergreen timber. When a deer is moving away quickly, I don't want to search for him. I want to see him in my scope the moment the rifle touches my shoulder. Higher magnification restricts the field of view in proportion to the power being used.

Because the 4× scope may not give me the detail I want on a buck, I use my binoculars as required. Once I make a decision to shoot, I let the binoculars slip down on their strap and make my shot.

If a deer flushes from cover and runs quickly, I never use binoculars, because there's often not enough time. I snap the rifle up, make a quick judgment, and shoot if the deer is what I'm looking for.

Many skilled hunters keep both eyes open when they use a scope. I've tried this but find it uncomfortable, so I use one eye. Since I'm so familiar with my scope, I can snap it up and instinctively spot a moving object.

Some scopes allow you to estimate distances by using the reticule as a constant indicator. If you know an object is a certain size and you know how big an area the dot covers up, you can judge the distance and elevate your sights accordingly. Some scopes have horizontal lines that allow you to estimate range by sizing up the quarry between the lines. Bushnell makes a scope with a Bullet Drop Compensator which assists in determining bullet fall and making correct allowances.

Some scopes are specially coated, and others have superior light-gathering capabilities. Try them out before you buy.

By far the biggest headache with a scope is its vulnerability to moisture. Rain and snow are the biggest enemies of a scope, and can turn a long-awaited hunt into a comedy of errors. I recall a moose hunt in Newfoundland many years ago that would have been a challenge for any scope on the market. I killed a moose early in the hunt, but a hurricane and never-ending rain made it a nightmare for my companions. One hunter had running shots at two different bulls, but each time his scope was miserably fogged. He never killed a moose.

Riding horseback through snowy timber can also render your scope useless, since the snow most assuredly finds its way into the scabbard and onto the rear lens.

The answer to these woes is a scope cap that fits over the lenses and protects them from moisture. Until I started using lens caps, I used several pounds of napkins, paper towels, and toilet tissue wiping my scope clean.

My favorite cap is the spring-loaded scope cover manufactured by Butler Creek Co. of Jackson, Wyoming. With a quick flip of your thumb the cover swings wide on a hinge and you're ready to shoot. If it's not available at your local dealers, write to Butler Creek at Box GG, Jackson, WY 83001. Since there are about 500 models of scopes in existence, tell them the brand and model you're using.

Some hunters like the option of having both scope *and* iron sights. If the scope is bumped hard or fogs, the iron sights can be used instead. Scope mounts are available that elevate the scope high enough to see the sights beneath. Other mounts swing off to the side on demand.

If you drop your rifle or have any reason to believe the scope's point of aim has been disturbed, by all means test fire your rifle just to be sure. Never take chances on your scope being on if you suspect it isn't. When you're hunting big game you *must* have confidence in your rifle's ability to shoot accurately. Don't be one of those unfortunate hunters who whimpers "my scope must be off" after missing a shot at a grand buck, or any buck for that matter.

If you're camped in game country and don't want to fire a shot, you can quickly bore-sight your scope to see if it's basically on target.

To do this, remove the bolt so you can look down the bore, and set a target at the distance at which you've sighted in the rifle. Carefully rest the rifle on a stationary surface, aim the bore at the target, and very carefully raise your eye to the scope to see if the scope is pointed at the target. If it is, the scope alignment is probably O.K., although this test is not as accurate as you'd want. If the bore and scope don't match, don't worry about disturbing game – resight the rifle. If people in camp object, head for the hills and do it where you won't bother the hunters. But do it, by all means.

If you're using a lever action or auto-loader, or any model where you can't look down the bore, forget bore sighting unless you've brought along a bore-scope or collimator that slips onto the muzzle.

If you're flying from home to hunt in the West, fire your rifle on a range before heading out to deer camp. Vibrations from jetliners could loosen the screws on your scope and cause it to perform inaccurately. A long vehicle ride might also adversely affect a scope.

Whenever you're sighting in a scoped rifle, make it easy on yourself and your ammo supply by knowing how to manipulate the elevation and windage knobs. If you're like most hunters, you say something like, "Let's see, I think four clicks equal 1 inch, or is it eight clicks?" Keep the manual that comes with the scope.

Another word of advice. Always sight in your scope personally. Don't let anyone else do it for you; everyone looks through a scope differently.

When selecting a scope, buy from a reputable firm. If you're on a hunt and your scope fails, your rifle is worthless. If you're lucky, you'll discover it is deficient *before* you need to shoot it. If you discover the problem after missing a shot, you'll cuss the day you bought the scope. A waterproof, fog-resistant scope is a must if you're hunting in rainy country. In most mule deer country, balmy days are the rule, but don't count on it. I can recall many days of hunting in fog, rain, and furious blizzards. If you're hunting in blacktail country where rain is common, be sure your scope repels moisture.

Be aware that when your rifle recoils, the scope does too. It hasn't happened to me yet, but one day my scope will get me. This happens when your body is in an awkward position and you must reach high with your shoulder to aim at a deer. When you pull the trigger, if your position is wrong, the recoiling scope zaps you around the eye, usually making a laceration around the eyebrow. If your position is *really* wrong, it socks you in the nose and bursts capillaries within, causing red corpuscles to spill on your clothes. Unless you want to join the fraternity of hunters who have been "bit" by their scopes, get your shoulder squarely behind the rifle stock and don't take shots from unwieldy positions. Very elementary advice, I know, but many skilled hunters join the fraternity every year. It goes without saying, too, that rifles with stronger recoil bite you harder.

Spotting scopes are simply telescopes used for hunting. Because they take a beating, spotting scopes are usually constructed so they can be handled roughly.

The weight and bulk of a spotting scope precludes carrying it long distances, although serious trophy hunters use one extensively. These scopes are used to scan far-off landscape for deer, and to show antlers in detail.

Because of their high magnification, spotting scopes must be used on a tripod or a mount that clamps to your vehicle's window. They can also be rested on the ground, but an elevated object such as a boulder or tree limb lets you look with more ease.

The magnification of spotting scopes range from 15× to 65×, with 20× being the most popular. The higher magnifications pose problems during hot days because of heat waves. This is a common problem in the West, especially in open country where rocks and shale reflect heat.

I like Bushnell's Trophy 16×-36× model because of its zoom capabilities as well as the protective rubber coating. The thick rubber coat protects it well when traveling horseback.

Take care when selecting optical equipment for hunting. It's mighty essential in the big open spaces of the West. You're doing yourself a big favor by purchasing quality material and learning to use it well.

The Trophy spotting scope by Bushnell has a rugged rubber exterior to withstand hard-knocks. They're especially good for horseback hunting. (Photo courtesy of Bushnell Optical Co.)

Scouting Deer Country

Every hunter worth his salt knows that scouting is an important prelude to successful mule deer hunting, but surprisingly few do it correctly — or at all. In the hunting world, scouting could be defined as a search for deer sign which ultimately leads the hunter to his quarry. Scouting can be done long before the deer season, just before the season, or during the season, depending on the time, enthusiasm, and skills of the hunter. For the most part, modern-day scouting is accomplished a day or two before opening day, if at all, and is generally part of a hunting trip rather than a separate trip made exclusively to look for deer sign.

Because we live in a fast world and time is all too precious, many hunters do not scout at all beforehand, but simply trust that the area they're planning to hunt harbors deer. Such trust is O.K. if you're hunting a familiar place that consistently produces game, but much hunting time can be lost by making a trip to a strange area and finding few deer, only to have to move somewhere else.

Skillful hunters who take the sport seriously scout well in advance of the season, ensuring that opening day will be more than an exercise in futility. They want to know they'll be in a good spot when the moment of truth rolls around, so they spend extra time checking many areas prior to the season, looking for the signs that spell success.

Kirt Darner, who I mentioned in the chapter on trophy hunting, is one of the super scouters of our time. Darner, who lives in southwest Colorado, has the distinguished honor of having seven mule deer in the Boone and Crockett book.

Checking a heavily used trail for sign. Leaves may mask or prevent imprints.

How does he do it? Scouting is the key to his incredible success. He spends all his off-time looking for big buck sign in the summer and early fall. He rides horseback through new country, always looking for clues of deer. He talks to a lot of people as he searches for tidbits of information that might lead to a big buck. Game wardens, road surveyors, foresters, and sheepherders are all good contacts who see deer during their regular course of work. Of them all, Darner likes to query sheepherders, since these men live in the mountains practically year round and are as intimate with game country as anyone.

Of course, most hunters aren't as dedicated as Kirt Darner, but he is a good example of a hunter who goes the extra mile to help his odds when deer season arrives. Too, Darner looks for big bucks exclusively, and spends more time scouting for that reason. Average hunters scout simply to find deer sign, and if a big buck is in the country, so much the better.

Pre-season scouting is based on the premise that deer will be in the same area when hunting season arrives. This may or may not be true, depending on the period of time the scouting is done before the season, and the weather conditions. Mule deer remain on a "home" range or territory, and normally don't move out unless disturbed by human intrusion or heavy snow that signals winter.

Not long ago I scouted my favorite deer country in Utah during late summer and found typical sign—plenty of deer and big buck tracks as well. On the day before the opener of hunting season, I drove to the spot and was appalled to see an oil rig sitting on my favorite ridge. A new road was scalped from the earth, and people were everywhere. A quick look around proved what I already had guessed. The deer were gone. Luckily, I knew another place a few miles distant, and the trip was salvaged. But had I scouted the first place later in the fall, I'd have discovered the oil rig and made other plans.

Another time I planned a hunt in an area that had always been good to me. It was about at 8,500 feet, with extensive quaking aspen forests on the ridgetops and scrub oaks on the sidehills. It had snowed a week before the hunt, but I had no idea how much snow had fallen in the area I wanted to hunt. I found out soon after leaving the pavement. The higher we climbed, the more snow we ran in to. Finally, when we reached our destination, 18 inches of snow layered the gound. Two days of hard hunting produced nothing but a few elk tracks. The deer had pulled off for lower county. Again, some scouting or at least inquiry with people familiar with the area would have prevented the fruitless trip.

If hunting pressure is heavy, scouting might be a waste of time, since competing hunters might beat you to places that you worked hard to find. This shouldn't discourage scouting though, because competition presents a special challenge. If you can find areas of heavy deer use, you might very well tag your buck under the noses of other hunters. If anything, heavy hunter pressure should stimulate your desire to scout. You need all the advantage you can get when the woods are full of hunters.

Sometimes the presence of other hunters stymies all the extra effort you've put into scouting, but that's part of the game. It's particularly frustrating when you've found heavy deer sign just before deer season, only to discover someone's tent or camp trailer parked smack in the area you want to hunt. Or to locate a well-used deer trail, only to have a pickup full of road hunters drive all around the area when you're trying to watch the trail. Such is the way of modern hunting. The only other option is to push back away from the beaten path.

It's one thing to scout deer country, but quite another to *interpret* what you're finding and translate it into useful information. How old are those tracks or groups of droppings? Are those larger tracks made by big does or bucks? How about those rubbed saplings you've been seeing, and the shrubs that have been browsed? These are some of the things to look for when scouting, and unless you know what they mean, you might be wasting your time.

Let's start with tracks. A worn-out saying in deer camp says something like "you can't eat tracks," but tracks betray deer unless the critters have devised a way of walking without touching the ground.

Some types of cover show tracks plainly, others do not. Mule deer walking in sagebrush or through pinyon-junipers, for example, make obvious tracks in the dusty soil, but deer walking across a quaking aspen forest littered with dead leaves or a lodgepole forest covered with pine needles do not. The absence of tracks, therefore, means little in some areas because deer aren't leaving them behind. The answer is to know *where* to look for tracks. The wet edges of waterholes, trails where the leaves are worn away, sidehills where the wind has blown away forest litter—these are the places to look.

The mere presence of tracks doesn't mean mule deer are in the general area. What it means is that a deer was occupying the airspace over the track. The next step is to determine the freshness of the imprint.

Lois Zumbo checks four-wing saltbush plant, a favorite mule deer forage species, for signs of recent browsing.

Tracks with sharp, distinct edges are generally fresh, made within the last 24 hours, but there are places where you can be fooled. Tracks imprinted into dusty soil during perfectly calm, dry days with no dew or frost may remain perfectly intact. As soon as a breeze stirs, however, the tracks tend to lose their crispness. The sharp edges crumble a bit and appear softer.

If it rains, tracks are either completely washed out, depending on the intensity of the rain, or take on a dull look. If sharp, well-defined tracks are located after a rain, they obviously were made after the rainstorm.

When tracks have forest litter such as bits of leaves and tiny twigs in them, they are probably older than the last good windstorm, since wind probably blew the particles in the tracks.

Snow is the best indicator of fresh tracks, but it's extremely easy to be fooled. Newly fallen snow is ideal, because every track is fresh, but snow that is days or weeks old may pose problems. A light layer of powder snow quickly dates tracks because the fluffy snow blows readily or crumbles into tracks. A heavy layer of powder snow is difficult to figure because when a deer lifts its leg from the ground the snow falls back into the depression, completely covering the foot print. Your only clue is a line of tracks, and sometimes it's impossible to tell which way the animal is going unless you find an imprint. In most cases, however, the sharp points of the hooves are distinctive enough in the print to tell which direction the deer is moving.

When winter days are warm, the tracks melt and widen. As the sun goes down, they freeze over again. This thawing and freezing wipes the ground clean each day, so new tracks will be obvious. If a track is newly imprinted on top of crusted snow, it was made since the snow last melted.

Once you've determined the freshness of tracks, you can get an idea of how many deer are using an area. Remember, however, that a relatively small herd of deer can make a lot of tracks when they're concentrated in feeding areas or around water.

The next step is to decipher what the deer were doing when they made the tracks, since that information helps lead you to where the deer are *now*, or tomorrow or whenever the season opens.

Tracks that meander about indicate a place where deer feed. That area, and areas like it, are good places to start looking during the season. If tracks are lined out straight, deer may be moving to water, bedding, or feeding areas. That might be a good place to try an ambush later on if there are enough fresh tracks to warrant your attention.

If you can figure why deer are heading in a certain direction and when they were traveling, you might be able to roughly estimate where feeding and bedding areas are. If you know you're walking toward a bedding area, you can adjust your technique accordingly. You hunt very slowly, looking for a stationary patch of fur or an eyeball that means bedded deer. If you know you're working your way into feeding areas and the time of day is correct for deer to be foraging, you can expect to see horizontal shapes off the ground or slight twitches that suggest a tail, antler, or moving head.

Another important aspect of scouting is to determine if any big bucks are in the area, if you're seeking a trophy. That brings us to two questions: How do you tell a buck from a doe track? How do you tell if a buck is big by the size of its track?

The answer to the latter question is simple—when you see the track of a big buck, there's no mistaking it. Mule deer bucks are much larger than

Bucks are preoccupied during the rut, a fact that may allow you to stalk to within a few yards.

does, and there's little similarity in size. But how about a medium-sized buck that isn't yet a heavyweight? Their tracks are similar to does, and there's no sure-fire way to tell the difference between the two, although a lot of expert writers and hunters think they can.

A deer hunter once told me that the presence of dewclaw tracks behind the hooves was a sure-fire tip that the deer was a buck. Horsefeathers! Both sexes have dewclaws, and both imprint them if the ground is soft enough to allow the deer's foot to sink a bit deeper than usual. The two small dewclaws behind the hooves are vestigial remains of what scientists believe was at one time a five-toed foot.

Another tale claims that bucks drag their feet more obviously than does, which is another misconception. Both drag their feet equally, though a big heavy buck might leave a deeper drag. Even so, it would be hard to determine in the wild.

Bucks are supposed to have wider hooves, or so says another story. Though scientists have shown that buck tracks might indeed be wider, the difference is in fractions of inches, and impossible to tell outdoors.

One of the best indicators of sexes is the number of tracks. A single, large track may indicate a lone buck; two or three large tracks may mean two or three bucks. Tracks of mixed sizes probably suggest a family unit made up of does, fawns, and very often one yearling spike, forked horn, or small three- or four-point buck.

The presence of tracks in country that deer share with antelope and domestic sheep can pose a puzzle, because inexperienced hunters can easily confuse the three.

Once while hunting with a beginning hunter in Colorado, we walked across a sage flat where my companion looked up from the ground and blurted, "Lord, this place is alive with deer. There are *thousands* of tracks." And there were—domestic sheep tracks. I looked up to a hillside and said, "There's what made 'em," and pointed to a herd of woolies. My friend suddenly lost interest, muttering unintelligibly.

Sheep and antelope tracks have a more squarish shape than deer, but they're similar enough that it's easy to make a mistake if the track isn't distinctive. Fresh tracks are much easier to tell apart.

A "rub" is another sign that indicates the presence of deer, but only bucks. Again, the rub means only that a buck was in the area at a point in time, and little more. But knowing about rubs, why and when they're made helps determine the general abundance of bucks in a given piece of real estate.

In August and September, bucks remove the velvet coating that has sheathed their antlers since they began growing in the spring. The velvety covering begins shriveling and sluffing off on its own, but bucks speed up the process by vigorously rubbing their antlers on saplings, brush, branches or whatever else is available. Because big bucks have more massive antlers to rub than small bucks, the size of the rub and the tree that bears rubbing scars often indicates the relative size of the buck. A 4- or 5-inch-diameter sapling with extensive rub marks usually indicates the work of a mature buck, but that doesn't mean a big buck won't touch up his antlers on a small 1-inch sapling.

A skillful hunter who scouts new territory and sees a large number of healthy rubs knows that he's found something worth looking into. The rubs don't mean, however, that bucks will be living in the precise area where the rubs are. Since most mule deer seasons open in October, rubbed trees are several weeks old. The bucks that made them could be long gone.

This shrub was shredded and broken by a buck. It takes a strenuous effort to rub the velvet off his antlers.

A rubbed tree made by a large buck as he polished the velvet from his antlers. Sign such as this indicates bucks were in the area in August and September.

Bucks don't seem to prefer any one kind of tree to rub their antlers on, though they may have preferred areas such as ridgetops, sidehills, and valley bottoms. I've seen rubs everywhere, and if there's a common denominator, it's only that bucks pick single trees a bit away from dense thickets or tight groups of trees.

I once watched a nice three-point buck go through the rubbing routine in Wyoming. He selected a tree and simply began raising and lowering his head, polishing an antler in an up and down motion. He worked at it for 15 minutes and then abruptly walked off, feeding as he went. I walked down to the tree, and was amazed at the pressure the buck had applied to it. Bark was completely peeled off on a section 2 feet long and 4 inches across.

Another type of rub that is more meaningful to hunters indicates the immediate presence of bucks, but it occurs after hunting season in most states. In late November and early December, bucks become lovesick and seek does. This is the breeding season, and although mule deer bucks don't become as violent with each other as do whitetails or elk, they still turn into ornery beasts that want little to do with each other. As part of the breeding display, they often hook and jab their antlers into handy trees and shrubs, leaving broken branches and deep gashes in bark. Now and then two bucks square off and actually fight antler to antler, but this is a rare event. My good friend Bill McRae, a well-known Western photographer, once photographed two bucks fighting a bloody battle. Few other people have witnessed such a confrontation.

If hunting season extends into the breeding period, the ravaged brush and trees scarred by rutting bucks are good indicators of recent deer activity. To carry the observation farther, bits of bark, branches, and twigs ripped by antlers and lying on top of fresh snow means the deer might still be in the same general area. Scouting efforts that turn up this kind of evidence should make the hunter's adrenalin flow.

There is yet another kind of sign that betrays the presence of mule deer. If a deer lives in an area for any length of time, it must feed there, and in turn must void digested food. Deer droppings are in the form of pellets, and are usually in a group rather than scattered about. As in the case of tracks, pellets need to be analyzed to determine their freshness. Pellets stay intact and appear fresh for long periods.

When the weather is cold, the freshness of pellets is easy to determine. Unfrozen pellets signify they've been there only a few hours. If pellets are moist rather than dry, they're probably less than a day old. Pellets lying on top of snow are a dead giveaway that they were dropped since the snow fell. If you're of the mind to do so, you can squeeze pellets to determine their softness. Soft pellets are generally fresh, although if deposited in the shade during cool weather, they may remain soft for days.

If pellet groups are abundant, you're probably standing in a feeding area, because deer void themselves often while standing and moving about. Don't fret about lack of pellets if other deer sign is visible. I've seen many big bucks in areas where pellets were scarce. Unlike tracks, pellets are seen only randomly and you simply might not have come across any in your hunting efforts.

If anything is worse than not enough scouting, it's too much scouting. Lack of scouting before the season might leave you unprepared to hunt certain areas. But, if you mosey around too much, you stand a chance of spooking bucks out of the country. Some hunters aren't satisfied with their scouting efforts unless they *see* bucks. This is fine if the bucks aren't unduly alarmed, but it's not uncommon for them to leave a basin, drainage, ridge, or mountainside because too many humans were poking around before the season.

Once I was hunting deer with my muzzleloader in a high-country area in Utah. My wife was with me, along with a pal and his wife. We set up a tent, gathered firewood, and decided to take a walk down a logging road to look for sign. The season opened in the morning, and the area was new to us. After walking only a half mile down the old logging road we had seen three bucks, all singles, along the road. My friend and I were ecstatic, because we figured the hunt would be duck soup.

It wasn't. We hunted 2 days and never saw another buck. The three bucks we had spotted from the road apparently left for safer areas. This is not a typical reaction, but it was an example of scouting too close to opening day. I guessed that since the bucks had seen so few people in the high-country forest they lived in, they were spooked enough that they retreated deep into the mountains. In that area, it was easy to do, since the hunting unit was within the High Uinta Primitive Area, a rough and wild place with no roads and few humans.

The trick to scouting is to look for sign, interpret it correctly, leave the area without disturbing deer, and then return to hunt with a strategy formed according to what you found while scouting.

Bowhunting

Mule deer do not suffer any lack of attention from bowhunters. Every Western state offers a special bow season where the archer can enjoy his sport with no competition from gun hunters.

In most states, bow seasons are well in advance of the firearm season. In Utah, for example, bow season starts the middle of August, which creates a much different set of conditions than later in the fall when most outdoorsmen are afield. Since a number of top mule deer states open their bow seasons early, this chapter discusses some of the unique opportunities at this time of year.

Everything is unique about bowhunting. Every skill you've ever mastered when hunting mule deer with firearms must be intensely honed and polished before you can confidently pursue a muley with a bow. Not only must you teach yourself the new rules of the game, you must also learn more about the quarry you hunt, for the axiom of bowhunting is to get close. Forget about those 100- and 200-yard shots, and running shots at deer in the brush that were common when you were toting a rifle. With a bow, those opportunities are gone. You must establish a more intimate relationship with a deer. And once you accomplish that, even a tiny twig or branch in your arrow's flight path can foul the shot. Everything must be nearly perfect.

Putting it all together is part of the challenge. With a firearm you learn how to line up two sights, or place the crosshairs of a scope on a deer. Not so with a bow. Hours and hours of practice are required to consistently drive arrows into an acceptable pattern. Not only do you need to shoot accurately at a target a known distance away, but you must also learn how to judge distances to allow for arrow drop. Alas, an arrow has no wonderful ballistics. It drops quickly to the earth as gravity pulls it down, requiring the bowhunter to compensate.

For many newcomers to the sport, becoming a competent bowhunter is exciting. As each practice arrow plunges closer and closer to the bull's-eye, you slowly become a disciple of this supreme hunting challenge. And when you're stalking your first mule deer and put an arrow into its vitals, you'll become an enthusiastic member of a fine fraternity of hunters. Though you might continue to use your rifle during the gun season as most bowhunters do, you will always anticipate eagerly the special season of the year when you can pit your savvy one-on-one with a wary buck.

Bowhunting is a fast growing sport, which leads one to ponder the rationale behind its upsurge in popularity. A number of reasons make this

Dean Derby with the Pope and Young world record nontypical mule deer he killed in Western Colorado. The buck scored 246 ⁶⁄₈.

so, a primary one being the opportunity to hunt longer each year, especially in states where firearm seasons are relatively short. This is true only in states that allow two-season hunting. Some states require the hunter to make a choice between hunting either with a bow or a rifle, not both. This "either-or" philosophy has drawn heavy fire from two-season hunters and some archery organizations and manufacturers. Advocates of either-or hunting are purists of both gun and bow hunting who do not want their ranks swollen with more competition. The purist bowhunter wants to reduce the number of bowhunters by barring those who also gun-hunt from going afield with a bow. Those that hunt only with a bow claim to wound fewer animals because of a higher degree of skill with a bow. Purist gun hunters feel likewise, wanting to keep their multitudes thinned as much as possible.

Besides the opportunity to hunt longer in two-season states, perhaps the most significant reason behind the increased popularity of bowhunting is the "return to nature" attitude that pervades much of our society. Many Americans are fed up with the conveniences and easy living of modern times. We pine for the basic things, things that challenge and stimulate us. Bowhunting is the most primitive means of hunting allowed by our rules (blowguns and slingshots are not yet legal), and it attracts people who want to do it the hard way. Bowhunting is without question the hardest way to hunt.

To hunt mule deer successfully with a bow, one must become an expert at two things: archery equipment and mule deer. Let's take them one at a time.

All of us know that primitive man used bow and arrow extensively to harvest game. Though the bows and arrows were roughly designed, they got the job done.

In the early 1900's, an event occurred that may have led to the bowhunting movement as we know it. On August 29, 1911, an emaciated Indian by the name of Ishi wandered into Oroville, California, practically dead from exposure and starvation. He was the last living Indian of the now-extinct Yana tribe, and was nurtured back to health by a number of concerned and interested people, including Dr. Saxton Pope, a man who took a great deal of interest in Ishi's way of living, especially hunting with a bow. Ishi taught Dr. Pope about bowhunting, and after the Indian died of tuberculosis, Pope continued his interest in archery. He not only became a highly skilled bowhunter, but he made archery tackle, and later

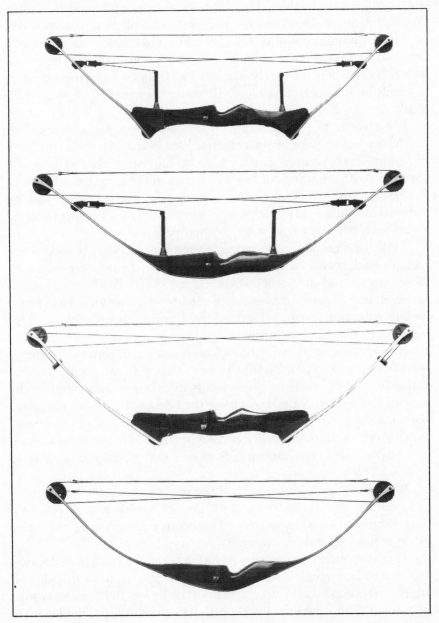

Various compound bows used by modern bowhunters. *(Photo courtesy of the Browning Co.)*

was considered to be the father of American bowhunting. With Arthur Young and others, Pope launched the sport of taking game with an arrow.

Later, during the World War II era, Howard Hill intrigued America with his unsurpassed trick shooting expertise and hunts for dangerous game. Because of his efforts, bowhunting was infused with renewed vigor. Curious hunters began seeing for themselves what the bow and arrow could do.

But it was in the 1950's and 1960's that bowhunting caught fire and took off. Many factors were responsible, but Fred Bear was perhaps the force that propelled bowhunting to new heights. Tall, affable Bear attracted the attention of the hunting public with movies and magazine articles about his bowhunting adventures around the world. I can remember looking forward to seeing Fred's articles, wondering when he was going to take a polar bear, grizzly, or tiger with his amazing bow.

In the next decade, bowhunting interest soared. Archery tackle business thrived, with new manufacturers entering the industry with new bows, arrows, and all sorts of gadgets and accessories. Bowhunting became so popular that game officials established separate seasons. Here was a way to provide an expanded recreational hunting opportunity to a large segment of America's sportsmen.

Archery tackle itself went through an evolution, or perhaps revolution would be a better word. Recurve bows, which were the mainstay of the industry until the early 1970's, suddenly lost their popularity when the strange looking compound bows made their debut. The switch happened so quickly that in the course of about 5 years more than 90 percent of America's bowhunters switched to compounds. The recurve bow was destined to become a faded memory. They were sold at garage sales, given to younger brothers, or stored in the attic.

Wooden arrows went a similar direction; few are used today. Aluminum arrows are now by far the top choice of bowhunters. Accessories, such as bow sights, bow quivers, and others are common items in sporting goods stores and archery catalogs.

The compound bow deserves attention because it has a special appeal to hunters. Featuring a system of wheels and cables, it mechanically and ingeniously decreases the draw weight of the bow at full draw from 30 to 50 percent. This means the hunter can draw the string and hold it at anchor position without needing biceps like a professional boxer. To illustrate, a 50-pound-pull recurve bow requires 50 pounds of finger pressure to pull the string back and hold it at full draw. A 50-pound-pull compound bow, however, requires 50 pounds of draw only about halfway back. After that, the mechanical advantage gained through the wheels and cables allows the string to be drawn and held at anchor position with from 25 to 35 pounds of pressure. As a result, the hunter can hold the bow at full draw comfortably for a longer period, allowing a more accurate shot at the quarry.

Because of the ease in shooting, becoming a skilled bowman with a compound bow is easier than with a recurve. And as arrows strike close to the bull's-eye, beginners see the results of practicing and become enthusiastic about the sport.

Compounds are said to shoot arrows much faster than recurves of equal draw weight, but tests show the difference isn't great enough to be significant. Recurves are less expensive than compounds, and require less maintenance. Another disadvantage of the compound is its nasty habit of snagging easily when the hunter is moving through brush. The cables and wheels have a way of catching every branch in the area.

Compound bows are not a panacea to hunters who shoot poorly, but compounds are easier to shoot accurately. Compounds come in a number of different models and styles. Before buying one, get advice from a bow-hunting friend or talk to your local archery dealer.

Once you've decided on a bow, be it a compound or a recurve, you must then make another purchase, which is the most important item of your bowhunting equipment—arrows. Make no mistake about it, the best-shooting bow in the world won't be worth a darn if the arrow isn't engineered to shoot straight. The arrow has four basic parts: head, shaft, fletching, and nock. Bowhunters usually concern themselves with the head and shaft, but every part must function properly for the arrow to fly true. Aluminum arrows are the hands-down choice of bowhunters. About 90 percent use them. The rest use fiberglass, and a few stubbornly stick to wooden shafts. Aluminum is far superior to all others. It's more accurate, tougher, waterproof, and available in many sizes. If you're confused by the array of sizes, talk to your archery dealer or refer to an arrow selection chart in sporting goods stores.

The days of feather fletching are about gone, too. Most hunters use plastic fletching because it is more durable, and waterproof.

There is much room for discussion about broadheads, but everyone agrees on one aspect: they must be sharp—sharp enough to shave with.

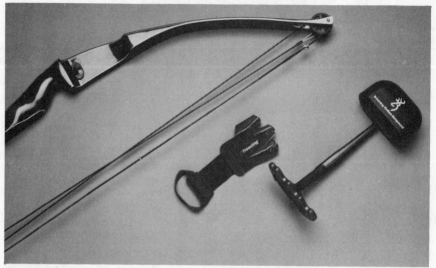

Bow quiver and finger tabs are two important accessories for bowhunters. *(Photo courtesy of Browning Co.)*

For mule deer, broadheads with at least three edges are popular, as are heads with razor inserts. Sharpening broadheads is a difficult and tedious task. Most hunters prefer factory-sharpened heads that don't require additional sharpening or touch-up. Arrows normally come in cardboard boxes with separators. Keep them there, they make good storage containers. *Never* leave sharp broadheads where children can reach them, or where you or another adult can accidentally get hurt with them.

Once you've settled on a bow and arrows, the next items required are an armguard to protect your arm from the sharp slap of the released bowstring, a finger glove to protect fingers from bowstring snap, and a quiver to hold arrows. Quivers come in three styles, a quiver that attaches to the bow itself, a hip quiver that can be worn on a belt, and a quiver that is carried on a sling across the shoulder. The bow quiver is the most popular. The shoulder quiver is fast disappearing from the scene. Arrows are hard to reach from it, they rattle together noisily, and they dull each other by constant wearing and abrasion.

Other accessories are available such as bowsights, rangefinders, stabilizers, bowstring silencers, and more. Once you've learned the fundamentals of archery you can add to your equipment.

With proper equipment, your next step is to learn how to use it. The best way is to enlist a friend to teach you the basics, or join an archery club or bowhunting organization.

When you understand the basic principles of shooting, don't stop just because you can loose an arrow and hit a target reasonably well. Practice. And practice some more. You owe it to your quarry to be able to hit a vital area and kill humanely. Don't be satisfied with shooting at known-distance targets all the time. Vary the range, and shoot from different positions to emulate real hunting conditions. Shoot from a kneeling position, a half-crouch position, a sitting position, until you can quickly assume any position and hit the target consistently.

Studies show that most bowhunters shoot deer at distances 30 yards or less. Concentrate your efforts at this range, but practice shooting at longer distances out to 60 yards.

Some friends of mine have a unique practicing session during the weeks prior to deer season. They walk through a relatively open wooded area and shoot target arrows at various objects such as stumps, a clump of grass, and trees. They also shoot down on targets from elevated hillsides, and between tree branches at targets beyond, trying to simulate actual shots they'd get while hunting. This is fine practice, because the distances and angles to targets are never the same.

As deer season approaches, step up your practice. An hour every day is not too much.

Because you need to get close to your quarry, you must take every precaution to remain unnoticed. That means blending in well with the surroundings. If your bow is brightly colored, camouflage it with commercial camo tape, bow-socks, or dull-color camo paint. Likewise with arrows, but if they're painted, allow the fletching to remain colorful so you can see the arrow in flight and find it afterwards.

Camouflage clothing is essential. Trousers, a shirt or jacket, and hat should be dull or camo colored. And don't forget hands and face. Gloves cover up the hands nicely; you can color your face with camo paints, chalks, and crayons, but I prefer a simple face mask with eye holes because it's not as messy and keeps bugs away from my face at the same time. Murry Burnham, the famous game call manufacturer, let me use one of his face masks while hunting turkeys in Texas. To me, it's the perfect answer to hiding the human face, which incidentally, is usually the part of the anatomy that catches a deer's attention first.

When bowhunting for mule deer, your best chances for a shot are when the animals are up and about. Trying to get an arrow into a deer bedded in thick cover is well nigh impossible. That being the case, you must be in the hunting area at the hint of dawn. If you're hunting from a stand or blind, all the more reason to be in place early.

If you're a stand hunter, you watch a place where deer are traveling, feeding, or watering. Mule deer don't use trails as much as whitetails, but in dense timber or brush they follow trails repeatedly. If sign is heavy, make your stand near a trail, but be sure you have plenty of room to thread an arrow through the trees. If you're going to construct a tree stand, do it well before bow season so deer become accustomed to it. When building it, try to determine the direction of the prevailing wind and put up your stand accordingly. Since most Western bow seasons are early in the fall, plenty of leaves should be on the trees to provide a screen. If you're comfortably in place in your stand, everything nicely camouflaged, and a freak breeze comes up and blows your scent toward the area you're watching, you might carry a small bottle of scent to mask your odor. I always use Burnham Brothers deer scent if I'm trying to sneak up on deer or if I'm in a stand and the wind changes suddenly.

If a mule deer approaches and you want a shot at it, move slowly. *Wait* until the deer drops its head or looks away before slowly raising your bow. Mule deer have remarkable vision and hearing, so you need to be ever so careful. If you get a shot, concentrate hard on the arrow in flight, since it's important to determine immediately if you hit or missed. A deer often jumps when it hears the arrow swish by or hears the bowstring twang. Deer also jump, lurch, or stagger when struck by an arrow, and many times it's difficult to tell if the arrow hit, even when it's driven into the vitals.

The first deer I killed with a bow gave no indication of a hit, or so I thought at the time. I was stillhunting in a glade of quaking aspens when a big lone doe appeared and began walking toward me. Does were legal, we needed meat badly, and deer herds were overpopulated, so I decided to take the doe rather than wait for a chance at a buck. I froze in my tracks and waited for the deer to walk closer. There was an opening in front of her, and I decided to make my shot when she walked into the open spot. She dropped her head just before she walked into the opening, giving me the chance to raise the bow and draw the string. I let the arrow fly from the Bear recurve bow and watched it go. The reaction of the deer was so swift and unexpected I wasn't sure if the arrow hit or not. I thought I saw the orange fletching disappear into her chest, but I wasn't sure she hadn't merely jumped at the twang of the bowstring.

She ran off into a thicket and I listened to her go, but suddenly the noise of her running stopped abruptly. I assumed she hit soft ground and continued on her way, unencumbered by brush.

I walked over to pick up my arrow, but it wasn't anywhere to be seen. Getting down on all fours, I looked for blood. If the arrow was gone, it must have stayed with the doe.

A tiny spot of blood as big as a BB told me everything I wanted to know. The deer was indeed hit. I got to my feet, walked in the direction she ran, but could find no more blood, and the aspen leaves were so deep it was difficult to see where she fled. I walked no more than 70 yards when

Max Stewart of Vernal, Utah, waits on a tree stand for a buck to walk by. Yes—you see correctly—Max uses a long bow for hunting.

Glassing is a big part of bow-hunting. Once the quarry is spotted, a stalk can be made. *(Photo courtesy of Rich LaRocco.)*

I found her dead in a little clump of trees. When I field-dressed her, I found that the arrow clipped the top of her heart and had penetrated completely through her body. I still hadn't found the arrow, and returned to the place where she stood when I shot. Finally I saw just a tiny part of the fletching under the leaves. The arrow had almost completely buried itself in the leaves.

I was stymied because the heartshot deer hadn't left a bloodtrail, but more experienced bowhunters told me that occasionally a deer struck in the vitals bleeds internally and suddenly falls to the ground dead. My doe mule deer had done exactly that. Even though an arrow kills by severing blood vessels and causing hemorrhage, external bleeding is not always the case.

Stillhunting for mule deer is perhaps the most popular technique. Bowhunters look for feeding deer, and try to approach unseen or work into a position so the feeding deer drifts naturally toward the hunter.

Dean Derby killed the world record nontypical mule deer by still-hunting in western Colorado. The huge buck, which is No.1 in the Pope and Young record book, was walking along a sidehill feeding when Dean first spotted him. Because the underbrush was noisy, he couldn't get close to the buck, so Dean made a circle and worked his way over to the sidehill well in front of the buck. Since the deer was walking on a trail, Dean located a bush that offered concealment and a good shooting position—if the buck stayed on the trail. It did, and Dean drove an arrow into its chest. The deer died quickly, and scored $246^6/_8$.

Trying to sneak within bow range of a feeding muley is no easy task. Mule deer aren't as nervous as whitetails, but their vision and hearing is good enough to warn them when danger is approaching. The trick of spotting deer first, seeing which way they're heading, and then maneuvering to a place where they'll walk toward you, as Dean did, is by far the best way to get within good range.

Mule deer in the sagebrush or other low cover are tantalizing targets, but are extremely difficult to approach. Sagebrush grows just thick enough to catch the bow repeatedly as you're crawling, and makes a lot of noise as you're trying to quietly squeeze through. I've seen muleys stand well out in the sage, practically defying a hunter to come closer. They don't seem to do that during rifle season, however.

Hunting in thick cover such as oak brush and tall sage is almost out of the question, unless you can set up an ambush where the brush thins out along a trail, or can get in an elevated position where you can shoot downward. One of the best options is to waylay a deer at a water hole.

Because most Western bow seasons are early in the fall, the high country is a popular place to hunt. An excellent technique is to slowly walk along old logging roads, especially through areas where visibility is a bit better and deer are often feeding. Thousands of miles of maintained trails traverse the national forests, providing an opportunity to walk and see a great deal of country.

Quaking aspen forests are usually green and in full leaf, offering more screening cover and quieter walking since leaves haven't yet fallen.

Cattle and sheep are often in the upper elevations during bow season. Because livestock are noisy and constantly traveling about, deer become conditioned to the noise and aren't as suspicious as usual when stock is in the general area. Take advantage of this situation to stillhunt and get close to deer. If you're hunting around stock, especially cattle, take every precaution to avoid spooking them. They automatically flush game in the area, and you aren't doing the cows or the livestock owner any good by running the animals about. Many cows in the forest are as spooky as deer, and crash through the timber as fast as they can when they see a human.

If you kill a deer during warm weather, take extra care to prevent the meat from spoiling. Skin the animal immediately, hang it off the ground, and wrap it in cheesecloth or a deer sack to keep flies away. Be sure it hangs in the shade during the daytime.

Mule deer killed in early seasons by bowhunters are usually fat and excellent eating, which is another reason to take up the sport.

The primary reason, however, is the satisfaction of taking an animal with equipment that requires you to do something more than aim and pull a trigger. Mastering the art of shooting shafts into small targets takes a great deal of effort. You must make a commitment and devote a lot of time and energy if you want to be successful. And when the day arrives that you find yourself in the big outdoors, you must then bring into play all the skills you've ever learned to get within bow range of a mule deer. After that is accomplished, and the arrow flies to the intended target, you perceive a strange sense of satisfaction, a kind that you never experience with a firearm. It is a unique sensation, with a special feeling that is enjoyed only when the bowhunter completes the full circle of learning the fundamentals of the sport, studying the habits of mule deer, and making the kill. To know these things, you must do them yourself. No words can describe the deep satisfaction of bowhunting.

Muzzleloading

Alpine firs swayed gently in the breeze as the afternoon sun peeked under a black cloud. The thunderstorm lasted only a half hour, but with it an intense rain and hail storm ravaged the Utah high country.

I had taken shelter under a granite boulder, part of a long talus slope that stretched above timberline. Despite the refuge, I was soaked to the skin from windblown droplets. I checked my flintlock and decided the powder in the flash pan was still dry. While the storm raged around me, I cupped my hand over the flint hammer to protect the fine powder from moisture. I didn't know it then, but my assumption about the powder being dry was dead wrong. In 10 minutes it would cost me a fine buck.

It happened when I rounded a bend along a deer trail and jumped a trio of bedded bucks. All four-pointers, they stared at me in surprise, but only for a split second. The deer crashed off through the timber, but one stopped behind a spruce blowdown. I had a clear shot at his chest, so I snapped the flintlock to my shoulder, pulled back the hammer and drew a fine bead. The chunk of flint struck the frizzen with a loud click, but the gun didn't fire. I drew the hammer back again, frantically hoping that the flint had merely failed to spark. Again the hard stone struck the frizzen without firing, but that time I saw sparks fly from the contact between flint and steel.

The buck wheeled and disappeared in the timber. I cussed, shook the obviously dampened powder out of the flashpan, then quickly grabbed the powder flask out of my possibles bag and poured a small amount into the pan. I thumped the stock gently with the heel of my hand to ensure that some of the powder would dribble into the touchhole.

Satisfied that the gun was primed with dry powder, I circled the ridge, hoping to ambush the bucks on the other side of the mountain. The deer never showed again.

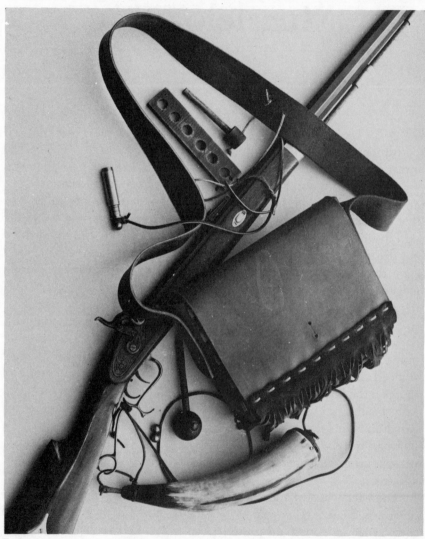

Everything a blackpowder enthusiast needs to hunt deer: muzzleloading rifle, powderhorn, starter, and possibles bag with patching, caps, and other accessories. *(Photo courtesy of Jerry Horgesheimer.)*

I hunted for the rest of the day and the next, but I was unable to get close to a buck for an accurate shot, though I saw several in the distance. Since I was a newcomer to muzzleloading, I had a self-imposed maximum range of 100 yards. At that distance I could punch holes consistently into a target the size of a volleyball, but anything over that was somewhat ambitious and hopeful.

I didn't score with a muzzleloader that year, and had to collect a buck later with my more trustworthy .30/06.

Such is the way of the muzzleloader hunter. But I wasn't disappointed because of my failure to score. Muzzleloading is much more than killing. Wonderful little rituals and traditions are part of the sport, bringing a special satisfaction felt nowhere else in the hunting scene. While it's certainly true that bowhunting is the most primitive means of killing a deer, muzzleloader hunting is more of a celebration of hunting. Much folklore is involved, as well as attendant garb and accessories.

My first impressions of muzzleloader enthusiasts were of delightful amazement. There was much interest in the different guns, powderhorns, and correct powder charges to use, and a host of other accoutrements and equipment. Everyone wanted to learn, to see, to know more about this ancestral way of life, for way of life is exceedingly important to many muzzleloaders. Many tan their own buckskins, fashion their own powderhorns, file their own knives, and perform other little duties that are part of their world.

Certainly not all muzzleloader hunters are tinkerers and traditionalists. Many shoot the guns because they are interested in the guns themselves, and are seeking more challenge in their hunting efforts.

To meet the growing interest in muzzleloading, many Western states have separate seasons for the sport, or reserve special units only for enthusiasts. Mule deer are being hunted more and more with these guns. It appears, by all indications, that the sport is here to stay.

The muzzleloader is called such because it is loaded from the muzzle rather than from the rear. Muzzleloaders are also called front-loaders, black powder rifles, and in the vernacular, front-end stuffers and smoke-poles.

The uniqueness of a muzzleloader is in loading the piece in separate steps rather than with a self-contained cartridge such as in modern rifles. Because of the loading process, only one shot can be fired through a barrel. Then it must be reloaded by the same process. As you can imagine, loading is a primary aspect of the sport. All sorts of gadgets and accessories are used, and there is no end to the debate and technique used.

All of us have seen movies of the U.S. Cavalry on the firing line shooting muzzleloaders, or Daniel Boone and Kit Carson stalking through the forest with black powder rifle in hand. Indeed, these were the guns of early America, and interest in them waned as repeating rifles and smokeless powder arrived on the scene. Throughout the first half of the 20th century, muzzleloaders were used primarily by some old-timers who loved the feel and performance of the primitive guns.

It was in the mid-1950's that the era of the muzzleloader replica came into being, largely due to the efforts of the Navy Arms Company and Centennial Arms Corporation. Soon, a number of firms entered the industry, and the era of black powder shooting was born. Outdoorsmen who wanted more out of hunting took to the sport quickly, and the rest of the story is common knowledge.

Though front-end loaders come in two basic styles—flintlocks and caplocks (also known as percussion firearms), the caplock is by far the favorite among deer hunters. It is much less expensive, generally more reliable, and simpler to use.

A series of events must occur successfully before the flintlock fires. First, the flint or hammer must strike the frizzen or steel, creating a spark. The spark ignites the fine powder in the flashpan, and this explosion travels

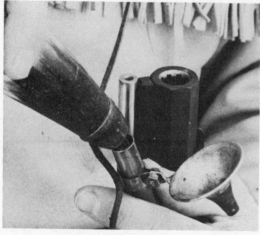

Muzzleloader is loaded first by pouring black powder into the measuring container, then into the muzzle. *(Photo courtesy of Jerry Horgesheimer.)*

Ball is seated on the patching
and started into the bore with
"short-starter." *(Photo courtesy
of Jerry Horgesheimer.)*

through a touchhole and into a chamber where it finally ignites the powder charge behind the patched ball.

As expected, the flintlock must be in perfect working order if it is to fire
consistently, or at all. A well-made flintlock is never guaranteed to fire
every time, since external conditions or malfunctions might prevent the
necessary sequence of events. The flint may fail to spark, or the spark might
fail to ignite the powder in the flashpan, or if the touchhole is fouled the
flashpan ignition might fail to reach the chamber powder. Or, in the case
of my high-country experience in the thundershower, a rainstorm or excessive humidity might moisten the powder, rendering it useless.

The caplock, on the other hand, depends on a much simpler chain of
events. A cap containing a fulminate of mercury is placed on the nipple
and the cap ignites when struck by the hammer. The explosion travels
through a vent hole and ignites the powder charge behind the ball. No
outside explosion occurs with the caplock, and the gun can be reloaded
more speedily than a flintlock since charging the flashpan with powder is
unnecessary. Instead, a percussion cap is simply placed on the nipple.

Both guns are loaded the same way with a ball. After the correct powder charge is poured into the muzzle, the ball is placed on a lubricated patch and driven down into the muzzle with a ramrod.

There is much controversy over the effectiveness and accuracy of a muzzleloader. Some critics claim the black powder guns are too inaccurate and shouldn't be used for deer hunting, while others say the guns are *too* accurate, comparing them to a one-shot .30/06. I disagree with both attitudes. In the hands of a competent shooter, the front-end loaders are adequate for hunting, but there are distance limitations. The ball drops rapidly in flight—anything much beyond 100 yards is questionable, al-

Patched ball is seated on top of the powder charge by pushing it down the barrel with the ramrod. Next, the cap is placed on the nipple and the gun is ready to fire. *(Photo courtesy of Jerry Horgesheimer.)*

though some very good shooters using high quality guns can do well at longer ranges. As far as comparing the muzzleloader to a .30/06, I'd amend that to read .30/30. Even then I'd have reservations, again depending on the skills of the person behind the gun. There is simply too much room for variation in loading the correct powder charge, seating the ball properly, and other factors.

Black powder rifles are made in different calibers, with popular ones being .36, .45, .50, .54, and .58, although there are others. Mule deer hunters should not use anything less than a .50 caliber rifle, even though many deer have been killed with smaller calibers. The proper velocities and energies are found in the .50 and bigger calibers.

To give an idea of the potential of a black powder rifle's potential, a .50 caliber Maxi-Ball shot from a Thompson/Center Hawken develops a muzzle velocity of about 1,400 feet per second when loaded with 100 grains of FFg powder. The slug produces about 1,600 foot pounds of energy, which is comparable to the performance of a .32 Winchester Special centerfire cartridge. The load packs enough wallop to drop any mule deer. I won't go into detailed data on other loads and ballistics, but be assured that the muzzleloader is a superb firearm to hunt deer with, as well as other big game around the world.

After my bad experience with the flintlock, I decided to buy a caplock, which I should have done in the first place. Most expert muzzleloader hunters suggest that the beginner learn first on the caplock, then go on to a flintlock if he wants a bit more challenge.

I bought a Navy Arms .50 caliber Hawken. The gun fit me well, and I liked its overall short length. It wasn't as cumbersome as my flintlock and was much easier to handle, especially when maneuvering through thick timber and blowdowns.

I broke-in the new gun by punching 100 balls through paper targets. When I felt like I had a good feel for the gun's capability at known distances, I took it out to the lowlands and shot prairie dogs. The first few shots were misses, but I settled down and concentrated. When I finally got the hang of it, I was able to hit prairie dogs with surprising consistency. I didn't attempt off-hand shots, only prone position shots.

The practice sessions paid off. When deer season arrived that year, I killed a nice buck with the Hawken.

To the uninitiated, muzzleloaders are bewildering and undependable firearms. The big belching cloud of smoke and sparks flying within inches

Dan Gardner shoots at a buck
during muzzleloading season.

of a shooter's face are far from being comfortable. Muzzleloading jargon is
unfamiliar, and the various accessories are strange.

I was typically apprehensive when I made my debut with a black powder rifle because I didn't know what to expect. I must confess that I closed
my eyes tightly when I fired the flintlock the first time. Much to my surprise the recoil was slight and the noise wasn't much. Instead of a sharp
crack, the rifle gave off a rolling boom.

As I learned more about the sport, a pile of paraphernalia slowly began to accumulate. I bought a "possibles" bag, which is essentially a pouch
that carries the tools of the trade such as percussion caps, patches, patch
lubricant, pocket knife, short starter, and other items, some needed,
some not. One of the joys of muzzleloader hunting is peeking into the
possibles bags carried by other hunters—you never know what might be
in them.

There are ways to load quickly with a minimum of movement. This is
an important requirement when you're deer hunting. A quick second shot
might spell the difference between success or failure. Percussion cap hold-

ers allow you to quickly slip a cap on a nipple in one fluid motion; you can use premeasured powder charges instead of taking time to measure and load; you can use precut patches that don't have to be sliced off after the ball is seated, and so on.

The best way to learn these tips is to befriend a muzzleloader enthusiast or join a club. You learn more from them in one day than you can from several books.

Black powder itself is a highly explosive, dangerous substance, and a number of safety rules should be followed. Here are some of them.

Never smoke when you're handling black powder. If a flintlock is being used, be doubly cautious. Remember, when the gun is loaded with a patched ball over a powder charge, all it takes to go off is ignition from the loaded flashpan. If an ash from your cigarette or pipe falls into the flashpan and ignites, the gun will discharge.

Don't pour powder from a flask or powder horn directly into a hot barrel. If there are any hot grains of powder in the gun, the new charge of powder could ignite. Always pour powder from a measure. I use the cap of my powder horn. Running a clean patch down the hot barrel to clean out hot embers is also a good idea.

If the gun misfires, give it sufficient time to rest before examining it. Otherwise a latent spark could trigger ignition when you don't expect it.

Don't even *think* about shooting any powder other than black powder in your muzzleloader, with one exception that I'll mention briefly. To try the smokeless powder used in modern cartridges and shells is to flirt with disaster. Be sure your mortgage and life insurance is paid if you decide to try it.

The exception I mentioned is Pyrodex, a revolutionary substance that is being used with increasing regularity each season. Pyrodex owes its existence solely to Dan Pawlak, a genius in explosives and pyrotechnic engineering. He achieved something that the experts said couldn't be done —making a black powder substitute that is safer to use, just as effective, and immune to the red tape and regulations applied to black powder. If you haven't heard about it already, you will. Pyrodex is becoming a household word in the muzzleloading field.

Black powder itself is classified into four different ratings: Fg (largest), FFg, FFFg, and FFFFg (smallest). This is a simple aspect of the sport. Unlike smokeless powder used in centerfire cartridges, the muzzleloader hunter has only one or two choices. And whereas the modern rifleman handloads cartridges with much precision and elaborate equipment, the muzzleloader fan need only shake a bit more or less powder into the barrel of his firearm. By varying balls and Mini or Maxi bullets, he can quickly obtain the kind of performance he wants.

The use of telescopic sights on black powder rifles is the subject of much debate and controversy. Proponents claim that if they help the hunter shoot more accurately, why not use them? Opponents contend telescopic sights are counter to the very roots of the sport, and render muzzleloading a hypocritic posture.

Jerry Horgesheimer, a black powder enthusiast, shows a nice buck he killed in the Utah high country. *(Photo courtesy of Jerry Horgesheimer.)*

I agree with the opponents. Any hunter who uses a black powder rifle should take it upon himself to learn how to shoot it to the best of his ability at ranges within his capabilities. If he needs an assist by way of telescopic sights, he's cheating, pure and simple.

Because the black powder hunter must get reasonably close to a mule deer to place his shot in a vital area, he should restrict his hunting to areas where close-in shots are typical.

I prefer oak brush and pinyon-juniper country for those very reasons. During early morning and late afternoon hours I hunt more open country when deer are feeding and moving about.

When I'm in brushy or heavily forested habitat I carry a small pair of binoculars to size up a deer in the brush. A buck's antlers can easily be concealed by branches and foliage.

Some states have special seasons for black powder hunters. Seasons may be statewide or restricted to special units. While some muzzleloader hunters scoff at such seasons and claim they don't need a special time to hunt because they're competitive with centerfire-rifle outdoorsmen, I must disagree with that attitude for a simple reason. Part of the lure of the black powder hunt is the quiet in the forest. Hunters aren't scurrying about everywhere, nor is there constant gunfire from every direction. It is a time to be alone, to slip quietly through the woods carrying a firearm similar to the ones used by mountain men who roamed those very woods long before I was born. While it's true that some accessories hasten loading time, or that some use binoculars (many purists do not) or other gadgets, the important thing is the peace one has within. That's what it's all about. And if a buck falls to the ball, there is a certain elation that isn't present with modern firearms. More and more hunters are finding that out every autumn in the West.

Horseback Hunting

This chapter is for hunters who have had little or no experience on horses. If you own a horse, or do a lot of horseback hunting, you won't learn much new here because I mention only basics.

If you're planning a mule deer hunt with an outfitter, chances are excellent you'll either hunt from a horse on a daily basis, or will ride into hunting camp on a horse as part of a pack train.

Many hunters come to the Rockies with apprehension about horses being part of the hunt. Some people are downright afraid of them, or just don't trust them, especially in rough country.

Most of those fears are groundless, because outfitters usually match clients with dependable horses that are mountain-wise and well broke. If an outfitter puts a hunter on a balky, skittish horse known to act up, he's taking big chances. First off, if he's honest and has a good reputation, he wants his clients to have a good, uncomplicated hunt. Second, he could be held liable if there's an accident, and third, no outfitter in his right mind wants more problems than he's already got. Rest assured, then, that you'll be teamed up with a good old steed to get you to camp and back safely.

The biggest worry to hunters with little horseback riding experience is soreness from extended riding. Saddle sores can't be helped much if your anatomy is tender and soft, unless you are able to ride regularly before the hunt.

This is one problem the outfitter can't help much with. If camp is a long way in, you'll have to grin and bear it. A couple of things can be done to alleviate soreness. First, be sure your stirrups are adjusted properly, or you'll have aching knees and legs as well. Most outfitters will check your stirrups to be sure they fit. If he doesn't, ask him to. Another helpful tip is to wear longjohns under your trousers when you're riding. They add a bit of cushion and keep your pants from rubbing against your legs.

Before getting on a horse, make sure the stirrups are wide enough to accommodate your boots. If not, change boots or stirrups. Your boot must slide easily out of the stirrup if you need to pile off the horse quickly. Of course, Western boots with pointed toes are the answer, but they're not much good for walking long distances if you're not used to them. When it's cold I wear pacs with leather uppers and rubber bottoms. Because they're wide and bulky, I make doubly sure they'll fit a stirrup well.

Before riding into camp, lash a heavy jacket to the leather thongs behind the saddle. It's easy to forget this if the weather is bright and lovely when you're preparing for the ride, but you'll be sorry if a blizzard or cold

Full panniers and packs lashed down! Wrangler leads horses into the high country.

wind bores down when you're halfway to camp. The outfitter won't be too excited about stopping on the trail and unlashing all the gear on a pack horse to get to your jacket in the bottom of a pannier or duffle bag.

Most outfitters employ a man to take charge of the horses. He's called a wrangler, and helps you whenever you need it. All guides should be horse experts as well, too. If you need assistance with anything regarding the horse, don't be shy about asking. Wranglers are used to "dudes," and are on hand to help. Don't feel embarrassed about asking, and don't take it upon yourself to fix something if you don't know what you're doing. If in doubt, ask. Wranglers have a lot more respect for you if you admit your ignorance, and are most definitely unhappy if you hurt yourself or the horse by doing something you had no business doing.

Your wrangler or guide helps you get started, and checks everything that needs to be checked, but he can't help you *ride* the horse. That's your job, and you can make it easier on yourself by relaxing at the very first. If you ride stiffly and are nervous, the horse will sense your insecurity. You must let him know who's boss from the beginning. Be firm, and don't let the horse get away with anything. If he wanders off the trail, rein him back on. If he settles into a slow walk and won't keep pace with the rest of the pack train, give him a jolt with your heels to get him where he belongs. If he persists, keep urging him on with your heels. Don't let him get the best of you, because he might try. Horses often "test" a new rider to see how much they can get away with.

If the trail gets rough with fallen logs, brush, and other obstacles, the guide or wrangler leads the way. If the horse balks, once again give him a bit of "heel" coaxing. If you're working your way off the trail through timber or brush, you can let the horse have his head a bit as long as he doesn't stray away from the lead animal.

Horses and new riders do funny things. One inexperienced rider was hunting deer when his horse decided to head back for camp. The rider sat helplessly, not knowing quite what to do. Horse and rider were 200 yards up the trail when the guide realized they were missing, and commenced to "instruct" the horse with a few well-chosen words and actions.

When riding, you're not supposed to hold onto the saddle horn as a matter of tradition, but if you feel better holding onto the horn, by all means do so. No one is going to kid you in the backcountry.

Now and then the trail might wind down a steep grade. If the guide gets off and walks the horse down, that's a signal to follow his directions. Oc-

Wyoming guide Tracy Barrus lashes a buck to a packhorse. This is a job for an experienced wrangler.

casionally a young guide will ride trails that should not be ridden. If your horse is slipping badly and on the verge of losing control, get off and lead him down. No reason to be shy about that, either.

Once in Montana while riding down the mountain into camp we had to negotiate a very steep, icy trail. The wrangler and all the hunters dismounted except for one rider. His horse took a nasty spill, but fortunately the man and horse were unhurt.

If you're riding up a steep trail, your horse needs frequent breaks to rest a moment. When the guide stops, make sure your horse comes to rest where he has good footing. Once when I was riding out of a steep canyon in Utah I stopped my horse on slick shale because the horse in front stopped quickly and I had no place to go. My horse started slipping, and I bailed

off in a flying leap, narrowly missing a free flight off a cliff edge into oblivion. When I was clear of the horse, it managed to regain its footing enough
for me to ease it up the slope.

Whenever you're atop a horse in the Rockies, you can figure on riding
somewhere that looks scary. You cross creeks, ride through narrow trails
in the timber, and negotiate trails up and down steep slopes or along
mountainsides. Trust your horse, but use good sense. Be prepared for anything.

If it's extremely cold, bundle up with everything you have. Riding a
horse offers no chance to exercise and keep warm. Unless you're well-
clothed, you're going to have problems ranging from mild discomfort to
frostbite. On a mule deer hunt in Montana last year we rode out of camp
on horseback each morning before dawn. The temperature was 20 degrees
below zero when we started. In addition to my regular underwear I wore
longjohns, a cotton shirt, two woolen shirts, a sweater, a heavy woolen
jacket, and a huge down coat with a coyote-ruff hood. For trousers over
the longjohns, I wore, as always, jeans. As the day warmed, I shed clothes
and tied them to the leather thongs on the front and rear of the saddle.

If it's raining and blowing, you can quickly become chilled and suffer
hypothermia. Always carry a slicker of some type for protection. Buy the
kind that folds into a compact size, but stay away from cheap brands. They
stay intact only until your horse brushes you into some branches.

Cold feet can be a big problem because they are off the ground where
plenty of cold air can get at them. I wear three pair of loose fitting woolen
socks in felt-lined Sorel boots, and seldom feel the cold. If I do, I get off
the horse and walk until my feet are warmed. At a normal pace, you can
comfortably walk as fast as the rest of the horses in the group.

You soon learn that horses like to be around each other. If you're riding out from camp with a hunting party and you split away from the group
with a guide, your horse will probably show his dissatisfaction by trying
to turn and continue with the main group. In that case, rein him where
you want to go, and let him know your boot heels are ready any time he
gets out of place.

Once I watched a hunter let his horse take him anywhere the horse
had a mind to, and at a slow pace. I was guiding at the time, and told the
hunter to control the horse with a bit of aggression. The hunter told me
he didn't want to kick the horse with his heels because he was afraid he'd

hurt the animal. I finally convinced him that a well-placed heel was akin to tickling a horse; it just reminds him that the human aboard is dominant.

If the weather is cold you should wear gloves, but most skilled horsemen wear gloves whenever they're riding. You can get a better grip on the reins, and if the reins brush into snow and water they can become cold and stiff.

If the weather is bitter cold and you're crossing icy streams, you might need to stop occasionally and chip away the ice that freezes under the horse's feet. Ice balls-up an inch or more thick and your horse has trouble keeping his footing. One night while riding to camp after dark we crossed a half dozen creeks while on a 7-mile ride to camp. We had to stop every time we crossed a creek to chip away ice. One man held a flashlight while the other chopped away chunks of ice with a hunting knife. It was mighty

Hunters look off into the distance for deer from atop the Continental Divide on the Idaho-Montana border.

cold work and we were happy to huddle around a warm stove when we reached camp.

When you come in to camp at night, most outfitters prefer that you tie the horses to a hitching rail and leave the job of unsaddling and unbridling to the wrangler and guides. Many hunters like to help, especially after a day or two when they understand what to do.

If you unsaddle your horse, make sure you use the same saddle in the morning. Your stirrups won't need to be readjusted, and you might have personal gear in the saddle bags or a jacket tied to the saddle. Keep the tack together, including bridle, halter, lead rope, and saddle blankets. (Tack, by the way, is the term used to define all the various gear used on the horse).

Whether or not your horse has given you a good ride, you should do him a favor by unsaddling and currying (brushing) him when you get back to camp. Tie him to a rail or tree with the halter rope and brush him thoroughly. He'll be well-soaked with sweat and his fur will be matted down. Currying helps him dry off quicker and removes dirt and debris.

The wrangler feeds grain to the horses before turning them into a corral or out to feed in a meadow. I like to grain my own horse if he's been good on the trail. I seem to grow close to an old cayuse if he's worth his hay. If he's given me problems, I still grain him, but not with a great deal of fondness. The way I figure it, if a horse packs me up and down mountains all day, he needs a little love and attention from his rider. I treat every horse as if he's my own.

Besides carrying hunters to camp, horses are used to pack gear. Except for tent ridge poles, everything in the typical hunting camp is carried in by horses. Before I tried packing in with my own horses, I thought it was a simple operation whereby you merely throw a sawbuck pack saddle on a horse, load up with gear, lash it down, and head for the boonies. How wrong I was. Immediately I learned that packing with horses is a science; that only long years of experience make a good packer. Knots must be learned and tied correctly, equipment must be packed so it won't break, and above all, the pack must be balanced. Some wranglers weigh the contents of the panniers to make sure the loads are equal on each side.

The packhorse needs to be a sturdy animal. There's a big difference between carrying a human and the dead weight of a pack. A person shifts weight when going up and down grades and through winding, narrow trails. A packload, on the other hand, stays in one position, always exerting the same weight.

In the Southwest and Mexico, burros or donkeys are used extensively for packing. In the northern states, horses and mules are preferred for packing. A big mule is a strong beast if it's in condition, and does wonders with a heavy pack.

A special pack saddle called a sawbuck is cinched on the horse. A pair of containers called panniers are lashed to the sawbuck. Panniers are essentially boxes that are made of a variety of materials; wood, canvas, buckskin, plastic, metal, or other material. With the panniers loaded and tightened down, the packer then piles other gear on top, such as duffel bags, tents, sleeping bags, suitcases, even the kitchen sink if one is used in deer camp.

Now and then a guide might ask you to hold the lead rope of a pack-horse behind you when you're riding along a trail. First, be sure you're wearing a glove, and don't wrap the rope around your wrist so snugly you

Loading panniers is tricky. They must be balanced evenly.

can't let go if the need arises. Occasionally the horse you're leading will stop abruptly while your horse is still moving. If you don't want your arm jerked out of the socket, you must let go of the rope quickly. Some outfitters who should know better dally (wrap) the lead rope to the saddle horn of the horse in front. This is a great way to induce rodeo in the wilderness, and maybe a serious injury or worse to horse and rider. Many wranglers "tail" the pack animals together by tying the lead rope to the tail of the horse in front. Tied correctly, this allows the horses to pull free if there's a problem along the trail. If you're holding the lead rope of the horse behind you, see to it that the rope doesn't swing under your horse's tail. He probably will become very upset and attempt to disengage you from the saddle with much vigor and energy.

Packing out a deer with a horse is a whole different ball game. Whereas gear can be balanced nicely and lashed accordingly, not so with a deer carcass. First of all, and most importantly, some horses and mules are not fond of the sight and smell of a dead deer. Therefore, not only do you have to contend with an unwieldy carcass, but with a balky horse that won't get close to it.

A Montana deer hunt illustrates the fun and games that can be had when packing with a horse turned off by a dead deer. I killed a five-point buck and had a packhorse that was new to the outfitter. Kevin Rush, my guide, wasn't about to take chances with the horse. Kevin grabbed a handful of blood and lung, wiped it across the horse's nostrils, and let the animal get used to the strange smell. The horse was tied to a small fir, and didn't object much except for a few wildeyed glances.

When we first approached the just-dressed deer, the horse took a whiff and did a little dance. Now, with the blood on his nose, the horse didn't know what to think. Before he could get his wits, Kevin quickly covered the horse's head with a jacket. That really made him mad, but Kevin wrapped the jacket tightly so the horse couldn't toss it off. Kevin and I dragged the deer to the horse and proceeded to load it with no problems. With the deer lashed tightly, Kevin took the jacket from the horse and led him down the trail.

Because the bronc couldn't see temporarily, he didn't know what was being loaded on his back, and the blood smeared on his nose prevented him from smelling the carcass. It was a slick operation, and I gained even more respect for those cowboy Montana guides.

The universal way to load a deer is to cut a slit lengthwise in the flanks

Montana guide Kevin Rush lashes my five-point buck to horse. Note Kevin covered the horse's head with a jacket to prevent it from seeing the deer while being loaded.

of the carcass, then heave the carcass up on the saddle so the slits fit over the saddle horn. With the carcass firmly anchored, the next step is to lash the deer tightly to the saddle and cinch strap. If the deer's head isn't removed, it should be turned back and tied so it's balanced in the center. Care should be taken so the antler points don't stick the horse.

When you're riding in deer country, you're apt to see a nice buck any time. Your outfitter will probably have a scabbard rigged to your horse. Never, but never, keep a live cartridge in the chamber of your rifle. In the excitement of leaping off your horse and jerking your rifle from the scabbard you could accidentally fire a shot.

Don't even *think* about shooting from the saddle. Not only will you no doubt miss the deer, but you might seriously injure the horse's eardrums. Worse, the horse might, and should, flip you off his back. Anyone stupid enough to shoot from a horse deserves a short flight to the ground.

If a shot is possible when you're riding, jump off the horse, let the reins
fall to the ground, grab your rifle, and run off a few yards from the horse.
Ideally, you should tie the horse to a tree if you think he might bolt and
run at the shot, but you seldom have time. Usually someone is with you
to catch the horse if it runs off. If not, it might be a long walk back to camp.

When hunting from a horse, I like to tie my animal well away from an
overlook and then walk up on foot and glass for deer. Horses are noisy
and quite handy at spooking deer. Too many hunters want to ride every
inch of the way, figuring to spot a deer from a horse and jump off for a
quick shot.

Sometimes, in thick country where elk share the real estate with deer,
you can get away with riding through thick timber to bedded deer. Apparently deer think elk are moving through the trees.

On a hunt in Wyoming I was riding through a thick Douglas fir patch
with my guide Tracy Barrus. I was amazed when we approached bedded
deer closely. I could have easily killed several bucks, but I was looking for
something special.

When I plan to be hunting all day from a horse, I take along a daypack
and fill it with accessories. I drape the daypack straps over the saddlehorn

Grant Barrus points out a deer drive strategy to one of the standers.

so it's within easy reach, particularly for cameras that I want to get at in a hurry. In the daypack I put an extra woolen jacket, flashlight, rope, fruit, cookies, first-aid kit, film, and other items. Saddlebags normally accommodate small items, but I prefer to use a daypack since I might leave my horse and walk for several hours. Sometimes a companion and I ride horses up a ridge, and I'll get off and hunt back to camp, taking all day. My buddy ties my horse in the shade and picks it up later in the afternoon on his way back to camp.

An advantage to riding horseback, if your horse has been in the country for awhile and knows the area, is knowing you'll not be lost. Most mountain horses can find their way back to camp in the worst possible conditions. If a blizzard hits or fog rolls in or you're just plain lost, give the horse his head and let him go where he wants. In most cases he'll eventually work his way to camp.

Horses are expensive to keep, but I wouldn't give mine up for anything. I have a white half-Arabian gelding and a big Palomino gelding. Besides their initial cost, they need to be fed, wormed, shoed, have their feet trimmed regularly, and otherwise well-cared for. Feed doesn't come cheap, nor does pasture rental, but fortunately I can grow hay in my own pastures. The fence is always needing repair, and gates have a way of being left open or knocked down every now and then. Grain and medication are always required, and just when I think everything is under control, a new crisis arises. And, of course, tack is the biggest expense these days. A new saddle costs about as much as a good horse. Add bridles, halters, lead ropes, blankets, etc., and you're looking at a sizable outlay. Furthermore, it's tough to find and buy a horse that fits into your hunting plans. The best horses usually aren't for sale; the knotheaded featherbrains are most often listed in the classified ads. And if you think you want to start off with a frisky colt, you'd better know a whole lot about horse training and be prepared to change your lifestyle. Finally, after you get your horse and tack, you need a trailer to haul him around in.

No, all is not simple when it comes to horses, but they're excellent for getting you back into the hinterlands and carrying your game out. Horses aren't for everyone. Many experienced hunters want nothing to do with them and would rather be afoot. That's fine and dandy, but as the years creep along and those mountains seem to get a bit steeper, it's nice to occasionally enjoy the finer things in life. Which, in the case of mule deer hunting, is a good mountain horse.

Getting Your Deer Home

The happy ending to a mule deer hunt is killing a mule deer. But, as the old saying goes, "The fun of the hunt ends when you pull the trigger." With the carcass on the ground, you are then faced with the necessity of transporting the meat from the woods to your freezer. The distance might be a few hundred yards if you're hunting in your backyard, a couple thousand miles if you live on the East Coast, or a distance in between.

First off, let's look at the job you're faced with in getting the carcass to a road, vehicle, or camp. The size of the deer may determine your choice of options. Generally speaking, a fawn dresses from 50 to 75 pounds, a yearling doe or yearling buck about 80 to 120 pounds, an adult doe from 120 to 150 pounds, and a mature to big buck from 130 pounds to 225 pounds or better. These are estimates; individual carcasses may be more or less than the weight suggested.

The next question is your physical condition and any assistance you need to get the carcass moved from the woods. Do you have a back problem that might be aggravated by carrying or dragging a deer? Or a heart or respiratory ailment that might act up from the sudden energy required? If so, dress the deer, drag it into the shade, and prop open the cavity so it will cool. Then find someone to help you get the deer out.

If you're alone but in reasonably good shape and the deer is relatively small, you might be able to drag the animal to a vehicle or road where you can drive to it. Before attempting to drag it, consider the terrain that you need to traverse. If you're in typical mule deer country, chances are good that the topography is up and down. Don't bite off more than you can chew, because you can seriously hurt yourself while dragging an animal. When going uphill, you're pulling hard, and using some back and arm muscles that will no doubt protest. If underbrush is thick or you need to negotiate a sagebrush flat, you can have double trouble. Every branch and root seems to be grabbing at you and the carcass as you tug the deer along. Snow helps the dragging process by offering a slick surface on which to slide the deer. It also makes it easier for you to slip, so be extra cautious when negotiating snow and ice.

Some ways of dragging make the chore much easier. Don't just grab a convenient part of the deer's anatomy and start to drag. If you've killed a buck, the antlers make obvious handles, but if the buck is a spike or small forked-horn a handhold is hard to get. If the buck is big, the antlers snag brush and branches. A word of caution when dragging a big buck, or any buck with long, sharp antler tines: be careful of those antler points when you're dragging the deer along, especially if a buddy is helping. If one of you stumbles, which is the norm rather than the exception, the momentum of the still-moving carcass could drive an antler into a leg, thigh, or

A pole carry is one way to transport a deer. Don't try it unless you have a strong back and shoulders.

other part of you. A serious puncture could mar the trip, and cause plenty of pain and discomfort as well.

If a long drag is in store, wear gloves. They give you a better grip on the antlers and prevent your hands from getting sore. Switch hands often to give each, as well as your wrists and arms, a rest. If a companion is helping you drag, change places often.

Don't drag any faster than you have to. Take plenty of breaks, and walk around during each break, swinging your arms to take the soreness and stiffness away from your tired and overworked muscles. Walk ahead in the direction you want to drag every so often to determine the best route. Try to stay on game trails and in the open as much as possible, even if it means losing a bit of elevation every now and then.

It's easier to drag a buck if you can lift his head well off the ground. You might tie a rope around the antler bases and form loops in the rope for handholds, or tie a strong stick to the rope just above where the rope is tied and hold on to each side of the stick as if it were a whiffletree. Some hunters tie the front feet of the deer up around the back of the head to keep them from dragging and getting in the way. I find it easier to simply cut off all four feet as soon as the deer is field dressed.

If you're dragging a doe or fawn or small buck with antlers too little to grab on to, tie a rope around the neck and drag with the rope.

Always drag with the grain of the pelt, which means head first. Otherwise you're in for a much tougher ordeal.

In the event you want to save the deerskin and have it tanned with the hide intact, *do not drag it at all.* Either skin the animal on the spot or carry it. Fur rubs off easily when pressed against the ground. Rocks, roots, and brush wears away chunks of fur, and you'll have an unsightly, and perhaps unrepairable, spot in the hide.

If you want to eat the heart and liver, you can place them in the chest cavity, but they might slide out, especially if you're dragging uphill. It's best to have someone else carry them, or put them in a daypack. Carry a plastic bag to put them in.

Another option of hauling a deer out of the woods is to haul it on your shoulders. To do so, however, you must have two things going for you: the deer must be small, and you must be strong. Few men can carry a mature mule deer, but every now and then it's done. There is a big caution if you try this. You *must* drape a large amount of orange flagging or orange clothing all over the deer so it doesn't look like a deer at all. Otherwise you might be executed by another hunter who saw deer antlers but not the hunter underneath them. In fact, any time you carry a deer or antlers above the ground, whether lashed to a pack frame or whatever, you should *always* festoon the animal with plenty of bright colors for safety reasons.

These Utah hunters team up to drag a buck out of the hills.

If two or three of you are helping, another way to transport a deer is to lash it to a stout pole and carry the pole on your shoulders. This technique may look simple, but it isn't. For one thing, finding a suitable pole isn't easy if you aren't in a forest. Most poles aren't sturdy enough to bear the weight of a big deer, and if they are they're probably much too heavy for you to carry.

Once I killed a big buck in Utah, and because it was getting dark and I couldn't drag the deer myself, I field dressed the buck and returned the next day with four pals. We tied the buck to a pole, but the pole promptly broke in two when we lifted it up. We found another pole which probably could have passed for a mini-log, and discovered it was so heavy we couldn't lift it and the buck both. Finally we found a suitable pole a quarter mile away and lashed the deer to it by tying its front legs and back legs together and running the pole through both. We labored long and hard to get the buck to a road, and ruined a half day's worth of hunting for my companions. We found out later the buck dressed over 200 pounds, which explained our sore shoulders and weary bodies. Had we known better, we could have cushioned our carrying shoulder by wrapping a jacket or down vest around the pole where it rested on our shoulders. Another thing we learned was that the deer must be securely lashed to the pole or it slides backward when carrying it uphill and forward when going downhill. Trussing the head to the pole keeps it from swinging about and catching on brush.

Another way to carry out a deer is to simply cut off the legs and head and simply stuff the carcass in a rucksack. This only works if you have a small deer and a big rucksack. As a word of caution, never sever the deer's head from its body unless you've first checked the laws in the state you're hunting. Some states or hunting units require that the head be attached to the carcass at all times until the animal is ready to be processed.

A litter, or stretcher, makes a fine conveyance for carrying a deer. An old blanket or sheet of canvas lashed or rolled onto two poles makes a dandy surface for moving a deer. Be sure the canvas or blanket is securely attached to the poles, or the weight of the deer collapses the whole contraption. You can carry a piece of canvas in a pack for just such a purpose, and find two poles in the woods. Some hunters have litters ready to go and keep them in camp or a vehicle until needed. If you don't have strong shoulders and a healthy back, don't try this method.

Back in the days before the wheel, Indians used a travois to carry their

Be sure to tag your deer in accordance with state laws. Don't forget!

goods and belongings from one place to another. The travois still works well, and makes a dandy vehicle to haul a mule deer, but it takes some time to put one together. If you're the enterprising sort, however, with plenty of rope and a small saw, you can make one. Constructed correctly, it transports a deer as well as any other primitive method. The long poles act as shock cushions and bounce readily over rough terrain.

Several years ago while I was hunting during Utah's muzzleloading season I came across a hunter dragging a deer on a travois expertly fashioned out of lodgepole pine. The hunter was wearing traditional mountain man garb, complete with buckskin clothes, moccasins, coonskin cap, and all the accessories that go along with the primitive hunt. If I had closed my eyes and opened them without knowing what century I was in I would have sworn that the man was a kin to Jim Bridger or another of his kind.

These days a lot of hunters use a one-wheeled cart to carry their deer. This is simply a lightweight aluminum frame with handles on each end welded to a bicycle wheel. The deer is lashed to the frame, two hunters grab the handles, and away they go. It's surprising how this rig negotiates rough terrain. Hunters who use them say they will never drag a deer again. I can't blame them. As far as I know, these cart affairs are jerryrigged with odds and ends.

I've never seen blueprints for carts, but a company could probably make a killing if they manufactured them in such a way that they could be easily dismantled and sold in sporting goods stores or through mail order houses. Each fall, just prior to the opening of Colorado's deer season, thousands of California hunters drive through my town, and I'm always amazed at the number of them toting wheeled deer carriers. I've often heard that California is first with innovations. Perhaps that explains it.

When you haul a field-dressed deer out of the woods, you'll be packing a lot of weight that you ultimately discard later. According to a study, here's how you can expect a small buck mule deer to end up if it weighed 114 pounds dressed: head—8½ pounds, hide—9½ pounds, fat and meat trimmed from typical bullet wound—25 pounds. This adds up to 43 pounds of waste. By leaving the discarded materials in the woods for the coyotes and magpies, you carry out only 71 pounds instead of 114. If you want to go one step further and bone out the meat, you can leave 11 pounds of bone in the woods and carry 60 pounds of usable meat.

To take advantage of this lighter load, you can quarter the carcass and lash the sections securely to a lightweight packframe. A sturdy hunter can carry 60 to 80 pounds, but this isn't advised for anyone without some stamina and strength.

You need a knife and small saw or axe to quarter the deer properly. I carry a Wyoming belt saw and knife for quartering game if I'm too far back in the woods to drag out a carcass.

If you bone the meat, work on a smooth, clean surface that you've wiped off carefully, such as a stump, log, or rock. Otherwise, you waste a lot of meat by having to trim away soiled edges caked with dirt, sand, leaves, twigs, and other debris. Boned meat can be carried in a rucksack or compartmentalized backpack. A friend of mine carries a wool sack and a packframe. He puts the boned meat in the sack and simply lashes the sack to the packframe.

When boning meat, cut off chunks as big as you can so you can make them into roasts and cut them into steaks later. Carry a small sharpening stone so you can touch up the knife edge often.

I like to wrap boned meat in cheesecloth to soak up excess blood and to allow air to circulate through it. Never put warm meat directly in plastic bags and keep it there for an extended time. Allow it to cool thoroughly as quickly as possible.

Another way to transport your deer, if you have the option available, is to haul it in a canoe, raft, or boat. There are no complications in using these conveyances, but take care when placing a deer in a canoe. Be sure the carcass is well balanced, and keep it as low in the canoe as possible. If a deer is big and the canoe wobbly in the water, pull the canoe up on shore and load the deer, then push it back into the water.

A horse is a great way to carry your deer, but it also is a great way to get hurt or have a frustrating incident that you'd rather forget. Horses do not like to be around dead deer. Some get nervous and prance around a bit, some perk up and refuse to approach the deer, and some go absolutely haywire, whinnying and raising enough hell to put a rodeo horse to shame. If you have never loaded a deer on a horse, absolutely do not try it unless you have an experienced wrangler with you. Besides the ordeal of preparing and loading the deer, it must be securely lashed and balanced so it won't fall off. Doesn't sound like a big project, but believe me, it is. As the

Approach downed deer carefully from the uphill side. Always be sure the animal is dead before you move in close.

owner of two horses, I can tell you it is definitely not all fun and games to haul a deer on a horse.

If you need to leave a deer in the woods and come back for it later, always assume that some bird or animal will try to feast on your prize. In mule deer country, magpies and ravens help themselves in the daylight hours, while coyotes, foxes, and bears work at night.

On a recent hunt in Montana I killed a fat five-point buck early in the morning. My guide Kevin Rush and I field dressed the deer and dragged it into the shade, and rode off on horses to look for elk. We left the buck's heart and liver laying in the snow under a sagebrush bush. When we returned just before sundown to pack out the buck, I saw two ravens and several magpies in the general area where the carcass was laying. I put my heels to the horse, urging him on, because I knew I was going to be unhappy with the way the deer had been treated and wanted to hurry over for a look. Sure enough, plenty was wrong at the scene. The entire heart and three-fourths of the liver were gone, and the birds had eaten away a pound or more of meat and fat from the buck's flank. Kevin and I cussed a lot, because we had planned to cook up a big pan of liver and onions that night. The birds foiled us, so we settled for less exotic food.

Just a few weeks before that hunt, I killed a big four-point buck in Utah just before sundown. It was too dark to get him out, so I field dressed him and left him for the night, hoping the coyotes would leave him alone. I worried about the deer much of the night and got back to him just before sun-up. Already a dozen magpies were preparing to have a feed, but they were just getting organized when I arrived. To my relief, the coyotes didn't visit the carcass.

The best way to protect a carcass from birds is to cover it extensively with brush. Thick pine boughs or juniper branches work well because they physically prevent the birds from getting to the meat. But cover it well, because if any of the body is exposed the birds will get to it.

When I killed my first mule deer, my father-in-law went to a lot of trouble to cover the deer with juniper branches. We had to leave the carcass for three or four hours to get a horse, and Dad worried about magpies. I thought it was strange to be protecting the deer from birds that I thought at the time were harmless, but now I know better.

Snow makes a handy protective covering from birds if enough is available. Cover the carcass completely, and pack the snow tightly over it.

Coyotes can make quick work of a deer carcass. A pack of the ever-hungry predators can turn a big deer into a mere bloodstain overnight. Even bones, fur, and innards are gulped down.

To protect a carcass from coyotes, you must get it off the ground well out of their reach. If possible, hang the deer high in a tree, at least 5 feet above the ground. Coyotes normally won't approach a fresh carcass because of lingering man-scent, but it's not wise to take chances. I know of several incidents where hunters returned to their deer in the morning to find nothing but coyote tracks and a bit of blood and hair.

If black bears are abundant in the area, then you have problems indeed if you must leave the carcass overnight. Since they climb trees, one of the few recourses is to quarter the deer and hang the quarters high from the ends of springy, pliable branches that the bears might resist walking out on. By hanging the quarters far apart, bears might get some but maybe not all of it. In grizzly country, any tree will do because the big bruins can't climb.

If the temperature is warm and you must leave a deer carcass throughout the day, flies will no doubt find it. You can minimize fly problems by sprinkling large quantities of black pepper on all exposed meat, as well as in the deer's nostrils and mouth. Flies lay eggs all over a carcass, particularly in moist places. A cheesecloth covering works somewhat, but enterprising flies find a way in. The best way to avoid fly contamination is to leave the carcass outside only as long as you have to. In the event you discover egg masses on the carcass within a day or so after they were laid, simply scrape them away. It doesn't take long for fly eggs to turn into maggots, however. I've seen maggots appear within 24 hours of the time the eggs were laid. If you see maggots, cut away and discard the infested portion. Then very carefully inspect the rest of the carcass because it will certainly be suspect. Unless you can move the carcass into a cooler for aging, have it processed as soon as possible.

I don't want to say this but I must. Another pirate is in the woods—a two-legged one. Though it's improbable that another hunter would steal your animal, it's a good idea to place the carcass out of sight if the forest is full of hunters. Your deer tag on the carcass establishes your ownership, but a few no-goods have been known to cut the tag off and defy that the deer is yours when you catch them dragging it off or find it hanging in their camp.

I use a trick that may stand up in court, but I haven't had to try it yet. If I need to leave a carcass in the woods for a period of time, I take pictures

In warm weather, a field-dressed buck should be hung in the shade as soon as possible.

of the deer and me from several different angles so the antlers are evident (my camera has a self-timer). If someone steals my buck and I catch them, I would sign a complaint and show the pictures to the sheriff, judge, or justice of the peace.

Another trick I've heard of but haven't used is to make a small slit somewhere in the cavity of the carcass and insert a coin whose date you've memorized. If the carcass is stolen, you can confront the guilty party with a game warden or sheriff and show the officers the coin that you placed in the deer when you left it in the woods.

Regardless of the way you transport your deer out of the woods, always be sure it is cooled as quickly as possible. That aspect is the primary step to ensuring a nice batch of meat when you get the carcass home.

Once you get the deer to camp or vehicle, then what? Let's look at the alternatives.

The simplest way to handle the carcass is to transport it immediately to a meat packing plant and leave the job to the butcher. He skins your animal if you haven't done so already, ages it properly, cuts it up to your specifications, ships it to your home, or you can pick it up when it's done. That's the easy way.

What if you've driven to the Rockies from a far-off place? If you have the time, you can wait for a meat plant to cut up your meat, quick-freeze it, and take it home packaged in dry ice. Don't count on fast service if you're hunting during the height of deer season. Packing plants are busy, and you'll have to wait your turn.

If you have a short drive, say less than a day, you can take the deer home intact by following a few simple rules. If air temperature is low and the carcass is thoroughly chilled, you can simply load the deer into a vehicle. Be sure the sun isn't hitting it, and allow for plenty of air circulation.

Because I live within an easy day's drive of anyplace in the Rockies, I usually lash my buck to the luggage rack atop my Ramcharger. If the temperature is warm during the day, I try to travel at night when it's cooler. I leave the hide on the buck to protect it from dirt and heat, and have never once had a problem with tainted or "gamey" meat. Of course, the buck is well-cooled when I load him for the journey home. If it rains or I must travel during the heat of the day, I haul the buck inside.

Many mule deer hunters who live in Texas, California, or other states a day or two away like to transport their deer in one piece and cut it up themselves. A good way to do this is to cut the head off the deer, skin it, and the carcass, and then cool the carcass by leaving it out where the night air chills it. Then, just before the trip home, wrap the deer carcass *tightly* in an old sleeping bag or heavy quilt that you've brought along just for that purpose. If you make an overnight stop and the night is cool, open up

Don't try this unless you have a mighty strong back.

the covering and let the deer rechill. Don't open it up if you've driven into a warmer climate, since the temperature of the carcass is probably still colder than the air will get.

If you kill a deer on the last morning of the hunt and want to head home immediately, you can wrap the carcass as I just described, but you *must* pack dry ice with it to cool it off. Otherwise it can spoil if wrapped tightly. If you can't get dry ice, don't wrap the carcass at all. Place it on a piece of canvas in back of your vehicle, allow air to circulate, and keep it out of the sun. This is an iffy proposition, because if you're faced with a lengthy drive in warm temperatures, the carcass may spoil. It's best to buy a cooler, or two coolers, cut the deer up into chunks, and pack it with ice.

Many outdoorsmen fly these days and are faced with a problem of getting meat home. This is really no complicated endeavor, because airlines are usually amenable to shipment of meat. There are several ways to do this. The best is to have your meat processed and frozen and put aboard as part of your luggage. If you expect lengthy lay-overs and will be traveling for 10 hours or more, dry ice should be packaged with the meat. Don Beeler, a taxidermist and meat plant owner in Rawlins, Wyoming, suggests using 10 pounds of dry ice per 24 hours. Airlines consider dry ice a restricted item. You must fill out a restricted article form, which is routine. All it does is ensure that boxes with dry ice are kept away from pets traveling in the same luggage compartment. Meat plants often pack meat in well-insulated cardboard boxes, so it is protected for extended periods.

Another way to ship meat home on an airplane is to make sure the meat is well chilled, cut it into large chunks, wrap it in cheesecloth and two large plastic bags such as the type used in trash containers. Place the bagged meat in a cardboard box, tape it tightly, and check it in as baggage at the airline counter.

Tim Irwin, who works for the NRA, killed a muley buck on a trip with me a couple of years ago and transported his buck back to Washington, D.C., in the manner I just described and had no problems at all. When he got home to Virginia the meat was still well chilled and ready to be cut up and packaged.

Another option, though expensive, is to leave your deer with a meat processor and have him ship it home to you either by air or on a bus. Figure it will cost about $50 if you live 1,000 miles away. I checked air freight rates at the Vernal, Utah airport, and found that Frontier Airlines charges $55 to ship a 100-pound container to Los Angeles and $49 to ship to Dallas.

One of my favorite options is to take the meat to a processor and trade it for delicious salami and sausage. One of my annual pleasures each hunting season is to take a carcass to Don Beeler and trade it for a variety of meats. Processors aren't allowed to sell wild game meat, but you can trade it pound for pound. Most processors have sausages and salamis already processed. All you do is give them your carcass, and pay for an equal amount of processed meat. That way you can have your salami and sausage in an instant without waiting for days or weeks. All the meat traded by hunters goes into a big pot and is ground and spiced uniformly, so it doesn't matter that you don't get back exactly the meat you brought in. You pay extra for the salami and sausage, even with the trade. Figure 85¢ to $1.50 per pound at 1981 prices. If you bone your meat before bringing it in, you save an extra boning fee. Because sausage and salami can withstand a short period without refrigeration, you can toss it in a duffle or suitcase. If you're flying, request an insulated container and check it as baggage.

Take care of your mule deer meat. It is among the best tasting big game you can find. And once you get it home, check the appendix in this book for recipes. Besides having memories of a Western hunt, you'll be able to partake of many culinary delights. What more could you ask?

From Carcass to Venison

When you pull the trigger and your deer is down, be sure its soul is in the Happy Feeding Ground in the Sky. If it still has life, it could injure you seriously or send you to the same Sky. If the deer is down but tries to regain its feet, shoot it once in the center of the throat just under the jaw. This is no easy accomplishment, no matter how close you are. Something is totally unnerving about finishing an animal. When I have to do it, I'm always rattled, and I've seen plenty of other experienced hunters come down with the shakes as well.

If the deer is lying still, examine it from a distance with your scope or binoculars. Look for a heaving chest or blinking eyes. If you see either, administer a killing shot. A sure sign of death is the tongue extended out of the mouth. When you make your final approach, slowly walk *downhill* to the deer from above and try to keep a tree or bush between you. This might sound overly cautious but on one hunt a big whitetail buck would have impaled me solidly if I'd approached him from below. The deer scrambled to his feet and charged wildly down the slope, slashing everything within reach. Luckily I was above, well out of the way. Hard-hit deer won't go out of their way to get you (although there have been a few rare instances), but they may stagger and fall.

Never attempt to kill a wounded deer with a knife. Leave this for Tarzan and other movie heroes. You can be hurt badly if the deer thrashes about with its feet or swings its antlers.

When the deer is dead, do not bother to slit its throat—unless you want the exercise. The only way blood flows is if the heart is beating, so the process becomes unnecessary. Bleeding a deer does nothing more than allow blood in the vicinity of the cut to flow out by gravity. Don't worry about blood. It drains when you remove the entrails.

Likewise, removal of the scent glands on the rear legs is a futile effort, because in no way can the meat be tainted if they're left alone. But if you touch them to cut them off, and then handle the carcass, your hands transfer the bitter odor to the meat.

Before touching the deer at all, throw a stick or rock at it, and bend forward and give it a prod with your rifle barrel or a branch. Always be positive the deer is dead. I heard a story once about a young hunter who dropped a buck and excitedly tied his hunting tag to an antler. The buck suddenly recovered, jumped up and ran off, and was killed by another hunter over the ridge. The boy ran up, got to the deer at the same time the other hunter did, and told the stranger he'd shot his buck. The man was skeptical until the youngster brushed away the leaves covering the antler and exposed the tag. The man shook his head in disbelief and wandered down the trail.

You must field dress the deer immediately after it's killed. The all-important priority in obtaining the best quality venison is to cool the carcass quickly. That means you don't run off looking for a buddy, or delay the job an extra minute.

If you're alone, position the deer in as flat a spot as you can find so it won't roll or slide. You might need to prop a log or some stones under the carcass to keep it steady. If you're on a steep sidehill, place the deer head-up. If it slides, try to entangle the antlers in some brush to hold it still, or tie the head to a tree.

Using a sharp knife, make your initial cut directly between the legs, holding them apart with your knees if you can. Do not puncture the intestines, but lightly slit the abdominal wall all the way up the middle of the underside from the anal opening to the rib cage. To help keep the intestines away from the knife point during this operation, form a "V" with your first two fingers under the skin, and press the intestines in while you guide the knife forward. If you're dressing a buck, simply detour around the penis and continue the cut. Don't cut off the penis or testicles if you're unsure of regulations in the state you're hunting. Some require you to leave evidence of sex (besides antlers) on the carcass.

With the entire underside slit up the middle, cut completely around the anus with the end of the knife. Don't poke the knife in too deeply, or you might puncture the bladder. Usually the bladder can't be reached unless the knife has a long blade, but be careful anyway.

With this done, you're ready to expose the intestines and organs. At the base of the rib cage, a thin sheet of muscle separates the organs from intestines. Slice this sheet (the diaphragm) away, and reach up toward the throat to cut the esophagus and windpipe. Be careful you don't accidentally slice a finger, because you can't see what you're doing and you're working in a confined space. Take a good grip on the windpipe and pull it down, cutting as you go. Slice the membranes holding the organs, and continue the gradual pull, freeing any muscles that connect the organs to the abdominal cavity. Reach up and pull on the intestines where they attach to the vertebrae area, and cut away any tissues that hold the viscera. Roll the innards out onto the ground, and gently ream the anal opening from the inside. Pull on the anal intestine, and very carefully extract the bladder. With the entire network of viscera on the ground, pull the deer away, and position it so blood flows out.

The job is done, and you're ready to move the carcass out of the woods or leave it and come back with help. If you leave it, drag it into the shade and cover it with branches to keep magpies and ravens away, but allow plenty of space for circulation. Prop open the cavity with a stick to let air in.

Tim Irwin skins a buck soon after it was killed. The quicker a carcass is cooled, the better it tastes.

If you're hunting mule deer in the Southwest in extremely warm weather and have no way to cool the meat, you might consider skinning it on the ground where you field dressed it. To skin it, lay it on one side in a flat area, and make a slit up the underside of the hind leg to the knee joint. Skin the upper side, work down the flanks and sides, and skin the front leg. When the skin is free from the entire upper side to the middle of the back, carefully roll the deer on to its other side and do the same. Take care not to soil the skinned carcass with leaves, dirt, and twigs.

When you get your deer to camp or vehicle, don't assume the job is done. You must constantly keep the carcass cool and free from flies. Hang the deer where it will be in shade all day. I can't emphasize enough the necessity of keeping the carcass cool. It is the key to good eating.

Studies prove that skinning a deer allows it to cool much quicker than when the skin is left intact. In one test, a mule deer leg with skin removed took 10 hours to reach 38 degrees during refrigeration, while a leg with hide took 14 hours to reach the same temperature. The test was under controlled conditions and was accurate. This doesn't mean, however, that you must rush to skin your deer if the nights drop down to temperatures in the 30's. By all means, leave the skin on, since the carcass will cool sufficiently with no loss of quality. There are other reasons for leaving the skin on, the primary one being to protect the meat from dirt and dust. Another is to prevent the skin from drying and glazing, requiring one to trim away otherwise good meat.

If the weather does *not* turn cool in the evenings, you must get the carcass to a cooler on the day of the kill. Say you're hunting for desert muleys in Arizona, and night temperatures get down to the 60's. You're flirting with trouble unless your deer meat is somehow cooled. An option is to have chest-type coolers with you. Cut the carcass into pieces and put them in the cooler. If you find dry ice in a nearby town, wrap the carcass and ice in an old quilt or sleeping bag. Best of all, take the carcass to a locker plant and pay them to cool it for you until your party is ready to leave.

Another chapter details various ways to get your meat home in good shape. Follow those instructions, and remember, the word is cool.

When you arrive home with your deer, you can hang it until it's ready to be cut up. A garage or basement is a likely place to hang a carcass, or you can hang it from a shady tree. If autumn days turn brisk and breezy, the carcass can be hung in the sun if it's left skinned or wrapped in canvas.

By all means, beware of neighborhood canines when selecting a place to hang your deer. Dogs will be dogs, and most love to dine on fresh venison. One year, I killed a particularly fat, juicy buck that required a small army of helpers to drag out of a steep draw. When I got him home, I hung him by his antlers from my garage rafter, and left the overhead door open about a foot to let cool air circulate. The next day, my wife called me at the office to tell me a neighbor's Irish setter had been feasting on the buck. I hurried home and found an entire hindquarter eaten away. It was too late to do anything but cry, but I learned a good lesson. Now I hang my deer by their hind feet so the antlers clear the garage floor by at least two feet or more.

To age or not to age? Most experts recommend aging a deer carcass for several days to allow it to become tender before butchering. Aging breaks down the muscle, and makes the meat much more palatable. If you hang your carcass in a room that stays about 40 degrees, plan to age the meat 5 to 7 days. If the temperature is warmer, shorten the aging time by a day or two. Keep a good lookout for flies during the aging process; wrap the carcass *completely* in cheesecloth. Some hunters wrap the body in cheesecloth and tie it off at the throat, leaving the head exposed. That's no hindrance to enterprising flies, because they find their way into the mouth, down the windpipe and into the body cavity, or into the nose or ears.

If you age the carcass without the hide, the exposed meat hardens and begins to dry inward. The longer the meat hangs, the more it dries, and the greater the waste. If at all possible, leave the pelt on until you're ready to butcher. You'll have moist meat and much less waste.

Make daily sniff tests as the deer is aging, especially around bloodshot areas where the bullet tore up meat. If you detect any sour smell at all, stop what you're doing, get out the knives and cutting board, and start in. Parts of the carcass have started to decay, and you must salvage the rest immediately.

Skinning a deer is no chore, because the hide peels easily. You can start from top or bottom, but I find skinning from the hind legs down to the head to be the easiest. When using your knife to sever tissue while skinning, take care to avoid cutting hair. A good skinning job leaves as little hair as possible on the carcass. No matter what you do, however, you'll have strands of hair on the carcass. When I'm finished with a skinning job, I use lukewarm water to lightly rinse the skin, removing every wisp of hair I see. Hair imparts a terribly bitter taste to the meat; you must remove every speck.

With hide removed, you next settle down to the meat-cutting operation. First off, find a comfortable place to work. My procedure is to wipe

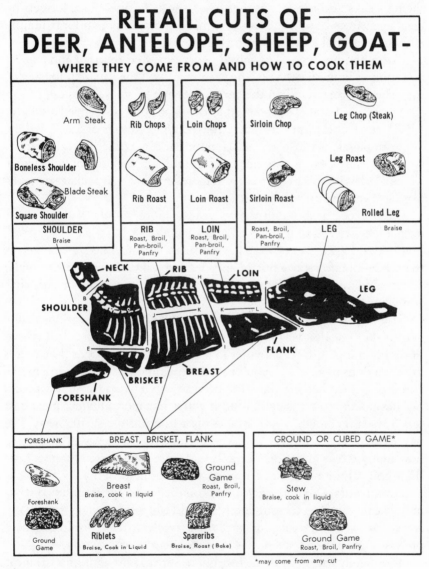

(Photo courtesy of Professor Ray A. Field, University of Wyoming.)

off the kitchen table, cut off a quarter of the carcass, and lay it on a 2-foot-square cutting board on the table. Sound uncouth? It isn't, if you've cleaned the carcass thoroughly. For tools, I use a meat-cutting saw, three butcher knives, and a sharpening stone. One knife has a long blade for slicing steaks and roasts, another has a short, flexible blade for cutting meat away from bones, and the other has a short, stiff blade for trimming fat, sinew, and bloodshot portions.

I keep handy a big roll of waxed-paper-type freezer wrap, and tear off two squares immediately, placing them nearby. One square is for steaks, the other for roasts. When the correct portion of steaks piles up, I wrap the meat, tape it, label it, and set it aside. Each roast is wrapped individually. When I label meat cuts, I describe the type of steaks or roasts within. For example, steaks are classified as round, sirloin, etc.; roasts can be front shoulder, rump, etc. I also include the state and the year of kill. (Don't wince. As I write this in the winter of 1981, I'm thawing a package of steaks from a Wyoming buck killed in 1978.)

If you expect to hold meat for a year or more, simply double-wrap it *tightly*. The trick is to seal it well and keep air out.

Besides the squares of wrap for steaks and roasts, I keep two pans on the table—one for stew chunks and one for jerky. If you want to make homemade sausage or burger, have a container available for cuts that you want to grind later.

The big question is *how* do you make the cuts for the various roasts and steaks? The best way is to ask an experienced friend to help if you've never butchered before. It's easier to watch and ask questions than to follow directions in a book. If you can spare the time and money, you might enroll in a meat-cutting class. I've been tempted to do this many times, but never seem to get around to it. If you're like most amateur meat cutters (myself included), you just dive right in and start slicing away. I've never cut up a deer, moose, elk, or antelope the same way. I just figure how many roasts and steaks I want, and start from there. Tougher portions go in the stew pot, and lean strips are used for jerky.

An advantage in cutting your own meat is the opportunity to wrap and slice it according to your family's needs. My teenage daughter, for example likes venison steaks cut extra thick, while my 10-year-old daughter prefers them thin. My teenage son wolfs them down regardless.

Your family will enjoy them, too, but be sure to start caring for the meat as soon as the deer hits the ground.

Hunting During Migration

When deep snow covers the Western mountains, mule deer must migrate to lower elevations where food is available. Hunters who are aware of migrations often make astounding kills when they intercept moving herds. Though anyone can blunder into a migrating herd, the hunter who understands mule deer migration behavior and patterns greatly increases his chances of success. And success it will be, if the timing is right. At no other period is a hunter likely to see as many deer as during migration.

Studies on migration show that deer begin their movement to lower country when severe weather strikes. The following statement from a study by the Utah Division of Wildlife Resources in the vicinity of Flaming Gorge Reservoir on the Utah-Wyoming border illustrates the point:

"On October 4, 1969, an extensive storm deposited 18 to 20 inches of snow throughout the study area, with greater depths recorded above 8,500 feet. In a few days, large numbers of deer were observed migrating east toward winter range. Does and fawns moved immediately with the advent of winter storms. Bucks generally migrated later from hunting pressure and effects of severe winter storms that occurred in 1969."

Snow is the ingredient that triggers migration, but a hunter needs to know several things before he can locate moving deer. First, has enough snow fallen to trigger migration? Second, where are the migration routes, and third, where is the winter range?

To determine if deer have started their annual movement, don snowshoes and start looking. If the snow isn't deep enough for snowshoes, prepare for tough walking. Snow that is deeper than 10 inches requires a strong mind and body to negotiate. If it isn't at least 10 inches deep, deer probably haven't begun to move to lower country. What you're looking for is a network of well-used trails showing an exodus of deer in more or less a general direction. Deer may feed on the journey, but are more interested in getting out of the snow to where better feed is. Thus the tracks are lined out straight.

Once you've satisfied yourself that the migration has started, you can execute a number of plans. You can stay in the high country, wallow around in deep snow and hope to ambush a buck that hasn't yet started down (remember, the study indicates does and fawns start down first); you can get on a well-packed trail and follow, trying to catch up to the deer; you can head for lower country and try to intercept them while they're moving down; or, you can go directly to the winter range and wait for them to show up.

Hoping to catch up to deer on a migration route can be a great exercise in futility. I tried it. When deer are moving out of snow, they don't dally. They might go several miles without stopping. If they're a full day ahead of you, you'll never catch them unless they rest to feed.

If you decide to stay high and waylay a stubborn buck that hasn't started down yet, you should be prepared for winter's worst. Biting winds and

Murry Burnham killed this Colorado buck during a December migration. Murry suffered frostbite on this bitterly cold hunt. (*Photo courtesy of Murry Burnham.*)

This herd of deer migrated from the high country to winter range. Note the nice buck with about a 26-inch spread. Do you see the little buck?

snowstorms could move in easily, catching you unprepared. A daypack and survival gear are a must. There's a special charm hunting in very deep snow. Trees are lovely with their heavily-laden branches, and there's a fresh sparkle in the forest. It's much quieter than normal, and you'll find plenty of solitude, perhaps more than you want. If you jump a bedded buck, you won't hear the usual thump as he pounds away, but muffled noises as he brushes by tree limbs and snow-covered brush. You must be extra alert in the whitened woods, because your quarry can see you more easily than you can see him. If you see a buck and try to follow him, don't be too ambitious if it's afternoon. You might find yourself far from a road or car as darkness approaches, and you're in for a rough night. Remember, dark comes quickly in the late fall. By 5 p.m. you're out of shooting light.

To intercept deer on their way down to winter range, do a lot of walking to find the migration routes. If the deer haven't made it down to where you're looking, obviously no routes are identifiable. If they've already passed, you might be no better off than you were in the higher country. The best bet, if you're serious, is to plan an entire day of walking and looking. You'll need to cover a lot of ground to find sign of migrating herds.

A tip-off to find migration routes is to query local residents about where herds of deer cross highways just after the first big snowstorm. Many will know, but failed to appreciate what was happening. If you can find such a place, check it out to see if deer have been by. If not, and your sources of information are reliable, park your vehicle and head upcountry where you can find a ledge or vantage point that offers a broad vista. Migrating deer don't necessarily stay in cover. They have a single mission in mind, and are liable to be marching across vast openings in the middle of the day.

Another tip-off is a sign along a highway that warns motorists of deer migration areas. The sign won't pinpoint the precise spot, but may say, "Warning, Deer Migration Area, Next 4 Miles." At least you have some idea where to start. If the country along the highway is public land, you can look anywhere, but if it's private, you need to ask permission.

The objective of the migrating herd is to get to the winter range. Most winter ranges are much smaller than the vast summering areas, but that doesn't mean you can walk right in and pick your buck. It may take deer weeks or months before they finally end up in the winter country. If the weather turns balmy and starts melting snow, migrations may temporarily slow down until a new storm sends herds on their way.

I had heard about migrations as soon as I came to the West in the late 1950's, but I never really appreciated the phenomenon until I experienced a 4-day odyssey in Utah several years ago.

I was hunting with Mike Perry, a professional biologist who is Director of the Utah Fieldhouse of Natural History in Vernal, and Earle Smith, a forester with the Bureau of Land Management. At the time, I was working as a wildlife biologist for the Bureau of Land Management.

When we drove to the 9,000-foot elevation area we planned to hunt, we found more snow than we figured. At least 20 inches blanketed the ground, and the only way we could negotiate the mountain road was to chain all four wheels on my pick-up and stay in the tracks made by other hunters. My camper was parked in the trees, since I left it there a week ago when the ground was dry. I hadn't yet killed a buck, and planned on finding something worthwhile on this trip. We had seen plenty of deer before the snowstorm, and I had no reason to be concerned when I saw the deep snow. If anything, I was delighted. I love to hunt in snow.

When dawn broke the next morning, we were on a high ridge that normally produced decent bucks. A solid stand of oak brush, mountain mahogany and serviceberry sheltered and fed a good deer population. I had never hunted the ridge without seeing plenty of deer.

We decided to still-hunt, so we split up and headed out in three different directions. I hoped to find a red-hot track of a big buck and line-out on him like a blue-tick on a coon trail. I wallowed through knee-high snow and walked along the side of a north-facing ridge. That side would stay shaded longer, and I figured I had a better chance of seeing bucks before they began bedding.

I plodded along for several hundred yards, and each step was torturous. In places the snow was drifted as high as my waist, and I had to fight it just to lift my boot to take another step. I hadn't crossed a deer track, and wasn't very confident about doing so when I suddenly came to a heavily used trail in the snow. I examined it, and saw many deer tracks, all heading west. I followed it for 300 yards, and saw where it merged with another trail, also going west. Again I followed, and before I walked one-quarter of a mile, found a half-dozen more trails. Without exception, every track was westbound, and it didn't take me long to figure out what was happening. Because I worked in the area, I knew the lay of the land and knew that McCook Ridge to the west was a major wintering area for the Book Cliffs region we hunted. Before me were the signs of a major migration, a sight that I'd never seen. I'd witnessed migrating herds on the move, but nothing this extensive. I estimated hundreds of deer piled off the high country in a matter of hours. If only I could have been there when it was all happening!

I couldn't believe all the deer had gone, so I left the trails and cut back upcountry. Perhaps I'd blunder into a tardy buck. The more I walked, the more trails I crossed. The deer had been on the move less than 24 hours, because we knew it had snowed until noon the previous day. All the tracks were made since it had snowed.

I found a place where eight separate trails merged into one. The amount of traffic on that major trail was incredible. If there ever was a massive migration, this was it.

I needed to evaluate my strategy. I hadn't seen an animal after 4 hours of hunting. Two possibilities presented themselves: keep working up, try-ing to ambush a buck moving down, or follow the deer west.

There was no choice. I couldn't resist the temptation to follow the trails. Too many huge tracks were imprinted among them.

As I headed west, I was astounded at the number of other trails that kept merging. I felt as if I was on a major ant trail where the main army had marched, with smaller battalions feeding in from the flanks. Because the deer had packed the snow, I could walk easily. Excitement built the farther I walked. I expected to see deer every time I topped a rise or rounded a bend. The country was beginning to open, and I could see several hundred yards in front. I could also see McCook Ridge some 12 miles away. It was frustrating to know that somewhere between me and McCook, several hundred deer were on the march.

The afternoon grew later, and I became more excited. I was so sure I was just behind the deer I began trotting to cut the distance. But nothing showed. Still the trails stretched ahead, filled with tantalizing tracks. With only an hour of daylight left, I topped a high ridge and looked across a huge, empty expanse that offered a view of more than a mile. With binoculars I followed the trails and saw them disappear far ahead. Empty, not a deer in sight.

It was too late to go any farther. I headed back to camp, amazed at what I'd seen that day. Mike and Earl had the same story to tell as I. Neither of them had seen a buck, only endless tracks heading for McCook Ridge.

Mule deer have recently moved into this winter range area from the high country. Note the abundant tracks.

Hunting during migration time can be a cold, snowy outing. Prepare for inclement weather and dress properly, as Mike Perry did on this Utah hunt.

We laid plans for the following day, deciding to hunt even higher. There just *had* to be some buster bucks back in the timber. If tomorrow didn't work, we'd pull camp and head for lower country.

The next day was a total failure. We stumbled around in deep snow, and gained nothing but sore muscles. More trails heading west, but no deer.

We hitched up the camper and pulled off to lower country that night. We drove for a dozen miles, found a place to set camp, and noted the snow was much more sparse, perhaps 10 inches.

Sign was encouraging the next morning. Tracks were everywhere — meandering tracks, which meant that deer were in the vicinity feeding. We didn't score that day, but the last day was a charmer. Before it was over, we put two four-points and a three-point to the ground. We had solved the riddle of the migration, and learned a lesson we'd never forget.

Mule deer migrate for long distances in many habitats. In the three-corner region where Utah, Wyoming, and Colorado join together, for example, deer from all three states travel to sprawling Brown's Park where winters are relatively mild. In Utah, a study with tagged deer indicated some had moved more than 80 miles to reach Brown's Park. Not even huge Flaming Gorge Reservoir stopped the migration pattern. Deer swim the big impoundment each fall and spring in the same places they had crossed the river before it was dammed.

Deer migrations may occur during the breeding season. If so, big bucks escort does. If the rut isn't into full swing, bucks may travel in groups.

One of the greatest success stories I've ever heard occurred during the middle of a migration in northeast Utah. Fifteen hunters were apparently in the middle of a migration route when a huge herd of deer appeared. When it was all over, 15 bucks wore tags on their antlers. The hunters said 20 or 30 more bucks were in the herd.

Deer migrations can transform deer-rich country into desolate regions overnight. The hunter who recognizes the pattern doesn't waste time hunting where there are no deer. Keep your plans flexible and be prepared to move. Get into the thick of a deer migration and you won't ever forget it.

Hunting in Aspen Forests

Quaking aspens are to the Rockies what the sugar maple is to New England. The autumn riot of color in Western forests is attributed almost entirely to quaking aspens. Without them, fall months would be somber and monotonous, hardly different than other seasons.

Besides their beauty, aspens are valuable for other reasons. A notable one is the attraction mule deer have for them. Perhaps deer aren't attracted to aspens, but live in them because the trees just happen to be there. Whatever the case, aspen stands are wonderful places to hunt mule deer.

Given the choice of hunting mule deer in any environment, I'll take a quaking aspen forest any time. Something is magic about slipping through the white-barked trees, of hearing the rustling leaves, of walking along a leafy trail when the sun is just a promise in the Eastern skies. My favorite mule deer hunting spot is a certain aspen grove high in the Colorado mountains. I wouldn't think of allowing a hunting season to pass without making my annual journey to this lovely spot in the Rockies. When I hunt in other states, my bias about aspens shines forth. I seek them every place I can.

Quaking aspens are a "fire type," which means they quickly invade an area after a forest fire has denuded it. Foresters call aspens an early successional stage because the trees are often the first to occupy a disturbed area. As years pass, aspens mature and are overtaken by tree species of later successional stages, such as Douglas fir, Engelmann spruce, and alpine fir.

Typical elevations for aspens range from 7,000 feet to 9,000 feet and

Murry Burnham (left) and hunting party relax near a heavy meat pole full of Colorado muleys killed in an aspen forest. *(Photo courtesy of Murry Burnham.)*

higher. They aren't in the high Rockies, but are at a somewhat intermediate level.

Mule deer thrive in aspens because all the elements are there—food, shelter, and water. Except for the winter season when deep snows drive deer to lower elevations, aspens are their home practically year round.

Brushy undergrowth is usually plentiful in and around aspen stands, especially when the trees are young. Various shrubs that mule deer love grow in profusion, creating ideal habitat for all sorts of wildlife.

Since aspens grow in mid to high elevations, water is seldom a problem. Creeks, springs, and water holes are generally abundant enough to satisfy the needs of deer.

There are all kinds of ways to hunt aspens, but my favorite is to sneak down well-traveled trails that snake along the tree-covered hillsides. By walking on trails, it's possible to move about with less noise, and there's always a chance that deer will be wandering toward you on the same trail.

A tough time to hunt aspens is when leaves are falling and the weather is dry. The dried leaves sound like brittle potato chips when they're stepped on. If nights are chilly, frost sometimes covers the leaves and silences them a bit until the sun dries them and renews their crispness. An optimum time to hunt is just after or during a rainstorm, or when soft snow covers the forest floor.

In aspen stands where visibility is good, long shots may be required. As long shots go, these aren't much—perhaps 100 or 150 yards. The difficulty lies in threading a bullet through the trees to the target. A 100-yard shot in the forest is akin to 300 yards or more in the open. I prefer a scope-sighted rifle in the aspens because the optics allow me to glass distant deer

Aspen forests are extensive in the Rockies. Mule deer use them for shelter and feeding areas.

that may be feeding, walking, or bedded. The scope is a disadvantage when trying to follow a running deer through the trees, but I've taught myself to pick an opening in front of the fleeing animal and shoot when it passes through it.

Deer normally bed just under the top of a hill so they can see below them. This isn't to say that deer don't bed in the bottoms of draws or on tops of knolls, but the majority I've come across like a small flat spot about 30 yards below the crest of a ridge.

My favorite strategy is to stillhunt just below ridgetops—just far enough down so I won't be skylined, and just far enough up to be above bedded deer. If a deer flushes above the hunter, it will likely run uphill and disappear over the top in a few quick bounds. But if it flushes below a hunter, it will normally run along the sidehill a bit and break for the top, giving the hunter a chance for a shot. It's important to remember that mule deer almost always run uphill to escape danger.

If you're hunting in aspens after the leaves have fallen, chances are good you might be able to see through the trees and observe nearby sidehills. Be extra cautious if this is the case, because a buck across a canyon might spook, yet still be within reasonable range for a shot. Don't be fooled by distances across draws or canyons, they're often longer than they appear to be.

A few years ago I was hunting a steep aspen sidehill when a pair of big bucks flushed from their beds across the canyon and ran up the mountain at an angle. The deer weren't in a hurry, but trotted along briskly, stopping every now and then to test the wind. I don't think they knew I was in the vicinity, just disturbed by a noise I'd made or a whiff of my scent. One of the bucks stopped in an opening where I could fire through the tops of the trees. I judged the distance to be about 300 yards, elevated my sights accordingly, and fired. The bullet smacked into a dead limb over the buck's back and the deer escaped unharmed. I looked the distance over carefully, walked to the area where the buck had been standing, and judged the distance to be no more than 150 yards. Had I known, I could have held dead on and scored.

If you can see a long way in the aspens, remember that deer can, too. They get nervous when a human invades their territory, and often don't wait long before moving out. In very open forests, deer routinely flush a long way out, making it tough to get a shot.

In hilly country, I like to walk along slowly and edge up to a rise, scanning the new country beyond. This is a fine method to spot a deer before it sees you, but be sure the wind direction is correct.

One of the biggest mistakes made by deer hunters is the speed with which they hunt. There seems to be an unwritten rule that the more country you put under your feet the more deer you'll see. That might be true, but most of those deer will be long gone or well out of range. Why not slow down, enjoy the delights of the woods, and call upon your skills to locate a deer close up? Hunters who walk fast commonly complain there are no deer in the country when in fact they've stirred up dozens of animals, most of which spooked unnoticed well ahead.

I look for deer movement in my favorite aspen forest. (Photo courtesy of Tim Irwin.)

When I sneak up to a rise with the intention of glassing the fresh land-scape beyond, the first thing I do is catch my breath if I've been climbing hard. I've missed deer because my scope raised and lowered too much when my lungs were working overtime for oxygen. To complicate matters, you'll see most of the deer just after or during a hard climb because muleys like to bed high. Once my breathing returns to normal, I peek over the crest and silently observe the area for a minute or two. If I see nothing, I snuggle into a comfortable position, and continue to observe, without binoculars, everything in sight. Basically I'm looking for movement, par-ticularly if it's early in the morning or late in the afternoon when deer are traveling to or from feeding areas. I don't look *at* the aspens before me, but *into* them. I slowly take in every detail, and concentrate on looking for forms and colors that spell deer. If I see nothing interesting, I stop the in-tensive staring and casually allow my eyes to wander about, looking for the moving head of a feeding deer, a twitching tail, or other signal.

If I still see no deer, I rely on binoculars to do the rest. I glass every pos-sible nook and cranny—everywhere a mule deer might be—and places he might not be. Patches of brush, blowdowns, water holes, weedy draws, and sagebrush flats are some of the places I glass intently.

When binoculars fail to show deer, I slowly top the rise with rifle ready. This is the time that hidden deer might jump from their beds and bound away. I want to be prepared for a running shot.

During a Wyoming hunt I was stillhunting along a series of pretty ridges blanketed with aspens. Deer were uncooperative, since most had spooked well in front of me. The wind was at my back, but I couldn't do much about it because my buddy was waiting about two miles away in the direction I was heading. We had agreed to meet at a pre-determined spot. While moving along slowly, I came to a small knoll. I knew the little basin be-yond it was a hot-spot for deer, and confidently sat next to a stump to give the area a thorough look with binoculars. Immediately I spotted six deer feeding in a small opening surrounded by aspens. One was a small four-point buck, but I was planning on something bigger. After 15 minutes of searching, I decided the six deer were alone in the basin. I got up from the ground, stretched weary muscles, and unwrapped a candy bar. Instantly a deer thumped away no more than 40 yards distant. It was a big five-point, and it wasted no time gaining ground. By the time I discarded the candy bar and snapped the rifle to my shoulder he was gone. Had I been ready when I stepped away from the rise, I could have had an excellent shot at him.

A disadvantage of hunting aspens is the difficulty of finding fresh tracks on ground covered with leaves. That means almost everywhere, except in places where wind has blown them away. There are other places that show recent deer use, however, such as water holes, roads, and bottoms of draws where well-used trails meander about.

Snow changes all that, and quickly betrays the presence of deer. The wonderful white stuff allows stalking, quiet travel, and makes deer stand out more vividly.

The only method I like better than stillhunting in aspens is following the fresh track of a big buck. It becomes an exciting challenge, one I look forward to each autumn.

One of my most memorable experiences occurred during a hunt in Utah a dozen years ago. I awoke to find 4 inches of powder snow piled lightly around my tent. It was the kind of day a hunter's dreams are made of. Snapping dead branches from some nearby aspens, I scraped a spot in the snow and soon had a brisk fire burning. Daylight was still an hour away, and I had plenty of time to savor a hot cup of coffee and fresh, homemade chocolate-chip cookies. I remember well that morning, with the tiny flames flashing off the trees and the smell of woodsmoke as it curled into the night.

I packed fruit, sandwiches, and cookies into my daypack, filled my canteen with water from a nearby spring, and headed off for a ridge where I'd seen a big buck the day before. He wasn't disturbed, and I felt good about finding his track. The ground was barren the previous day, and any tracks in the new-fallen snow would be just hours old.

By daybreak I was a half mile from camp. Elk tracks were evident, but deer sign was scarce. It was a good omen, because I figured deer had been holing up during the storm and would feed well into morning.

An hour later, I cut a single track that spelled big buck. The prints were long, wide, and deeply cut into the snow. This was a buck to respect, and I was all for tying my tag on his antler. The big buck I had seen the previous day appeared to be a typical four-pointer, with a high, symmetrical rack. There had been no chance for a shot at the deer then. He had given me only a quick look before disappearing into a brushy draw just minutes before shooting hours were over. I hoped the tracks before me in the snow were made by the same animal.

I took up the trail and followed for 2 hours. The deer led me across three ridges, always staying in the aspens. He wandered about to feed, but didn't stay very long in one place. While trailing him I saw dozens of other deer, including a small four-point, two three-points, and several forked horns. None were interesting to me.

About 9 a.m. I discovered where the buck had bedded. His body heat melted a depression in the snow, and it looked as if he had left his bed just minutes before. His tracks showed he was in no hurry to leave, but I suspected he knew I was in the area and simply sneaked off.

His tracks were lined out toward a deep, rugged canyon, and I had a hunch he was headed there. This crafty deer knew what he was doing. I knew I had to catch up soon, so at the risk of blundering into him and spoiling the chase, I trotted along his trail, hoping to catch him slipping through the aspens ahead.

A half-hour later I finally saw him, 600 yards away and walking briskly forward. The deep canyon was just before him, and I watched the big animal disappear from sight. I considered following, but gave up the idea when the top of the buck's antlers momentarily appeared between two

Aspen is a "fire type," which means it grows in quickly after a forest fire. Note the young saplings growing only 3 weeks after fire burned this area. Mule deer are already feeding on the plants.

boulders. The antlers were whizzing along, and I knew the buck had finally decided to put me far behind. Once in the canyon, he bolted and crashed straight down. I gave him a salute, and wished him health. Then I turned and headed back into the aspens. While trailing the buck, I crossed another interesting track that required investigation!

Deer drives work well in quaking aspens if the trees are thinned out. Drives work where aspens are thick, too, but more standers are required to effectively cover the forest.

Since deer normally prefer to escape by running uphill, small drives are best designed by placing standers on ridgetops with drivers working up from the bottom. On long drives, a good strategy is to put standers in a saddle where deer are apt to cross from one drainage to another, and along the flanks of the area being driven. Be sure each stander is at a vantage point where he has a broad vista. It's surprising how much you can see when leaves are off the aspens, especially if you're on a high slope looking onto a hillside below or across from your location.

Standers need not be at high vantage points all the time. Deer like to run up, but sooner or later they come to the end of the climb and start down again to gain the next ridge. If it's easier for the hunting party, you can space standers down low on the backside of a mountain or ridge being driven and hope that pursued deer top the crest and travel down near the standers.

Drives that take in more than a half mile are seldom consistently successful, because a flushed deer can make plenty of unexpected moves in that distance. Once in awhile, though, the method works.

I'm reminded of a hunt in Colorado during the mid 1970's. I was camped in an aspen forest, and met a party of congenial hunters from Arkansas. They were a friendly lot, and invited me to share tales with them around their fire that evening. We discussed the deer we'd seen and drank steaming cups of black coffee, and the hunters said they planned an all-out drive the next day. They had killed only two bucks, but had been seeing lots of does and fawns. I was invited to hunt with them, but I had seen a pair of big tracks that day and I wanted to give them my undivided attention next morning.

By daybreak the following morning I was deep in a drainage, about a half mile from where the drive was being held. Because the aspens were patchy and thin, I could see hunter-orange-clad figures moving along a distant ridge. The party from Arkansas was in action. Though the drive was being conducted a long way off, I decided to sit and wait. Finding a comfortable spot, I unscrewed the top of my thermos and poured a cup of coffee. Maybe a stray buck would move out ahead of the drivers and wander into my lap. It was worth a try.

Fifteen minutes later I heard the unmistakable sounds of deer rustling through an aspen thicket just below me and on the other side of a small creek. The thicket was practically impenetrable, and the deer couldn't take a step without making noise. I peered into the tangle of trees and brush with my binoculars, but couldn't make out a thing. Finally, a doe and fawn emerged and stepped into a brushy swale. The doe turned her head, looked directly over in the direction of the drivers, and trotted off down the creek. Presently eight more deer walked out, including three medium-sized bucks. There was nothing that excited me, so I watched them move off down the creek. No other deer showed, so I got to my feet and headed up the ridge, looking for a buck with something enticing atop his head.

Around the campfire that night, I told the hunters about the deer. They elected to make the same drive the next day, but this time two hunters would cover the thicket next to the creek. It was a wild chance, but it worked. Each killed a buck—a modest four-pointer and a lovely five-pointer. Apparently the deer headed routinely for the thicket when they were spooked.

Why didn't they remain in the thicket where they'd be hidden? A good question, and if I knew the answer, much of the excitement about mule deer hunting would be gone.

I wish aspen forests were overlooked by other hunters, but they're not. I'm not the only person attracted to them. Indeed, hundreds of thousands of other hunters hunt aspens for mule deer. The reason is simple. Aspen forests are productive and fun to hunt in.

Don't let the presence of other hunters dampen your enthusiasm for aspens, however, unless you're the type that likes solitude and few gunshots echoing about the hills. There are ways to capitalize on the presence of other hunters.

A good way is to find a ledge, rocky outcropping, or other overlook that offers a view of landscape that harbors deer. Next, make yourself comfortable and prepare to sit as long as you can. Sooner or later something is bound to happen. If you stick it out, it may happen when you're there.

I know a ridge in Utah that is mobbed by hunters. Each year, just like

A buck I killed in an aspen forest that has provided a buck for
me 5 years in a row.

clockwork, men, women, and children leave their camps on top of the
ridge and head off down the hillside. Predictably, deer are stirred immediately and head for cover elsewhere. Nearby is a small knoll that offers a
view of the sidehill. If a hunter takes the trouble to walk to the knoll before
daybreak, and it's a rugged walk, he's almost assured a shot at a buck.

The ploy doesn't work every day, however. Usually only the first one
or two days of the season are productive. It doesn't take a deer long to
figure he better leave if he wants to keep his hide intact.

I don't mean to imply that quaking aspen forests are traditionally crawling with hunters. Quite the contrary in areas where roads are few. These
days the majority of hunters don't travel far from their vehicle, so if you
can find the backside of a mountain where access is only by shank's mare,
investigate it and give it a try. Chances are good you'll stumble into a buck.

In some mountain ranges, aspens grow in patches with open meadows
between them. The patches can range anywhere from a few to several
hundred acres. If cover in the meadows is sparse, deer will use the aspen

timber for shelter. Many of those timbered patches require an uphill climb, but are worth the effort. Wyoming offers some of the best of this type of habitat. I know several mountains where it's practically impossible to hunt a patch without seeing deer.

. Aspen forests are often intermingled with evergreen trees, especially at higher elevations. These are old aspen stands, about to be overcome by the more hardy pines, firs, and spruces. Foresters use the word *tolerance* to classify tree species. Tolerance means the ability of a tree to withstand *shade*. Aspens are not as tolerant as most evergreens, and slowly give way as the firs and spruces top them and shut out sunlight. When enough sunshine is blocked, aspens die and evergreens take over. This is natural succession in the forest, and goes on everywhere that trees grow. The aspen cycle is renewed only when a major disturbance such as fire or logging eliminates the evergreens. Then aspens reappear and start a new succession all over again.

To a mule deer hunter, the aspen-evergreen forest is a much different environment to hunt than the classic pure aspen stand. Visibility is severely limited, and new challenges are presented. Successful hunting techniques include deer drives, watching the edges of the forest when deer are moving about, stillhunting, or watching a water hole. This forest produces some of the biggest bucks of all, because they can easily avoid hunters. Snow is a big help in the aspen-evergreen forest for obvious reasons. It not only makes for quieter walking, but it also indicates the presence of deer and makes it easier to see them.

If aspens are present in the area you like to hunt, give them a hard try if you haven't already. You might never go back to any other areas again.

Hunting in Pinyon-Juniper Forests

Pinyon-juniper forests blanket an amazing part of the West, covering about 50 million acres. The bulk of the forests are in Colorado, New Mexico, Arizona, Utah, and Nevada. Such forests are commonly referred to as the "cedars" or "P-J" forests by locals. It is the characteristic vegetative type of the southern Rocky Mountain foothills, the mesas of the Colorado Plateau, and the mountains of the Great Basin. On good sites with adequate moisture and growing conditions, the trees of the pinyon-juniper forest often reach heights of 40 feet.

Several species of pinyons and junipers make up the forest, the most common being the Colorado and Singleleaf pinyon, and the Utah juniper. Junipers generally grow in the lower elevations with low precipitation, while pinyons tend to grow higher where water is more abundant. For the most part, the pinyon-juniper forest thrives in areas of relatively low rainfall, light snow cover, and poor soils. Shale layers much of the forest floor in P-J country.

To knowledgeable mule deer hunters, P-J forests represent deer — lots of them. It's no secret that many of those deer are big bucks. Note that all five states with P-J forests are tops for mule deer. Ironically, countless hunters drive through P-J forests to hunt areas higher up, blissfully ignorant of the prizes roaming the trees.

Pinyons and junipers are evergreens, retaining their foliage year-round. Because there is no leaf fall, visibility is limited in dense stands. Hunters get no break in the autumn as they do in forest stands where deciduous trees expose their innards. P-J stands are perhaps the toughest cover to

Lois Zumbo looks for deer
tracks in the shaly floor of a
pinyon-juniper forest. Tracks
are difficult to see on shale rock
fragments.

hunt in much of the West, and killing a big buck in them is a challenge.

Layers of shale rock commonly carpet the forest floor, which poses
another problem for hunters. The rock clatters and crumbles when stepped on, and noise becomes an important factor. For that reason, I like to
wear light hiking boots to "feel" my way about. Tennis shoes would be suitable in good weather, but there's always the danger of stepping on cactus.

Because the P-J forest often grows in the foothills of mountain ranges,
or at relatively low elevations, it receives little precipitation compared to
nearby higher altitudes. Most precipitation is either snow or rain during
high-intensity, low-duration summer storms. Water is often scarce, afford-
ing few drinking places for deer. Obviously, water holes are prime spots
to look for mule deer during hunting season, or are at least places to *begin*
looking. Deer may travel a mile or more to water, and frequently drink at
night well after shooting hours are over.

Nonetheless, by using a waterhole as a central spot from which to hunt,
a strategy can be planned to eliminate areas where water is nonexistent.

How do you find waterholes if you're unfamiliar with the country? A dead giveaway is the presence of livestock. If cows are around, you can bet your boots that water is close by. Another way is to simply ask people familiar with the country you're hunting. If you spot a rancher passing by, flag him down with a friendly wave and inquire. Ranchers, more than anyone else, know where every last spring or water hole is located. Government employees are also helpful, especially conservation officers.

Once a group of us headed to unfamiliar country and intended to hunt an expansive P-J forest that was rumored to have big bucks. We had no idea where deer were watering, but we met a game warden who volunteered information. The forest we wanted to hunt was perhaps 10 miles by 15 miles square. The warden said three water holes were in the southeast quadrant of the forest and two in the southwest, but none in the north.

We split up on opening day, three of us hunting the north area, and three the south. By sunset, two bucks were killed, both in the south area. The north sector was practically barren of deer, and only a few tracks were seen. Two days later we each had a buck, all of them killed within 2 miles of the water holes.

On another occasion, my son Danny and I camped near a water hole in Colorado adjacent to a thick P-J forest. We had been hunting doves, and planned on an early shoot over the water hole at dawn. We spread sleeping bags on the ground, but slept hardly a wink for fear of being trampled by thirsty deer. During the night, I estimated that at least 100 deer visited the water hole. It was interesting to note that this was an area where deer were not particularly abundant.

A hunter who set up a stand near this particular water hole obviously would be wasting his time if deer continued to drink only during the night. But by knowing about the water, he could concentrate his hunting efforts close by, confident that a number of deer were in the general area.

In the event you locate a water hole, try to determine the direction most of the deer are going when they head for bedding or feeding areas, because that's where they'll probably be during the time you're hunting them. It's not unusual to score near the water during the first minutes of daylight or just before dark. This is especially true if the area is undisturbed and hunting pressure is minimal.

If snow is present, forget about water holes, since deer usually eat snow and avoid free water unless it's close by. Of course, if the temperature is bitterly cold, water holes freeze over and are useless to deer.

Don't be fooled into thinking that P-J areas without obvious water holes are barren of deer, however. I've been in dozens of places where I was puzzled by plentiful deer sign, yet I couldn't find water anywhere. The only two explanations were that deer were drinking from a hidden water source, or weren't drinking.

The latter possibility sounds preposterous, but could very well be true. Allan Whitaker with the Colorado Division of Wildlife made an intensive study of mule deer on the Mesa Verde National Park in southwest Colorado. Whitaker proved conclusively that deer can survive in arid climates without drinking. Their water needs are satisfied by succulent forage. Whitaker does not imply that mule deer everywhere do likewise, but that certain populations have been conditioned over the years.

What this all means is that deer are attracted routinely to water, but in some areas can exist without it. Don't be surprised to see deer where water is absent.

There is often little feed in the P-J forest, because much of the available

A modest "meat buck" that was killed in a pinyon-juniper forest while moving from feeding to bedding area.

moisture is used by the trees, leaving little for herbaceous forage that mule deer feed on. Precious sunlight is blocked by trees, and the abundance of shade also hinders underbrush growth. Consequently, deer must daily leave the shelter of the forest to find feed elsewhere. Deer often travel considerable distances to feeding areas, and this necessity makes them vulnerable to hunters.

A workable strategy is to set up an ambush on a well-used travel route. Deer seldom use a particular trail unless the cover is extremely dense. More likely, they meander about on general paths, but always in the direction of feeding areas, or bedding areas, as the case may be.

Some P-J forests are riddled with brushy sagebrush draws that make ideal feeding areas. These are prime places to find deer early in the morning and late in the afternoon, and are often the only feeding spots within a herd's home range.

To increase your chances of success, visit the open feeding grounds during mid-day when deer are bedded and won't be disturbed. Look for fresh tracks and signs of feeding on the brush. If deer are using the area, try to learn the direction they're coming in by scouting for tracks in the adjacent forest. If you find their travel route, check the wind direction, and look for a vantage point where you can see as much of the feeding area as possible. If the terrain is hilly, choose an observation point where you can easily see the edge of the trees where you suspect the deer will exit. Deer may often loiter in the forest until the final minutes of shooting light, then ease out into the opening at the last moment. You must be ready, since light might be poor and you'll have only a few minutes to spot a buck and make a well-placed shot. Make absolutely sure your shooting position is well concealed and that you can't be seen by approaching deer. When they step out into the opening from the protection of the forest they're apt to be nervous and will spook at the slightest provocation.

I learned a good lesson the hard way while hunting deer in a feeding area in Utah a few years back. The P-J forest I hunted was fairly dense, and I knew a small herd of deer were feeding daily in a large bitterbrush patch. The tracks indicated at least one and maybe two of the deer were good bucks. I found where a tree had fallen into another in the middle of the patch, and used it as a blind. Darkness was approaching quickly, and I was about convinced that the deer would not come out until shooting hours were over, when a doe and fawn walked out to feed. I raised my binoculars to look for more deer in the trees behind them, but my arm

Three big bucks feed in a chained area. The buck on the right is a dandy.

movement spooked the doe and fawn. I caught a flash of movement just forward of them and saw a fine buck racing into the cover of the forest. Somehow the buck worked his way into the brush without me seeing him, and my careless movement sent him flying into the trees.

Hunting feeding areas just at daybreak is sometimes more effective than watching them in late afternoon because few hunters are in position at this critical time. It's necessary to use a flashlight on your way to the feeding place, unless a moon lights your way. If you can see to shoot before you get to the feeding area, you're too late. Try again the next morning, but set the alarm clock an hour earlier. That extra cup of coffee or few precious moments in the sleeping bag might be pleasant, but those luxuries could cost you a good buck.

Stillhunting the P-J forest during the day when deer are bedded is one of the most difficult ways to hunt mule deer. Because walking the forest floor is often noisy due to shale rock, it's difficult to sneak up to a bedded buck. I can remember only a few instances when I successfully stalked deer in their beds.

Branches that brush against clothing also betray human movement through the trees, particularly if the forest is dense. I like to wear wool or cotton shirts or jackets because they are quieter than synthetic fabrics.

Another problem facing the hunter in P-J forests is the lack of visibility. Trees do not self-prune themselves as they often do in taller forests, and branches run down to the ground. Deer form a low profile when bedded, and it's practically impossible to spot them before they flush. Yet they can easily detect humans walking through the trees.

Stillhunters must move at a snail's pace to keep disturbance to a minimum, and it's important to watch where each foot is placed. A tiny slip could easily alert a big buck bedded nearby.

Besides stealth, the eyes have it when hunting slowly. A cursory glance in front and around you won't do it. You must pick each limb, log, and stump apart with your eyes, looking for a telltale sign that spells deer. Don't allow your eyes to wander about, *penetrate* deeply into the trees with all the concentration you can.

What do you look for? Most deer experts suggest looking for horizontal shapes since many objects in the woods are vertical. A deer normally projects a horizontal outline, and can be spotted by a skillful observer. In a P-J forest, however, the trees are often short and rounded, with many horizontal limbs and logs to confuse the pattern. Better to look for a slight movement, such as the twitch of an ear or tail, or a gleam of light flashing off an antler.

Some years ago, my daughter Janette and I were quietly walking through a P-J forest, hoping to spot deer moving from feeding to bedding areas. It was about 8 a.m., and I figured some of the deer might be unsettled and still traveling through the trees. Suddenly I saw movement in the pines and signaled to 11-year-old Janette to be still. I eased my binoculars up and made out a doe just as she was lying down. At the same moment I saw a deer's ear twitch 5 yards away and knew she wasn't alone. Though chances were good the other deer was her fawn, I couldn't be sure and decided to wait and see. Other hunters were nearby; I had a hunch the deer would be spooked before the hour was up.

Janette and I didn't have long to wait. Fifteen minutes later the doe lurched to her feet and walked briskly toward us, followed by a fawn, another doe, and a small three-point buck. I was ready for the buck, and squeezed the trigger the moment I saw antlers. He made a fine addition to our freezer.

At times, deer disturbed by hunters walking nearby won't spook, but will hold their ground and stare at the intruders, especially if they're screened by limbs. This behavior allows hunters an opportunity to glass a motionless deer and determine if it wears antlers. Of course, if you have an either-sex permit, no distinction needs to be made.

The density of the P-J limbs and low-growing branches often creates a maddening situation. A deer that decides to remain motionless is usually uncooperative about moving its head in order for antlers to be spotted. In this case, the only option a hunter has is to change position and hope for a better view through the branches. Or, he can wait and try a running shot when the deer breaks and antlers are discernible.

Many years back, a member of our hunting party spotted a good buck standing behind a juniper tree. The buck stared intently, and the twisted branches of the juniper completely blocked the deer's body. The hunter waited for 5 minutes, but the buck never twitched. Finally, not able to take the stand-off any longer, the hunter fired a shot directly into the tree, hoping the bullet would exit and strike the buck. Juniper wood being what it is, the bullet penetrated little and the buck dashed off unscathed. As the man told it later, he could have made a head shot, but didn't want to ruin the cape or hit the antlers accidentally.

Another time I was hunting a P-J forest in northwest Colorado for a reasonably good buck. I had already killed a nice buck in Idaho that year,

Lois Zumbo still-hunts in an old burn in a pinyon-juniper stand. Deer often feed in these openings.

and could afford to be fussy. Lots of deer were in the forest, and I knew big bucks were in there with me.

The first two hours of stillhunting I jumped at least 30 deer. The plentiful shale rock was brittle, making it almost impossible to walk quietly.

As I often do in a P-J forest, I slowly lowered myself to the ground and carefully panned the landscape around me, penetrating intently every tree and log. By holding my head close to the ground, I could see under the branches. Only a wall of trees was visible if I stood erect.

A big sagebrush bush caught my eye, because something wasn't quite right about it. There were too many vertical objects under it, but I couldn't put the pieces together in my mind. I concentrated harder, demanding that my eyes see into the brush, and slowly I detected a gray color that didn't belong. More penetration, and I saw the unmistakable brown eye of a deer. The vertical objects that puzzled me were legs, and the gray was its pelt. I tried to find antlers, but the deer's head was totally confused in the limbs.

A moment later, the deer snapped its head just a fraction to direct its attention to a noisy magpie squawking close by. The movement was all I needed. Antlers flashed 15 inches above its head. I knew what to do, and after adding up the body parts I could see, I focused on the spot where I suspected his lungs to be. Nothing blocked the bullet path except the soft tips of the sagebrush, so I drew down on the imaginary circle and fired. A splendid four-point buck fell heavily to the ground. The shot was a bit high but took him in the vertebrae, killing him instantly.

A deer drive is effective in the P-J forest, but luck plays a major part. Spooked deer are difficult to see because of the brush, and many will stand still or circle behind the drivers. There are few vantage points for standers, which means that a deer needs to show himself in an opening to be seen.

Because of the low elevation where P-J forests grow, some are inhabited by few deer until winter snows drive animals from higher country into winter range areas. Forests that contain sparse numbers of deer could be swarming with animals overnight.

In order to improve forage production on pinyon-juniper forests, land managers use a technique called "chaining." A huge chain from a ship's anchor, often 100 feet long with links weighing 90 pounds each, is dragged between two large bulldozers. The chain rips the trees out of the ground as if they were bamboo shoots. When the area is completely chained, the uprooted trees are either wind-rowed and left to decompose, or burned.

The chained area is then seeded with various forage species beneficial to livestock and wildlife.

The Bureau of Land Management, a Department of Interior agency, does most of the P-J chaining in the West. In the early days of land improvement, the BLM was basically concerned with livestock and did little for wildlife. Consequently, they seeded many of the chainings with crested wheatgrass, a fine feed for cattle, but practically worthless for mule deer. As the years passed, the agency was taken to task for its livestock priorities, and was required to consider wildlife as an important resource in land improvement projects. Now, when the BLM or any other government agency makes a chaining, wildlife will enjoy a variety of forage plants as a result.

Chainings are excellent hunting areas, but some special problems exist. Access to chained areas is usually very good because roads are constructed to bring bulldozers and vehicles to the project areas. Hunters recognize the value of chainings, and are quick to pursue deer in the newly fashioned environment.

A hunter glasses for sign of a bedded deer in a pinyon-juniper stand.

However, since chained areas are fairly open, deer quickly learn to avoid them unless there is little or no human disturbance, or to feed only after dark. This is especially true when chained areas are close to well-traveled roads. Many hunters overlook small chained patches hidden in a draw or over a ridge. These are the places that appeal to deer. If the chained area is small with plenty of surrounding cover, deer are apt to feed during daylight hours.

Pinyon-juniper forests burn like the dickens when conditions are right. Forest fires often consume entire forests, leaving nothing behind except for a few charred logs. Land agencies often reseed burned areas, creating optimum feeding areas for deer.

Two years in a row I killed big bucks in P-J burned areas. One was a nice five-point and the other a fat three-point. Both were shot within 20 yards of the same spot and both were feeding on saltbush when I spotted them. Saltbush is a favored mule deer plant that grows well in disturbed areas such as old burns.

The message of this chapter is to discover pinyon-juniper forests. The largest-antlered mule deer I've killed was taken in a P-J forest, and plenty more just like him are out there. One might be waiting for you.

Hunting in Evergreen Forests

Every state in the West has evergreen forests, almost all of them in what is known as "high country." Many of the forests grow on the 86 national forests of the Western states, and with the exception of coastal forests in Washington, Oregon, and California, all such forests are home to the Rocky Mountain mule deer.

Evergreen forests are just what the name implies. They stay green permanently, unlike deciduous trees which lose their leaves each fall. Evergreens do shed their needles, but only a small portion at a time so it's not noticeable.

The most common evergreen trees in the Rockies include Douglas fir, ponderosa pine, lodgepole pine, alpine fir, and Englemann spruce. Pinyon pine and junipers are also evergreens.

These trees do not grow just anywhere. They have very definite growing requirements, and often grow in "pure" stands, which means only a single species grows in a forest stand. As with other plants, they also have elevational preferences. For example, alpine fir and Englemann spruce grow at the very highest elevations, often up to 12,000 feet and better, while lodgepole pine, Douglas fir, and ponderosa pine grow at lower elevations. Since these trees are so important to mule deer and mule deer hunters, we'll discuss them separately or group them as required.

Lodgepole pines commonly grow in extremely thick timber stands, so thick that often no underbrush grows beneath them because of lack of sunlight. Foresters often refer to them as "doghair" thickets because the trees are said to grow thicker than hair on a dog's back. Lodgepole pine is called a "fire type" because it rapidly takes over a burned-over area, and is often the first tree species to grow after a forest fire denudes the landscape.

Because lodgepoles grow in thick stands, mule deer spend much time bedding and loafing in them during daylight hours, but seldom feed in the timber because there's simply no food. They must leave the shelter of the trees daily to find forage elsewhere. The distance they need to travel depends on the proximity of forage. They may have to walk just a few yards to the edge of the forest, or a mile or more to a brushy sidehill.

The key to hunting muleys successfully in lodgepole pine stands is to locate their feeding areas and wait and watch. That means plenty of scouting to determine where they're living and what their feeding patterns are. Water is seldom a problem in lodgepole forests because creeks and springs are common in the upper elevations where lodgepole pines grow.

If the pines aren't growing too tightly together, a hunter can often

A young mule deer buck in velvet stares from his evergreen forest environment. *(Photo courtesy of Mike Perry.)*

Open areas alongside thick evergreen timber attract deer because of the abundant forage. These places are best early in the morning and late in the afternoon.

walk silently if there isn't a lot of forest litter on the ground and he doesn't snap branches off tree trunks while brushing past them. Most lodgepole forests offer a surprising amount of visibility because the tree trunks are self-pruning, meaning the lower branches die as the sunlight is slowly shut out by the upper branches. Consequently, skilled hunters often slip up close to deer by sneaking slowly and using trees as screens.

Snow is often on the ground during deer season, adding yet another advantage. If snow is powdery and soft, it allows quieter walking. It also helps outline deer, but keep in mind it also helps outline the hunter.

In some lodgepole forests, feeding areas aren't easy to locate. Here's a tip to help. In practically every forest, logging operations are either going on or have been completed in the past. Logged-over areas, especially those that have been cut within the last 10 or 15 years, often produce a great deal of browse. When trees are cut out of a dense forest, the sudden burst of sunlight stirs dormant seeds in the ground that have been patiently waiting for just such an occasion. Other seeds are carried in by birds and animals, or are blown by the wind. In no time, the ravaged area blossoms with succulent plants, and mule deer are quick to move in and take advantage of the new-found paradise.

You can locate old logged-over areas by asking forest personnel you meet in the woods or by visiting forest offices and inquiring. Every Forest Service Ranger District office should have maps showing details of the forest, and though maps don't normally depict logged areas, forestry personnel should be able to mark some on a map.

Logging operations in progress also attract deer, but there might be restrictions on hunting where loggers are camped or working.

Old burned areas are also popular feeding places for mule deer. As in logged-over areas, browse plants quickly invade areas that have been opened up by forest fires. Again, you can get information about the locations of old burns by visiting forest offices.

I know of an old burn near my home in northeast Utah that continually attracts deer. Two years in a row I killed bucks there on opening morning. Each time I walked to the burn well before daylight and took up a vantage point where I had a good view. Just like clockwork, deer were feeding in the burn when shooting light rolled around. All I had to do was pick the biggest buck and squeeze the trigger.

In some lodgepole forests, deer move around longer in the morning because feed is sparser and it takes them longer to fill their bellies. Likewise, they come out earlier in the afternoon to feed. This is especially so in forests where human activity is light.

In the 20-odd years I've hunted mule deer, four or five truly magnificent bucks are indelibly etched in my mind. One of them, a massive four-point, came trotting along a trail on the Ashley National Forest near my home and ran within 30 yards of me and a companion before spotting us and almost turning inside-out trying to change course. My friend and I were hunting elk in a lodgepole forest, and were talking in low tones when the

This buck is emerging from the thick evergreen forest to feed in an opening in late afternoon.

buck appeared. Though I only saw the deer for a few seconds, I'm convinced he'd make the record book. Big bucks are not uncommon in forests, and knowledgeable hunters do very well in the lodgepoles by figuring the patterns of deer. Although I've seen many more deer in other types of cover, such as aspens and oak brush, lodgepole pines offer a different type of challenge, one that makes hunting interesting each autumn.

Ponderosa pine trees offer a completely different type of mule deer hunting in areas where the trees grow far apart and expanses of grass and shrubs lie between. The openness of the woodlands often allows long-distance shots. There is seldom a lack of feed in the open country, so deer can be anywhere. Look for them feeding and moving to bedding areas in the morning, but take care that deer don't see you first. Ponderosas are often big, overmature, trees up to 3 feet or more in diameter. A sneaky hunter can stalk deer by slipping up behind trees, using the thick trunks as screens.

Once I spotted a buck in open ponderosas about 600 yards away. I wanted to cut that distance at least in half before making a shot, and knew I'd have my work cut out for me. The deer was feeding, walking slowly away from me. I charted a course, and moved from one tree to another. Between trees, I half-crawled, and half-crouched, depending on the cover. When I reached each tree I peeked around to find the next one, and hot-footed it along, always keeping track of the buck's location. Finally, after 15 minutes of playing cat and mouse, I was 250 yards away from the deer. I laid my rifle across a log and collected a fine piece of deer meat and a nice set of horns.

Muleys may bed anywhere in the open ponderosas, but generally like to surround themselves with cover. Blowdowns, small thickets, creek bottoms—all these appeal to deer. When approaching a dense area, be ready for a quick shot at a bounding deer.

Ponderosas also grow in heavily timbered stands, but never as densely as lodgepole pines. When ponderosa trees are young, they're often called "blackjack" pine by foresters, and commonly grow fairly close together. They aren't as self-pruning as lodgepoles, but walking between them isn't necessarily a noisy effort. Since lower limbs often extend low to the ground, deer can be bedded anywhere. Be ready for a shot anytime.

Douglas fir is the "bread and butter" tree of the American timber industry. It is the major tree species in the great logging states of Washington, Oregon, and California, but it grows throughout the entire Rocky

Mountain system. A mule deer in high country forests could hardly avoid Douglas firs.

Forests made up of Douglas fir range from very dense to moderately open, depending on the site. Like lodgepole pine forests, these trees often provide plenty of shelter for muleys, but little food. The same techniques that work in lodgepoles work in firs. Hunting in old burns and logged-over areas is an effective way to see deer in fairly open areas. Otherwise, Douglas fir stands are hard to hunt because tree limbs generally grow close to the ground, and visibility is poor.

Englemann spruce and alpine fir are the highest of the high country tree species. These spire-tipped trees withstand incredible weather extremes, from several feet of snow to temperatures of 30 to 40 degrees below zero or lower.

The spruce-fir type is often extremely thick, dotted with fallen logs, young trees in dense thickets, extensive blowdowns, and limbs that grow completely down the trunk to ground level. A snap shot at a running deer is often the only opportunity available.

Of all the forest types, the spruce-fir regime is most apt to have snow during deer season. Tracking a big buck through fresh snow is an exciting way to spend a day in the woods. If the wind is blowing, which it often does in the upper elevations, chances of sneaking up on a bedded deer are better.

Note the lack of forage in the lodgepole forest. Deer move out of these timber stands to seek feed elsewhere.

I killed this buck in a burned area in the midst of a thick evergreen forest. The deer was crossing from one timber stand to another in the early morning.

Some skillful mule deer hunters believe the biggest bucks hang out in the spruce-fir zone. I won't argue with that philosophy, because I've seen too many giant bucks in these high forests.

Perhaps an explanation centers on the fact that spruce-fir forests are farthest removed from humanity. Disturbances are few in the upper elevations, and big bucks prefer solitude. Deer are usually not plentiful in these forests, which might be another reason spruce-fir is sought out by big bucks. Old monarchs often retreat to areas where they can be alone. Occasionally big bucks band together in twos and threes, but loners seem to be the rule.

Because you see fewer deer in the high-elevation forest, and the ones you see are likely to be mature trophy bucks, you need to use every bit of woods sense you have. Outsmarting a 4- or 5-year-old deer is a task not equal to the casual hunter, especially in the rugged spruce-fir jungles that wary deer live in.

In many high country areas, spruce-fir trees grow to timberline. Rocky ledges and rimrock are ideal hang-outs for trophy bucks, and deer commonly travel from the forest to the barren rocks. Truly big bucks like to bed in the rimrock where the world unfolds below them. This is no-man's land, a place where only dedicated hunters care to seek deer. With elevations of 11,000 to 13,000 feet and steep, dangerous terrain, one can understand why many hunters stay away from places above timberline. Horseback hunting is a popular way to hunt these high areas. Trails are surprisingly common in this land of rocks and snow, but many are dangerous in spots. Horses do stumble on the rocky trails, requiring plenty of careful negotiation.

The area known as the timberline is the line where trees stop growing, usually because of thin, unfertile soils, and steep, rocky terrain. Often trees at timberline are stunted, no more than 5 or 6 feet tall. Bucks frequently use the midget spruces and firs for bedding areas because of the low, dense cover.

Glacial cirques and tarns in the timberline zone are also fine places for bucks. Hidden basins, rocky outcroppings and other broken real estate features are just what a big buck likes. He's at the top of the world, and is never far from cover when danger occurs.

During the 1980 deer season, I hunted on horseback with Gabby Barrus in Wyoming's Greys River country. Grant Barrus (no relation to Gabby) was our outfitter, and each day we rode high up into the spruce-fir zone from base camp. Gabby and I were searching for 30-inch bucks, and had passed up a number of smaller bucks.

One afternoon, while we were riding just at timberline on the edge of a cirque, I turned around in my saddle to look up at a high basin when I saw two deer bounding for all they were worth from a small stand of stunted, windblown firs. They were a full 600 yards away, but I didn't need binoculars to spot the huge racks they were carrying. Gabby saw them at the same time, and we just sat in our saddles, mouths agape. They were the kind of bucks we were after. The deer clambered up into a steep rocky sidehill and trotted out of sight. Though Gabby and I tried to follow, it was too rough for the horses and too late in the day to track the deer on foot, even though there was plenty of tracking snow. We hunted that area afterward, but never saw the giant bucks again. I estimated the width of their antlers to be 34 to 35 inches after looking them over with binoculars just before they disappeared from sight.

Hunting in the evergreen forests, whether they be lodgepole pine, Douglas fir, spruce-fir, or whatever, is only good when the deer are there. A logical statement, but often unappreciated by hunters. When the weather turns bad and snow starts to pile up deep in the high country, deer begin to move lower, and so should hunters. Some big bucks linger behind in deep snow, but eventually move out when feed becomes scarce.

By the same token, during balmy, hot fall months, the high country might be crawling with muleys. Hunters pursuing deer too low might revise their strategy and head for the higher country. As a rule of thumb, deer are usually in the highest elevations until winter starts the migration downward.

Access is seldom a problem in many forested areas. In national forests, road systems are often extensive. Besides main forest roads, logging spurs and secondary roads allow access off the beaten track. Nowadays most national forests have a travel map that indicates restricted areas. Be sure you're driving where it's allowed; some roads are closed to vehicles.

Backpacking is an excellent and challenging way to get into remote forest areas where you can get away from other hunters and enjoy the solitude of the woodlands. If you're healthy and savvy the outdoors, you might consider this hunting aspect. Few others are as rewarding if you're seeking the total outdoor experience, as well as a big buck.

In most Western forests, mule deer share the land with elk. Interestingly enough, areas that support big elk herds often have few deer, but this isn't the case everywhere. If you've been hunting an area hard and see plenty of elk but few deer, consider changing your hunting location. Try higher or lower, or another part of the forest.

It might seem ridiculous to point this out, but many first-time mule deer hunters have trouble telling the difference between deer and elk, so be absolutely sure you can identify each before setting out on a hunt. Bucks and bulls are so different they should never be mistaken, and the same with cow elk and doe deer. Yet every year, hunters unfamiliar with Western hunting take to the woods, never having seen either animal in the flesh.

Once, while hunting in Colorado for mule deer, I happened to be in a party of hunters from the Midwest. While riding down a trail on horseback, a huge buck jumped out from a brushy creek-bottom and trotted up an open park. The hunter directly in front of me piled off his horse, withdrew his rifle from the scabbard, and drew a bead on the buck that had stopped just behind a clump of firs. Plenty of the buck was visible, and

I waited for the shot, but it never came. I had already killed a deer, so all I could do was observe. Finally the buck spun, took a long bound, and was gone from sight.

"Why didn't you shoot?" I said to the hunter.

"Shoot? That was an elk. Why would I want to shoot an elk?" he replied.

"That was no elk," I answered evenly. "It was a hell of a big buck deer."

The man looked at me as if I was crazy when the outfitter, who was riding the lead horse, turned and rode back toward us.

"Why didn't you shoot?" he said to the hunter. "That was as big a buck as you'll ever see."

The miserable hunter muttered something to himself, obviously distressed at the missed opportunity, and rode the rest of the way to camp in silence. I felt a bit sorry for him, but had he done some homework and studied pictures and descriptions of deer and elk, he'd have killed a fine trophy. As it turned out, he settled for a forked-horn buck 2 days later.

One reason many forest areas are lightly hunted away from roads is because hunters are afraid of getting lost in the tall timber where landmarks are hard to see. Another chapter covers ways to hunt comfortably without wondering where you are, but it's a fact of hunting that most of the pressure from other hunters occurs fairly close to access roads. Of course, it's easier to transport an animal to your vehicle if the deer is killed close to it, but some of the best hunting is just beyond the ridge, or in the next basin, or somewhere up ahead where few hunters have looked. In

I glass openings in an evergreen forest for sign of feeding deer in late afternoon.

forests, mule deer simply move farther back from roads when hunting season begins, so it's only logical to try those hideouts if deer are scarce.

If you're a typical mule deer hunter, you no doubt have hunted the evergreen forests at one time or another. Besides being scattered throughout the West, many of them are on public land, road systems are adequate with plenty of access, and mule deer live in them everywhere. That's about all a hunter can ask for.

Hunting in
High Brush

This chapter describes mule deer hunting in high brush, which essentially means oak brush, mountain mahogany, serviceberry, and other shrubs that grow 8 feet or higher. The techniques and opportunities are so different in this environment that it warrants special attention. Most importantly, this cover consistently harbors enormous mule deer, and no book would be complete if the high brush country of the West was not thoroughly detailed.

Oak brush is the most widespread and best-known of the high brush regime. Although this shrub grows in the Rockies and across to the West Coast, its area of greatest importance in mule deer hunting is Colorado, New Mexico, Utah, and Arizona. The plant is a true oak, and is also called Gambel's oak and scrub oak. It prefers sunny slopes, and although it withstands surprisingly little moisture, it does best during wet years when spring rains and stormy summers provide generous amounts of water.

Being a true oak, the plant produces acorns, and therein lies one of its primary attractions to mule deer. Acorns provide starches and carbohydrates, and are one of the key food plants in much mule deer country. Biologists often base the condition of a deer herd on the abundance of acorns. Oaks don't produce heavy acorn crops each year, but according to a cycle. This is so regardless of weather, although the high part of a cycle could be reduced by a prolonged drought.

Oak brush grows at intermediate elevations, from 6,000 feet to 8,000 and more. At its highest elevations, it mixes with aspens, at its lowest with pinyon-juniper, although these transitions depend on local conditions.

Hunter Burnham, Murry Burnham's son, with a 30-inch-plus
buck taken from Colorado's oak
brush country. *(Photo courtesy
of Murry Burnham.)*

A healthy oak brush stand is higher than 10 feet, and so dense that a
person has difficulty walking through it. Often the tree has an umbrella-
like shape, allowing a hunter to squeeze through the twisted stems. The
best way to travel through oak brush is to follow game or livestock trails
that wind about.

Being a deciduous tree, oaks lose their leaves each fall. Visibility is increased somewhat, but the dried leaves often cling to the branches well into
winter, creating an effective screen for deer. Dried leaves on the ground
make for noisy walking, which often prevents stalking opportunities.

I have yet to see an extensive oak brush stand that did not harbor a
herd of deer. Muleys have everything they need in the oaks, though they
might leave temporarily for water. Yet that need has been disputed by
Allan Whitaker of the Colorado Division of Wildlife, who found that
mule deer may condition themselves to exist in some areas without water.
This was discussed in the chapter on pinyon-junipers, but oak brush was
the primary plant in Mesa Verde National Park in Colorado where Whitaker made his study. According to Whitaker, Mesa Verde is one of the
most thoroughly searched landscapes in the West. Because it is an important Indian ruin area, virtually every foot of ground has been investigated
by scientists seeking artifacts. In the entire park, only a few small springs

have been confirmed, but a large herd of mule deer thrives without drinking readily available water unless it rains or snows. Allan does not imply that muleys everywhere do not need water, but his study proves that at least in some areas this is the case.

Hunters often shun oak brush because it is extremely difficult to hunt in, even though mule deer are fond of the cover. For one thing, even if one is physically capable of penetrating the brush, it's a frustrating experience when deer flush all around you but they can't be seen. Deer drives are the obvious answer, but stillhunting can be an ultimate challenge. Every now and then a bedded deer remains quiet instead of bounding away. This happens just enough that I like to occasionally slip along in the oaks and try to spot a bedded deer before he bolts and runs off. In other chapters I've indicated the importance of penetrating with all the concentration you can muster. Oak brush is the place to try those eyes.

A few years ago I was hunting along a mountain range in Colorado, doing my best to find a bedded buck in an oak brush patch that held plenty of deer. I jumped two dozen deer in the course of 3 hours, but caught only glimpses as they glided through the brush. Then the wind freshened and muffled my footsteps, giving me the break I needed.

A half hour later, I saw a movement 30 yards downhill from me. I crouched on one knee and glassed the spot with binoculars. A doe was standing, feeding on acorns. I saw more movement off to the left, and knew a herd of deer was within stone-throwing distance. For a full 10 minutes I watched, hoping to find something with antlers, but only three does and two fawns were evident.

Suddenly, while watching the deer, my eyes sent signals that something was strange about a branch between me and the deer herd. I had been looking past it all that time, but nothing registered. I focused on the branch, marveling at how it forked twice, just like the tines of a four-point buck. The realization of what I was looking at hit me like a brick, especially since the object of my attention was a mere 10 yards away.

I traced the so-called branch down, and smiled to myself. A big fuzzy ear and two eyes were under the branch, and I knew I was looking at a nice buck. The animal had me pinned down cold, and was riveted to his bed. I never saw a buck with the nerves this one had. I searched every branch around him with my binoculars, but I couldn't see another part of his body. I had no choice but a head shot, unless I wanted to jump him and shoot him on the run. Since only a quick leap would put him out of sight, I decided to take him where he was.

Ever try to shoot a buck at 10 yards with a scope-sighted .30/06? I hadn't, and wasn't sure just what to do. The target area was as big as a baseball, because the only spot I could see was between the eyes. I didn't want to damage his skull to the point where it would split, so I decided to hold on the top of his head, just taking out the top of his brain. It would be a humane shot, and I wouldn't ruin one gram of meat.

What followed is something I'll never understand. I had a dead aim, absolutely calm, and when I touched off the round the buck jumped high into the brush. He never stopped. Incredible, I thought to myself. A 10-yard shot, Zumbo. How could you have blown it? I was sure the buck simply ran off to die, but no such luck. I crawled around on the ground where he bedded, looking for anything to indicate a hit—a spot of blood, strand of fur, chip of skull—but there was nothing. Then I circled the area, and after 2 solid hours, I was convinced I missed him clean. A buddy who is a gun expert told me later that the parallax difference of the scope sitting over the muzzle probably did me in. At that close range, the bullet

I approach a Colorado buck killed in a serviceberry patch. This plant, called "buckbrush," shelters many muleys.

wasn't going where the scope indicated. Maybe so, but I'll never forget it. And the buck probably won't, either.

Deer seem to feed longer in oak brush, perhaps because they feel safer in the cover. From a high vantage point, it's not beyond the realm of possibility to see deer feeding in the brush. Early morning and late afternoon is the prime time to see deer moving about.

During a Colorado hunt, I spent 2 days hunting the oak brush in vain. Plenty of deer were about, but they ran around me easily, giving me no chance for a shot. Trails in the area were imprinted with hundreds of fresh deer tracks, some of them made by big bucks. I knew that deer were using the trails daily, so I decided to be in the best area at first light. The spot was a half mile from a road. I knew I'd have to fight through the brush by flashlight, but a big buck was worth it.

The next morning, my son Danny and I left camp an hour and a half earlier than usual. We hurried to the brushy mountain, but took longer than we expected to find the right spot to park the vehicle. Daylight was approaching quickly as we started into the oak. I knew we'd be late, so I started trotting, dodging and twisting through the gnarled branches. Danny, who was 11 years old at the time, whispered every now and then to slow down a bit. I was running by instinct, shining the light only on the ground ahead instead of in the air. I didn't want to risk spooking deer. By keeping the crest of the ridge on my right, I could pretty much navigate my way to the place I wanted to be.

As we neared the area, I slowed down and moved slowly, staying on a well-used trail to keep noise to a minimum. Suddenly a doe snorted and bounded away. She was just ahead of me, standing on the trail. Shooting light had arrived, and I was disgusted with myself. If we had been 10 minutes earlier I might have seen a buck.

At that moment, I saw something move farther up the trail. Immediately I made out the form of a deer. I was a fraction too low in the brush to see well, but by standing on tip-toes I quickly saw three deer standing looking directly at me. One was a dandy buck. Without thinking about it, I raised up on tip-toes again, threw the rifle to my shoulder, and pulled the trigger the moment the rifle hit my shoulder. The buck went down in a heap, hit in the center of the neck. Danny and I ran over and admired the big four-point. I was delighted, because we had capitalized on knowing what the deer were doing and when they were doing it.

"You had it planned out pretty good, Dad," Danny grinned. "When we

were running through the brush I thought you were crazy, but you knew
what you were doing, huh?"

"Sure did, son," I said proudly, when in reality I was just hoping. Yet,
although I believe in a certain amount of luck, I also believe that if a hunter interprets deer sign correctly, he puts himself in a much better position
to make luck happen.

An abundance of deer sign keeps enthusiasm high, but sometimes little or no sign doesn't mean deer aren't in the area. I can't remember how
many times I've hunted in a likely looking place, but seeing no sign I started
leaving for another spot when a buck jumped out and startled me witless.

Such was the case a half-dozen years go while hunting in Colorado
with my wife Lois. We had walked all day, passed up a dozen small bucks,
but couldn't find a good one. Lois complained of a blister, and decided to
wait in the truck while I walked over a couple of ridges to have a look.

An hour later, after wandering through an aspen-covered mountainside, I hadn't even seen a doe when I topped a ridge and looked down into
an oak brush thicket that blanketed a sidehill. I stayed high on the ridge
just on the edge of the oaks, but couldn't cut a fresh track. I traveled another half-mile and almost blundered into a deer feeding in the brush below me. Its head was down behind an oak tree; all I could see was its body.
I wasted no time getting down and taking a dead rest over a log because
the size of the body spelled only one thing: big buck!

Moments later I saw a long antler tine move well above where the
deer's head was. It was all I needed. The rifle roared and the buck collapsed
in the bush it was feeding on. I ran over excitedly, because I knew he was
a *very* big buck, but I didn't know just how big. As I neared him, I saw
massive beams with long tines, and knew I had a beauty. He had four
points on one side and three on the other, and I judged him to be quite
old. I took a moment to look at his teeth, and saw he was at least 5 years
old. I field-dressed the deer, tied my tag to his antler, and ran to get Lois
to help drag him out. Besides, my cameras were in the car and I wanted
plenty of pictures where the buck lay. Before leaving the deer, I stuck a
square of pink toilet tissue high up on a branch so I could find him again.
There were no landmarks to pinpoint his location because he was in the
middle of a thicket that looked alike from one end to the other.

Lois and I returned with ropes and cameras, but we couldn't find the
buck. At first I shrugged it off because I figured we'd eventually stumble
across him, but after 20 minutes I began to have serious doubts. Where
was that confounded piece of tissue?

We looked for 10 more minutes, and I was beginning to get frantic when I spotted a magpie flying over the brush. The carrion-eating bird lit in the top of a bush and squawked. Ah, wonderful magpies. I knew exactly where my buck was. I walked directly to the tree the bird had been sitting in and found the deer, exactly as I had left him. The pink tissue had blown off the bush and was lying on the ground. Lois and I had missed the buck by a mere 10 yards.

After pictures were taken we had to get the buck from the mountainside to the road. Suffice to say it was one of the worst deer-dragging ordeals I ever experienced. Though we found a wide, well-used cow trail that led down to the road, the trail was not as much down as we hoped. The ups were rather profound, and it was almost more than we could stand. When we finally got the buck in the vehicle, we drove directly for camp. A pair of T-bones and a bottle of good Scotch went untouched that evening. Nothing could compete with a sleeping bag, and we were asleep as soon as our heads hit the pillows.

Driving deer in oak brush is, at best, a gamble, but it pays off now and

I killed this nice buck in the middle of an oak brush patch in 1973.

then. A well-organized group of hunters can often rout deer and drive them to nearby standers. The trick is to find drivers willing to get into the worst of the brush where most of the deer are.

Once I was sitting on the side of a canyon, just enjoying the view and relaxing after a hard morning's hunt. Two pickups came into view across the canyon, and six hunters got out and walked to a big oak brush thicket. The brush was directly across from me, and I had a clear view of it.

The hunters huddled and pointed in various directions. Soon they split up, and it was obvious I was going to see a drive. Three hunters skirted the oaks and took up positions on the far side from where the drivers were. It didn't take long for action to begin. The drivers hadn't walked 200 yards when I saw five deer sneaking along in front of them. Though the brush was at least 700 yards from my vantage point, my 10-power binoculars enabled me to see the deer in detail. Two of the five deer were bucks, one a nice four-point and the other a very fine five-point. I could see the other deer only when they moved, otherwise the brush swallowed them up when they stopped. The drivers seemed unaware of the deer, and continued their march.

A moment later, seven more deer showed up, a three-point buck and does and fawns. The first five muleys had scattered, with both bucks slipping along together and the does and fawns going along another way. The bucks circled the drivers until they were directly behind them, and disappeared in the brush. I never saw them again. The single buck in the group of seven deer stayed with the herd, but quickly made a break and dashed out of the brush and down the canyon, obviously unseen by the hunters. The two herds of does and fawns suddenly milled about and broke up, running helter-skelter through the brush. Some ran back toward the drivers, some past the standers. I thought perhaps one of the so-called does or fawns might be a spike or forked-horn buck that I couldn't identify over the distance, but no shots rang out. The three bucks were still alive and well.

Later in the day, I ran into the hunters, and we made small talk about deer. They told me that they had put on a drive, but had seen only does and fawns.

"The bucks are all gone in this country," said one. "Damn game department is to blame. Huntin' gets worse every year."

"It ain't the game department," another said. "It's the damned coyotes. Hell, you can't go anywhere without seein' coyote tracks, and you know what they're eatin'."

The hunters climbed back in their trucks and headed down the road. I looked off into the oak brush alongside the canyon and smiled, and wondered if the three bucks were doing the same.

The unsuccessful drive brought back plenty of memories, because I spent lots of time in the oaks playing hide and seek with bucks without ever seeing them. More than once I drove a buck to a stranger, and once I had a buck driven squarely into me by another hunter. I had already filled my tag, however, and had to practically dive off the trail into the oaks to keep the buck from running over me.

The problem with oak brush is the simple fact that you must work

This muley, with antlers similar to a whitetail's, was killed by Murry Burnham in a small opening in the oak brush. *(Photo courtesy of Murry Burnham.)*

hard to find action once the sun rises high and the deer bed down. You might get lucky by sitting on a rock and waiting for someone else to drive the deer to you, but that's not very likely. It's fine when it works, but when it doesn't, wallow around in the brush and take your chances.

Mountain mahogany and serviceberry grows at about the same elevation as oak brush, and is just as nasty. But again, mule deer make their homes in it, and skilled hunters aren't unwilling to work it hard. Both shrubs are sought out by muleys as feed, and deer often have all the comforts they need without leaving.

Mountain mahogany often grows on rocky ledges and ridgetops, and is a natural place for big bucks to hide. I saw one of the best four-point bucks I've ever laid eyes on in a mahogany thicket where I was hunting elk. The buck had been feeding when I surprised him, and gave me just a split-second look before crashing into the heavy cover. I promised to come back for him when deer season opened. I did, but never saw the buck again. The sight of him, even though it was for only a fraction of a second, is one that is permanently etched into my mind. I shall never forget that grand buck.

Serviceberry shrubs often grow in sagebrush expanses, and is often referred to as "buck brush" by old-time Western hunters. This shrub sometimes grows in sparse clumps, and deer love to bed around them, but there are plenty of places where serviceberry grows extremely thick. When that happens, I'm drawn to the thicket like a chunk of iron to a magnet, because I seldom fail to see deer wherever serviceberries grow.

The high brush country of the West takes some muscles and willpower to hunt, but the big bucks are in it. That's why I don't mind sweating and cussing a little when I'm crashing around in it, or sneaking through it. Maybe that dream buck will show under the next bush!

Hunting in Sagebrush

Sagebrush is the symbol of the West. It is symbolic of lonely, dusty places where cowboys punch cattle and Indians attack cavalrymen. Much romance is associated with sagebrush, as in Zane Grey's work, *Riders of the Purple Sage*. Gene Autry, Hopalong Cassidy, and Roy Rogers smelled the pungent odor of sage in their day, and so do hunters today.

Sagebrush is often called the lifeblood of mule deer. Without it, muleys would be in big trouble. In the winter, when snow piles high in the upper elevations, many mule deer herds migrate to the low country and head for sage flats where they feed through the cold, wintry months. This is the time sagebrush is important to mule deer. No other period is as critical. If a deer survives the winter, it overcomes the primary mortality factor affecting its kind in most northern latitudes.

Modern wildlife biologists have made enlightening discoveries about the relationship of sagebrush to mule deer. One of the most significant is their preference for certain subspecies of sagebrush over others.

Sagebrush goes by the Latin name *Artemisia tridentata*. *Artemisia* is the genus, *tridentata* the species. The plant is further divided into subspecies. One of them, *vaseyana*, is highly preferred by mule deer, so much so that deer avoid other subspecies only inches away from *vaseyana*. Many of the subspecies look exactly alike, but deer somehow identify it and select it exclusively. Biologists are attempting to learn more about this peculiar attraction, and hope to improve mule deer habitat with favored forage plants such as *vaseyana*.

This big buck is almost hidden in the high sagebrush. You need to be up high or close to see him.

Sagebrush is not well-liked by many Western cattlemen. Because sage grows in arid climates, water is critical in the growth of range plants consumed by cows. Sage competes too successfully with grass, which is the staple food of range cattle. As a result, stockmen eliminate sagebrush by burning, railing, disking, or applying lethal herbicides. The conversion of sagebrush areas to grasslands has a negative impact on mule deer, and much prime deer habitat is being destroyed to make more livestock feed.

Because sagebrush is an exceedingly important food plant for deer, biologists use it as a key in studying winter range. Hunting harvests and antlerless seasons are often based on the well-being of sagebrush.

Besides being an important plant during the winter, sagebrush is often the year-round home for countless deer herds. That's where knowledge of deer behavior in and around sagebrush helps the hunter.

As I detailed earlier, the first and heaviest mule deer of my life fell to a bullet in an expanse of sagebrush. The deer was walking down a draw heading for a spot to bed down. I marveled at the region I hunted, because there were no trees and I couldn't believe deer would inhabit such "barren" country. I was raised around whitetails, and couldn't conceive the treeless terrain as deer range. As I learned that memorable day some 20 years ago, I couldn't have been more wrong.

On good soils, sagebrush often grows extremely high, as much as 8 feet or more. Big sagebrush is the common name given to this tall subspecies. Hunting in it is a challenge of its own, completely unlike hunting in "regular" sage in which plants grow 2 or 3 feet high. Generally, big sagebrush grows in the bottoms of draws, in valleys, and in other well-drained, fertile places. Plants normally grow close together, forming a jungle-like thicket. It's impossible to see a mule deer standing in this cover. Even the antler tips of a high-racked buck don't stick out over the tops of the sage.

The only way to kill a deer in big sagebrush is to waylay one outside it, or be very lucky and have one almost run you over in the midst of the cover. To kill a deer outside the cover, you must either jump them out on purpose or spot one moving into or out of it.

If big sagebrush grows in a canyon bottom or draw and a ledge or hillside is adjacent, use this high vantage point to observe from. The higher the better.

Several years ago a buddy and I hunted a patch of big sagebrush that nestled in a canyon. We flipped a coin, and I won the option of standing while my pal made a drive through the sage. A nearby sidehill made an ideal spot to watch from.

My companion had barely entered the innards of the thicket when a dandy buck slipped out the edge. Before I had a chance to find him in my scope, he ran back into the high sage and was totally lost from sight. I had the entire patch of tall sage in view; in no way could the deer sneak out without me seeing him.

Ten minutes later my pal walked out of the sage and signalled to me that a deer was in the brush. I nodded vigorously, held my hands over my head to signal big buck, and motioned him to go back in.

Presently the deer reappeared, but I caught just a flash of him as he ran through a tiny opening. Unless he came out of the big sage, and it seemed he wasn't going to, I'd have no chance at him. But I had an idea.

A lone cottonwood tree grew next to the sagebrush. If I could climb it, I might have enough elevation to see down into the sage. I waited for my companion to emerge again, and told him about my plan. He helped me up the first 6 feet of the tree to where I could use branches to climb on, then he went back into the tall sagebrush to keep the buck moving. I hoped he hadn't left while we were discussing our plans.

I climbed as high as I dared, amazed at the new angle. I could practically see the ground in places in the sage. I found a secure position, placed the rifle where I could shoot easily, and waited for something to happen. It didn't take long.

The buck dashed down toward my end of the sagebrush patch and promptly did the unexpected. He ran out into the open and up an open sidehill toward the safety of the ridge. I wasn't prepared for a shot at that angle and almost fell out of the tree in my haste to turn and get a shot. By the time I was in position, the buck was 200 yards away and going like the wind. As luck would have it, a big branch completely blocked my view, but I'd have a shot sooner or later. Finally, when the buck was 300 yards out he was in the clear. I adjusted for the distance and squeezed the trigger. The bullet powdered a rock just in front of the buck's chest. There was no way to quickly chamber another cartridge because of the awkward position I was in, so I watched the deer disappear over the knoll.

Meanwhile, my pal walked up to the tree, grinning like a Cheshire cat. "Well, where is he?" he said.

"Where is who?" I responded as I shinnied off the tree.

"The buck! You didn't miss, did you? You were looking right down his throat," he exclaimed.

"I missed. Plumb damn missed," I answered.

My friend muttered some unprintable words as we walked up the draw. He calmed down when I pointed to the place where the deer was when I shot. But he allowed that I should have killed the buck regardless.

Three hours later, the tables were turned. My buddy missed a shot at a buck standing broadside. We didn't have much to say while sitting around the campfire that night.

Most sagebrush is of a lower type, knee to waist high, and this is the type most hunted. Although many sagebrush areas harbor plenty of

A hunter draws a bead on a buck he jumped out of the sage. Deer often bed in the middle of a sage flat.

deer, few hunters take advantage of it. I suspect that most hunters aren't aware that a big, empty-looking expanse of sage could be a fine place to kill a buck.

Because of the blue-sky situation in sagebrush country, deer don't expose themselves any longer than they have to. Most are bedded when the sun begins to climb, and they remain in their beds without moving most of the day.

Once I watched a herd of deer in a big sagebrush flat as they were preparing to bed down. I had a ringside seat on a big rock on the side of a canyon. About 7:30 a.m. a big doe pawed at the ground with her front hoof, then laid down. Two fawns did likewise about 20 yards away. Two more does and a fawn bedded a moment later, followed by a small three-point buck that made his bed about 40 yards from the group. When the deer were all down, the sagebrush looked placid and empty. If I hadn't seen the deer melt into the sage, I would have taken bets that there wasn't a deer within a mile. Deer season was closed, or I would have tried a stalk on the buck. One of the greatest thrills in mule deer hunting is watching deer bed down, then stalking them. It's an exciting event, knowing precisely where the quarry is and knowing that you're going to get a shot; very rough on the nervous system.

Obviously, one must rise early in the morning to see deer in the sage. Few hunters ever watch deer bed because if the hunter can see the deer, the deer can probably see the hunter. When deer know humans are close, they leave for an area where they won't be disturbed.

So it follows that if you want to watch deer pick their beds and make a stalk, you must be sneaky. Get to your vantage point when the stars are still shining, well before daybreak. Find a high place in the middle of an expanse of sage and glass for deer everywhere you can. When you see a herd of deer, watch them if any look interesting enough to wear your tag. If they bed down, try to mark the area in your mind by remembering a shrub near the deer, or a rock out-cropping—anything dissimilar from the rest of the terrain. When you make your stalk, consider wind direction above all else. In most flat sagebrush country you have plenty of ways from which to make your stalk. Keep in mind that deer often bed with their heads almost even with the top of the sage. You need to stay very low to get close, and at that you'll be lucky to get much closer than 100 yards. Sagebrush is noisy to walk through. If a slight wind is blowing, you're in good shape. If the wind is sporadic, move only when it blows, and remain quiet when it stops.

Dan Zumbo with his first buck. Dan killed the buck in Colorado after spooking it out of its bed in the sagebrush.

If you're simply hunting randomly through sagebrush, you can wander about until you flush deer. As a rule, I walk in zig-zag fashion, stopping frequently to make hiding deer nervous. If you walk in a straight line with no variation in your pace, a bedded deer might stay down and wait for you to pass.

No sagebrush flat is entirely uniform. Washes, pockets of taller brush, small knolls, and other features should be carefully investigated. If the sagebrush area you're hunting is typical, it has a road running through it or alongside it. Get as far as you can from roads, and check out every corner.

Tall vegetation in a sagebrush patch is always inviting to deer. On a Colorado mountain not far from the Utah border, small groups of serviceberry bushes grow in clumps on top of a big sagebrush plateau. I can practically guarantee that deer will bed under those serviceberries. Apparently they like the extra brush overhead as shelter.

Ravines and deep arroyos that trickle through sagebrush areas should always be inspected closely, particularly if brush grows in them.

Many years ago while hunting with my father-in-law in Utah, we came across a little brushy draw that meandered down a sagebrush sidehill. Dad walked to the edge of a draw, picked up a rock, and tossed it into the draw. Nothing happened. He did it again, and still nothing happened. I thought he was a bit touched by the hot sun when he continued to walk along the edge of the draw, throwing every rock he could find into the bottom. Five minutes later, as I was chewing on a juicy apple, I was startled to see a little forkhorn buck bust out of the draw. The deer tore across the sagebrush flat like he had been branded with a red-hot iron.

"I believe a rock hit that little guy," Dad said grinning. "Too bad his daddy wasn't in there with him."

Too bad is right, I thought, but maybe he's farther up the draw. Or maybe in that draw over yonder. I pidked up rocks, threw them into draws, and had a heck of a time the rest of the day, even though a doe and fawn were the only results of my efforts. Oh, and a sore arm.

Dad told me later that he'd killed many a big buck by flushing them from draws. I can understand why, since they offer plenty of concealment.

Hunting from horseback is the most effective way to hunt sagebrush for two very good reasons. You can cover a lot more country from a horse, and you're high enough off the ground that you can see well. There is a notable disadvantage as well: when a deer flushes it's always a mad scramble to fly off the saddle, grab the rifle from the scabbard, find a dead rest, and shoot at a deer—by now 500 yards away and running like hell's afire.

That scenario isn't always the case, but it seems to happen to me so much that it's becoming a bad joke.

One important piece of advice: *never*, but never, shoot from atop a horse. At worst, the beast will throw you to the ground in fright and you will die of a broken neck, or the horse will have its ear drums seriously damaged by the rifle report. At best, you will be thrown to the ground to live a long life, promising you'll never again shoot John Wayne-style from the saddle. An old cowpoke once told me that the only horses you can shoot from live in Hollywood.

If a deer flushes and you're atop a horse, drop the reins *to the ground*, grab your rifle, take a few quick steps away from the horse, and make your shot. Don't try this with a green-broke horse or one that spooks at loud noises since you might be spending the rest of the day—or weekend—trying to catch the confounded nag.

Some sagebrush country is relatively barren of deer until snow drives them out of the high country. If you see lots of discarded antlers but few deer, you're probably on a winter range. Deer hunting there might be restricted to a small herd of locals that lives there year round.

If your state offers hunting seasons in late November and early December, by all means give the lowland sagebrush a whirl, but only if sufficient snow is in the mountains. As I write this chapter in December, I can look out my front window at Utah's High Uinta mountain range that exceeds 14,000 feet. Only the tops of the mountains are white, and ridges running to 9,500 feet are dry and snowless. Only a few deer are in the sagebrush foothills, because most are enjoying the balmy upper elevations. But let the snow come deep, and the sagebrush is alive with muleys.

Because sagebrush offers winter survival to mule deer, concentrations of animals are often spectacular. It's not uncommon to count 1,000 deer or more in a single day when conditions are right.

There are many, many places in the West where entire mountains are blanketed with sagebrush. Whether you're hunting early or late, your chances of getting close to deer are minimal because they can see you. Deer drives in the sage are not popular, but can be extremely effective. During one drive I saw at least 70 deer trotting rapidly ahead of their pursuers. Four standers who waited on a hillside collected four beautiful bucks as the herd ran by. The hunters knew what they were doing, and capitalized on that knowledge.

It doesn't happen as much as it used to, but mule deer sometimes take comfort if they are some distance from humans. A buck may stand in the open sage several hundred yards away from humans, thinking he is safe. A flat-shooting rifle spoils his plans, but bowhunters and muzzleloaders need to get up close. Another reason why hunting in sagebrush is such a challenge.

Road hunting is becoming more popular each year, especially in high-visibility sagebrush country. Human nature being what it is, it's much more comfortable to sit in a heated vehicle and drive about, looking for deer. Whether or not you condone this type of hunting, it is extremely effective. This is my least favorite form of hunting, and I bristle when I see it go on with the frequency with which it does, but it deserves mention in this chapter because it's such a widespread practice. I've been guilty of jumping out of a vehicle to try a shot at a nice buck, but I don't road hunt on purpose. Personally, I'd rather be walking the sage, smelling the good smells, looking for tracks, and finding deer on my own. Yet the environment of the mule deer, particularly sagebrush, makes them vulnerable to road hunting. The increased access into the backcountry as well as the boom in off-road vehicles has led to more of this type of hunting. Mule deer have responded by staying away from roads, and fewer are killed from vehicles each year, especially big bucks that know the dangers of being seen by the occupants of a vehicle. By and large, yearling bucks are most susceptible to road hunters.

If snow covers the ground in a sagebrush area, you can try some exciting hunting by finding fresh tracks and following. Unless deer leave the sage and head into more rugged country, chances are good of catching up

This little spike was taken in a sagebrush flat while feeding in early morning.

to the quarry, especially if you're on a good fresh track. When snow covers the ground for days, it's often difficult to figure where the deer are since they can make plenty of tracks in a few nights. If the days turn balmy, tracks get mushy quickly in the course of a few hours, making it difficult to determine the freshness of tracks.

When snow is deep—more than a foot—walking through sage is often an ordeal. It's practically impossible to walk a straight line, because you must navigate around and over individual plants. Sagebrush branches seem to reach out and grab your boots at each step, and you soon learn how much of a hunter you are.

Wherever you find sagebrush, whether it grows alone, or with pinyon-junipers, aspens, or whatever, always take a close look to see if deer are feeding in it. It's easy to see deer sign in sagebrush, because the range floor is generally dry and dusty if there's no snow. Deer tracks imprint easily, and the lack of ground cover makes them easy to spot.

Although this chapter describes hunting in sagebrush, the techniques I've described work equally well in similar forms of vegetation. Bitterbrush and four-wing saltbush, also excellent mule deer foods, grow fairly low to the ground and offer good hunting possibilities.

Don't discount the low shrub rangeland the next time you're looking for a buck. Give it your best shot and surprise yourself. You might do exactly that if you've been a disbeliever or simply unaware of the bounty using those "barren" sage flats.

Hunting the
Riverbottoms

Some of the greatest rivers in North America flow through the West, and many offer excellent mule deer hunting. The rivers are touted for wonderful fishing, recreational floating, and marvelous scenery, but few people realize their potential as places to hunt mule deer.

Rivers flow through canyons, farmlands, rugged stretches of back-country—all sorts of terrain. The gouges they carve in the earth range all the way from steep, vertical cliffs to gentle, rolling breaks. Mule deer live in most riverbottoms, except those dammed by concrete and converted into massive reservoirs.

Rivers offer something no other type of real estate does, an opportunity to experience a unique hunt by floating. Besides the potential to kill a big buck, riverfloating is relaxing, and you'll see some of the most gorgeous country in the West. It's not always a relaxing adventure, however, because it often takes hard work to find your buck and kill him.

Not all rivers are navigable, of course. Some are too small to float a raft, and some are much too dangerous for anyone but skilled boatmen. Some rivers require permits from federal agencies, and others have quotas on the number of boats that can float them.

Floating is only one way to hunt a riverbottom. There are others, all of which are described in this chapter.

Floating requires more preparation and planning than most other hunting trips. Not only do you need a dependable craft to safely carry you down the river, but also specialized gear to keep your equipment dry. And, of course, there's a logistical problem of parking a vehicle down-

Dewey Haeder glasses a sidehill in Idaho's Salmon River Canyon. My buck lays alongside. Riverbottoms and adjacent slopes often offer excellent mule deer hunting.

Inflatable rafts are the top choice for most mule deer hunters who float rivers. They navigate rapids well and are roomy enough for plenty of gear as well as deer.

stream from where you're hunting, or the coordination of another party to pick you up when the trip is over.

Rubber or neoprene rafts are commonly used to float Western rivers. They're tough, can withstand a lot of abuse, and are roomy enough for plenty of gear. For the deer hunter, they're ideal for carrying carcasses after a successful outing.

Be aware that rafts are classified according to the number of people they can carry, such as four-man or six-man. Don't ever believe those capacities, especially when figuring on the room you'll need for your equipment and deer carcasses. A good rule of thumb is to divide the rating in half. For example, figure no more than four people in an eight-man raft, three in a six-man, and so on. Even at that, space might be tight.

I won't attempt to explain how to maneuver rafts. If you own one or are planning on buying one, you'll know how to pilot one. Suffice it to say that although they aren't as maneuverable as canoes or river boats, they respond remarkably well. I always figured they were clumsy and hard to manage until I got behind the oars. I was pleasantly surprised, although afterward my back and arms weren't exactly delighted.

Water is always with you on a float trip, and besides being an ally, it becomes the enemy when you try to keep items dry such as sleeping bags, food, cameras, clothing, and guns.

Always have adequate waterproof containers to keep equipment dry. Nothing ruins a trip quicker than soggy gear. All sorts of waterproof containers to protect everything from cameras to much larger items are for sale these days. However, I have yet to find a suitable way to keep my rifle dry; I want it where I can reach it quickly. I usually concede when it comes to my rifle, and simply wipe it down each evening with gun oil and solvent. Better that than have it unavailable when a big buck spots you around the river bend and runs for cover.

When preparing for your float trip, make sure you double-check your list of equipment. Once you're on the river, you won't be able to pick up an item you've forgotten. Plan your meals carefully, and bring more than you need. If weather turns bad or hunting takes longer than you've scheduled, you might spend an extra day or two on the river. Of course, when you kill your buck, you'll have plenty of fine meat to sizzle over the campfire. Try to stick to your timetable if you've arranged for someone to pick you up downriver. Tell your relatives or friends that you might be an extra day or two so they won't worry. It's no fun waiting for an overdue raft party. All sorts of undesirable thoughts are conjured.

If you have room, pack plenty of clothing, because you'll get plenty of it wet, especially boots. A survival kit is essential. Flares, waterproof matches, a first-aid kit and other items should be part of your list. Take along a fishing rod, but be sure you're licensed and the fishing season is open.

Rope is an item that must be in good supply. You use rope for all sorts of chores, from camping along the river bank to lashing deer and equipment to your raft.

A tent is always a good idea, regardless of long-range weather reports that predict balmy days for your trip. Western weather is fickle in the autumn. It doesn't take long for a lovely star-studded night to turn into a miserable stormy adventure. Small mountain tents that fold into a small compact size don't take much space. Some hunters like a big wall or Baker tent. Use whatever you like, but plan carefully so there's plenty of room in the raft.

When selecting a camping area, make sure you find a dry site that won't pose problems if the river rises unexpectedly. If you're camped below a dam you shouldn't need to fear flash floods, but water levels can change several feet in a matter of minutes when water is used for hydroelectric purposes. Flash floods are always possible on rivers if the area receives prolonged and intensive rainfall. Bear in mind that flash flooding can occur far downstream of the actual area that is receiving the storm. You might be enjoying fair weather while the upper drainages of the river system are taking a pounding from storms. Weather forecasts usually predict flash flood danger, but unless you have a small portable radio or hear the report before leaving you might not know about it. I like to make camp at least 5 feet above the water line, if possible. In some areas it's tough to find a spot this high because the riverbottom slopes gradually up and ends at steep, abrupt mountainsides.

Many years ago I had a horrible experience while floating a Utah river by canoe. It had been raining hard for 3 days, with lightning flashing constantly and frequent thunder claps. The final evening, my companion and I had had just about all we could take. We were drenched, and had given up being warm. All we looked forward to was getting out of there.

I check for fresh tracks along a wide riverbottom.

With darkness quickly approaching, we looked in vain for a campsite. Every bend we rounded showed nothing hospitable, only boulders and driftwood along the shore. A sheer cliff met the river on each side, precluding us from getting well up from the river. Both of us were worried about flash flooding.

Finally, with just a few minutes of daylight left, we beached the canoe and quickly pitched the tent in the only possible spot. It was just 3 feet higher than the river level.

Lightning flashed and rain beat down all night. Every half hour I sat up in the tent and shone my flashlight outside to check on the water level. It was rising, but very slowly. By dawn, the canoe was floating free, tugging on the tether rope. The river had risen 2 feet. We hastily broke camp and headed downriver, just in time to beat a surge of water. The river rose 2 more feet in the next 2 hours, but we got out in time.

The mere act of floating aimlessly down the river does not mean you routinely kill a deer, especially a big, wary buck. You must use some strategies to put meat in the raft or canoe.

In the case of river systems with brushy bottoms, there are all sorts of ways to score. The easiest is to simply float along and see a deer feeding or drinking from the river. A shot from the raft, provided it's floating smoothly with no jiggling, might very well be all you need. But it might not be that easy. When you're floating, you travel at the speed the river allows you to. Obviously, you can't observe all the best places during the first hour of shooting light because they might be too far downriver on your route. So you hunt according to the schedule of the current.

During the first minutes of shooting hours, deer should be visible, especially along rivers that are reasonably remote with little traffic. For the first hour or so, use your binoculars to glass the slopes leading down to the water. If you're moving along faster than you'd like, beach the craft every now and then so you can take all the time you need to look.

If you spot a deer, by all means take your shot from a steady position. If the raft is steady and moving slowly, it might offer a solid rest, although you'll have to swing with the animal to keep up with the current. I've never been able to take a shot from a canoe, regardless of the smoothness of the float. Even in calm water a canoe is wiggly, so I wouldn't try a shot. If there's any question about too much boat movement, beach it and draw down on the target from shore, or use the side of the raft after it's moored.

Chances are good of being spotted quickly by feeding deer, because

These deer live all winter in a riverbottom, driven down by snow in the high elevations. Note the bucks in this herd.

you'll be in the middle of a river and easily seen. If you know deer are looking at you, keep your cool and continue down the river until you're well out of sight. Then quietly beach the craft and make a stalk toward the deer. They usually resume feeding soon after you've disappeared and are in the same place you first saw them.

Even on the most remote rivers, deer see floaters every now and then, and seldom react by immediately breaking for cover unless hunting pressure is heavy. Most simply stare at the intruders until they pass out of sight.

Several years ago, two friends of mine, Mayo Call and Don Duff, were rafting a river in Utah hoping to kill some big bucks. They were drifting along Huck Finn-style enjoying the scenery when Mayo made a profound explanation.

"My God, look at that buck," he said.

Don thought he was kidding, and said, "Yeah, sure."

"I mean it," Mayo retorted. "There's a heck of a buck bedded in the rimrock just under that ledge."

When Mayo paddled frantically for shore, Don began to believe his partner wasn't kidding. They glassed the sidehill, and the big deer stared quietly at them. Don quickly became a believer. A quick consultation was in order, because the deer obviously had them spotted. He was not wearing those huge antlers by allowing humans to come close, and Don and Mayo were skilled enough to appreciate the problem. The buck was at least 450 yards out, and there was no way for the hunters to shorten the distance. The river turned away from the buck downstream, and there was no cover to make a stalk. Don was using a handgun, but Mayo had a rifle. Since he spotted the buck first and had the equipment to do the job, Mayo was elected to try for the deer.

Mayo found a comfortable position on shore, figured his elevation, and squeezed off. At this point I should mention that Mayo was born in big buck country, Afton, Wyoming, and was no novice at killing big deer under all sorts of circumstances. So it wasn't a great surprise that he drilled his bullet into the vitals of the great buck. The deer made a lunge from its bed and died in the rocks.

That part of the hunt was easy. The worst was yet to come, because the buck died in a place that was almost impassable to humans. Mayo and Don worked 5 hours just to get to the buck, and had to use ropes to pull themselves over the ledges. By the time they reached the deer, field dressed it, and lowered it off the steep cliff, it was practically dark. Mayo made the shot at midmorning, and spent the entire remainder of the day retrieving his prize. They were understandably pleased to crawl into their sleeping bags that night.

Deer often bed where they have a view of the river, and consequently can often be spotted by sharp observers. Too frequently hunters are absorbed in the relaxing atmosphere and scenery to tune their senses to the task at hand. Concentration is a must.

Mule deer commonly bed in brushy bottoms as well as hillsides. When they do, they're practically impossible to spot and must be jumped and flushed into the open.

Another option is available to river floaters that sometimes works like a charm. When you see a wide spot downstream that is brushy enough to attract deer, beach the raft well up from the spot and let half the party out. If you make noise, no problem. In fact, it might help. Then, the rest of the party floats downstream, being absolutely silent, and beaches the craft below the place you suspect deer are bedded. The downstream party slowly and quietly climbs as high as possible to have a good vantage point, or if there is no sidehill, they make a stand where there is some visibility. The upstream party makes a noisy drive through the brush, and if all goes well, the odor of gunsmoke is soon evident.

Since rivers flow through the lowest elevations, they might be somewhat scarce of deer until snow pushes muleys out of the mountains. Many riverbottoms are great winter range, but support few deer during the fall.

This fact became evident about 15 years ago when I was guiding for Don Wilcox, an outstanding outfitter in Utah's Book Cliffs country. Three clients wanted to hunt mule deer along the Green River in the Desolation Canyon area. They explained they were interested in the solitude the river offered, as well as the uniqueness of the hunt. Don told them that deer might not be as plentiful as they liked unless heavy snow drove them into the river canyon. The hunters elected to try, and the hunt was on.

The day before the hunt, another guide and I led a packstring of saddle horses and mules into the river canyon. It was a hair-raising experience, because the trail was anything but good. Much of it was just barely the width of a horse.

When we finally made our way into the canyon, we cleared away an airstrip along a big sandbar for the pilot to land and drop off the three hunters. By the time the airstrip was cleared and we had tents pitched, we heard the drone of a low-flying plane. I looked downriver and saw the plane in the corridor of the canyon. To make the final bend in the vertical canyon, it was practically flying sideways, completely vertical. I swear the wing of the plane was no more than 5 feet from the cliff wall. I wasn't worried, however, because legendary Jim Hearst of Green River, Utah, was behind the controls. If anyone could land an aircraft in an impossible spot, it was Hearst.

When the plane landed, some of the hunters were obviously shaken. One of them immediately confided in me and said, "I don't know how the hell you got those horses in here, but I'm going back out with you. That pilot has guts, but I don't."

After three days of hard hunting, we saw only one decent buck, but no one had a shot at it. We had a conference, and decided to ride the horses back up to the main lodge, which nestled in an aspen forest. Don suggested we return to the lodge and hunt in the aspens if we had no luck in the riverbottom.

The next day, after an even more harrowing ride up the so-called trail, on which my horse slipped and almost sent us headlong into oblivion, the hunters killed bucks as soon as they climbed up out of the river canyon.

Which all goes to prove that riverbottoms, like other mule deer winter ranges, might be vacant of deer one day and swarming with them the next.

As I mentioned before, one of the nicest things about hunting in river corridors – especially those that are somewhat remote, is the opportunity to enjoy the hunt without a lot of competition from other hunters.

One of the prettiest rivers I've ever seen is the Snake. The river is born high in Wyoming mountains, then flows into Idaho and across the entire state to its borders with Oregon and Washington, where it finally flows into the Columbia.

A few years ago, I was fishing for sturgeon in the Snake with Norm Riddle, who owns a lodge in the canyon and runs jetboats in the river. After catching, photographing, and releasing a big sturgeon, we tried some bear hunting in the drainages that fed the river. I couldn't believe the beauty of the country, and though we saw only one bear, a good number of deer were in the side canyons and on the hillsides overlooking the

From high on a ridge, I check a riverbottom for deer late in the afternoon.

river. Norm said he occasionally took deer hunters, but for the most part, pressure was light. Some rafters who were brave enough to float the raging rapids were about the only hunters who tried for deer. Our sturgeon and bear trip was in the spring, and I promised myself I'd go back for a buck. So far I haven't, but one day I will.

Some Western rivers, like the Snake, flow through canyons that just roll away into steep but climbable hillsides. The famous Salmon River is one that fits the description.

A half-dozen years ago, I hunted deer along the Salmon with my close friend Dewey Haeder, a college classmate. Dewey and his son Tommy headed in one direction, and I the other. We had driven to the top of the river canyon and planned on dropping down along the brushy sidehills to hunt.

"Don't kill a buck too far down," Dewey grinned as we split. "There ain't but one way to get him out, and that's up. A very tough up."

Two hours later and a half mile straight down the canyon, I stood over the carcass of a fat three-point. I just couldn't resist the shot. Dewey appeared just as I finished field-dressing the buck. Because Tommy was with him his language was civil, but I knew what my buddy was thinking.

We should have quartered the buck and packed him out in pieces, but we were feeling feisty and strong. Four hours later, we made it to the rim, but not without a lot of blood, sweat, and tears. We dragged the buck, and urged ourselves ahead by tossing a jacket a few yards up the mountain. When we dragged the buck to the jacket, we rested and caught our breath, then threw the jacket a few more yards and made another drag. All the while I looked at the sparkling Salmon River below, wishing for all the world that we had been floating and hunting from the bottom up instead of the top down.

In the last 30 years or so, a nuisance shrub called tamarisk has invaded many Western river systems. The plant was introduced from Asia, and is cursed by Westerners, especially stockmen. The shrub grows so dense, it is almost physically impossible to walk through it, but deer use it extensively for cover.

Hunters have realized its value for harboring deer and hunt it by making drives. Because of tamarisk's shelter value, riverbottom areas seem to be producing more muleys in some areas, although that's only a personal observation. One needs to be careful when talking about any advantages of tamarisk, especially in saloons frequented by big, nasty cowboys.

Many of the big Western rivers flow through public land, so access isn't a problem, but smaller rivers often flow across private land. Before embarking on a trip down a river where ownership is in question, check the laws in the state you're hunting to determine navigation rights. Some states have laws which give landowners the right to deny access down a river if he owns both sides.

If you're a serious mule deer hunter, do plan a float trip before you hang up your rifle. It could very well be one of the best hunts of your life.

Hunting in Agricultural Areas

When we think of farmland deer, we often think whitetails are the only species associated with agricultural areas. Mule deer have always been considered to be deer of the mountains and lonely places.

Times are changing. Muleys discovered cropland when the first settlers plowed land and planted it, but the deer seem to be becoming more noticeable in agricultural areas.

Farmlands may appeal to mule deer year round, but winter is an especially active period. This season usually has little importance to hunters because most deer hunts are over, but farms being ravaged by muleys is often a profound problem.

Alfalfa, corn, and wheat are among the chief crops in the West, and mule deer are fond of all three. During winter months, high-country deer often move in to an agricultural area and help themselves to valuable crops. Haystacks are unsafe unless extensively fenced, and farmers have little or no love for the four-footed raiders. Various repellants are used to drive the pesky deer off, but control by shooting the herd is often the last resort. Game wardens move in and systematically execute the deer.

Most states have game damage payment programs which compensate the farmer for crop destruction by wildlife. Compensation can be in the form of cash, or the wildlife department might replace the damaged crops directly by hauling in an equal amount of forage, wheat, or whatever the case may be. Some state agencies have farms that raise crops expressly for the purpose of compensating farmers. To prevent abuse of the game damage payment program, state legislatures usually set ceilings that put a maximum payoff to farmers. As expected, the entire program is controversial, especially when revenue for the damage compensation comes from hunting license funds. When Utah recently raised the game damage payment maximum limit, farmers predictably asked for more money, which in turn wreaked havoc with the wildlife budget, forcing many cuts in fish and wildlife programs. A few years back, Wyoming tacked an extra $5 fee on all nonresident license applications, earmarking the $5 for game damage payoffs. Interestingly enough, only nonresidents foot the bill for compensating Wyoming's farmers and ranchers.

With all the damage suffered by landowners, you'd think they'd be delighted to allow hunters on their property to reduce deer numbers. Right?

Wrong. Posted signs abound over much of the West, but this is not to say that the great majority of lands are off-limits to hunters. Compared to the Midwest or East, an enormous amount of private land is available to Western hunters, but those acres are dwindling each year. Nonetheless, hunting on farmland is a productive opportunity, and most deer harvested are fat and tasty.

To hunt on farmland, you first need to have permission of the owner. Plenty of hunters are shy about walking up to a stranger's house and asking for permission, but there seldom are other options. Having relatives or friends who are farmers or know farmers helps, but many of us aren't that fortunate.

Before asking permission, find out who owns the land you want to

This beautiful buck lives on a farm within sight of a building.

hunt. You'll save lots of time visiting farmhouses. Rural country store owners and gas station employees can often tell you the ownership of every acre in the community. They might also tip you off about the landowners who are apt to let you on their property, as well as those who won't.

When you ask permission, be polite, and always respect the wishes of the farmer. If he says no to your request, give him a genuine smile and thank him anyway. Once, when I was denied permission to hunt muleys on a Wyoming ranch, I tried to be as gracious as possible and thanked the rancher anyway. As I left the porch, I saw a newspaper laying on the ground. I picked it up and handed it to the rancher. That simple act must have triggered sympathy, because he called me back and said something to the effect that I looked like a pretty good guy and offered me the key to his gates.

If you're offered permission, be sure to confirm the farm's property boundaries. It's easy to trespass off a property if you don't know the land ownership patterns. If the owner tells you not to cross a creek or a fenceline, don't be tempted if the "grass looks greener" on the other side. Abuses like these increase conflicts between hunters and landowners.

Likewise, if a farmer tells you to stay off cropland, obey his wishes. Many landowners do not want people walking through standing corn or wheat for obvious reasons. Respect those instructions.

In some states, landowners need not post their land. It's up to the hunter to determine if he's on private land or public property. Wyoming is a good example, and I had an experience there a couple years back that illustrates the problem. I was driving along, looking for a place to hunt deer in an area that I'd never hunted before. A chunk of land looked interesting, and I was almost positive it was federal BLM land. There were no fences, no sign of cultivation, just dusty acres that looked typical of BLM land. My map showed a great deal of BLM land in the area, but it wasn't detailed enough to show precise boundaries. I decided it was federal land, and drove in a quarter mile and parked my vehicle. Three hours later, after walking across several ridges, I returned to my truck to find two men sitting in a pickup parked near mine. They were polite, but firm.

"Do you have permission to hunt from Mr. so and so?" one of them asked me.

I told them I hadn't, and asked them to look over my map. They pointed out where I was, and said the federal land was just over the hill. However, if I'd simply ask the rancher for permission, he'd probably let me on, according to their guess. The men worked for the rancher, and said he allowed hunters if he knew who they were. The men pointed out the ranch house down the valley.

I drove down, pulled into the front yard, and met the landowner working on a tractor next to the barn. He was friendly, and easily offered permission. He wrote a note to this effect on the back of my hunting license, and told me some of the better hunting areas. That evening, I killed a fat buck as he was coming out to feed in an alfalfa field.

Farmlands are often sleeper areas. Many hunters are amazed when they learn about big bucks killed in agricultural areas, particularly close to urban centers. One day, while driving along a highway with a friend who was an experienced deer hunter, we passed the carcass of a nice buck that had been hit by an automobile.

"I'll be doggoned," my friend said. "Wonder where that buck came from. Nothing around here but cornfields and farmhouses."

A farmland buck walks into a brush patch to bed for the day. Small brushy creek bottoms that flow through agricultural areas are likely places to jump deer.

His curiosity aroused, my pal asked a highway patrolman if many deer were struck by vehicles in the area.

"Sure enough," the patrolman said. "Two or three every year."

Our attitudes changed about mule deer and farmlands, and we began looking into this new possibility. With gas prices being what they are, the nearby agricultural areas offered a close-in place to hunt.

Mule deer are seldom seen around agricultural areas because they move about under the cover of darkness, whenever possible. The sounds and disturbances by people and farm machinery usually keep deer in cover most of the day. Places far from the ranch house are quieter, and deer may be seen there in fields more so than in busier areas.

A cornfield being ravaged by mule deer is a sight to behold if they've been at it awhile. Deer knock down big patches of corn in their daily behavior, whether feeding, bedding, or cavorting about. A farmer once told me he watched two young bucks sparring in a cornfield. The man was intrigued at the display, and allowed the deer to continue their fun. When the mock battle was over, a quarter acre of standing stalks had been knocked over.

When mule deer decide to take over a cornfield, they often make it their permanent home, leaving only for water. They bed right in the corn, and seldom come out into the open.

Farmers take a dim view of this destruction, and are understandably eager to have the culprits eliminated. If a farmer isn't reserving his land for himself, friends, or relatives when hunting season arrives, he might give you permission to hunt. A good way to learn where deer damage is occurring is to contact the state wildlife office and inquire.

Once you have permission to hunt corn, the next step is to convince the deer that cornfields are not conducive to their health. A well-organized drive is practically the only hope ofnmaking deer show. If the cornfield is bordered by a brushy creek, patch of woods, or other cover, put the standers on that end. Deer are more apt to leave cover only to run into more cover, and almost any other kind of vegetation is easier to hunt than standing cornstalks. There are always exceptions, however. A friend of mine told me about an elusive mule deer buck that claimed part of a western South Dakota cornfield as his exclusive territory. When hunters tried to rout the buck with a big drive, the deer busted out of the cornpatch, ran down the main farm lane, directly past the front door of the farmhouse, and across a well-traveled highway. A farm boy on an adjacent farm spotted the buck, ran for his rifle, and killed the deer as it crossed an irrigation ditch. The fat buck dressed at 290 pounds.

I recall another time when I was crossing a cornpatch to set duck decoys at the other end. Halfway through the corn, I heard a rifle shot directly ahead of me. When I got to the end of the field, I saw a hunter bent over a deer carcass. It was a pretty four-point muley.

"Thanks, buddy," the man said. "You kicked this buck right to me. Been watching him for 2 weeks, but never expected to get him."

I looked at the buck, then my duck decoys, and mused about the choice I'd made for hunting that day. Maybe another buck in the cornfield needed looking into.

In crops other than corn that are short and offer no shelter, another technique must be used. Obviously, deer must travel to and from these fields from adjacent places that offer protection.

Many years back, my father-in-law and I decided to try for bucks that were feeding on a big alfalfa field. The ranch had suffered enormous deer damage over the years, with upwards of 150 deer in the field at one time. It sounded like an easy hunt, but there was a major problem. Because the deer had been harassed for years, they operated only at night. Furthermore, a series of rugged ledges were adjacent to the ranch, and heavy pinyon-juniper cover offered plenty of concealment for the marauding deer. The ledge area was public land, so we elected to ambush bucks leaving the field for their bedding area. To do it, we had to be on stand at the hint of first light.

Before setting out to hunt, we spent a full day looking over the ledges. We found several major deer trails, but were puzzled because we couldn't find where they were crossing a vertical razor-backed ridge. We finally located four small passes that appeared to be natural crossings. Even at that, the deer had to jump about 5 feet off a vertical rocky wall to make the crossing.

The next morning, Dad and I positioned ourselves where we could see the passes. The hunt appeared to be duck soup, but the joke was on us. Only a dozen deer crossed, but all were does and fawns. Even the little bucks eluded us. All was not lost, however, because later in the day we jumped nice bucks in the pinyons and dropped a pair of four-points.

The crossing was a mystery however, and I asked the rancher about it. He told me the biggest bucks wandered into the alfalfa about 8 p.m., fed for several hours, and left for the ledges at least 2 or 3 hours before

Deer do substantial damage to crops and haystacks. Farmers often allow hunting when deer cause problems.

daybreak. Apparently we had the right idea, but the bucks beat us across the passes well before legal shooting hours.

If deer are strictly nocturnal in their feeding habits on farmlands, often your only choice is to jump them where they bed, as my father-in-law and I did in the pinyons.

Since farmlands are often in valleys, creeks are often part of the landscape. Mule deer love to spend the daylight hours basking in the shelter of creekside vegetation such as willows, cottonwoods, and other plants that grow near water. Many of the mule deer in western Kansas, Oklahoma, and the Dakotas, in fact, live much of their lives along brushy creeks that meander through farmland. Whitetails often share some of this environment, and more than one whitetail hunter has been shocked to see a huge muley buck bouncing out of a creek bottom.

I'll never forget an experience I had while hunting pheasants in Utah. The season was a few days old, and most of the young birds had been shot, as is typical with pheasant hunting. The best opportunity was in the thick tangles of brush where wary birds hid. I walked a mile of weedy irrigation ditches with my German shorthair Pepper but couldn't find a rooster. A brush-choked stream ran down one side of the barley field I was hunting. It usually paid off when birds were scarce. I didn't relish hunting the creek, however, because it was a nightmare tangle of wild rose, Russian olive, and other godforsaken thorny shrubs that could make a grown man cry.

Pepper minced into the cover, not liking it at all, and did his best to find birds. He disappeared down the creek, and I followed along with all sorts of branches tearing at my clothes. Suddenly I heard a loud crashing in the brush across the creek, and looked over to see a big mule deer rack swiveling around above the brush. The buck looked back at Pepper, then stared directly at me as if to say, "What in heck are *you* doing here in my hideout?" At that the deer made a strong leap out of the tangle and scrambled up a rocky sidehill.

I asked the farmer afterward about the buck, and he told me the deer had been in the area for 2 years. Several people tried for him, but no one got a shot. I wasn't surprised.

Some Western farms and ranches are in the lowlands where water is scarce, and places with free-standing water are often good spots to watch for deer. Stock tanks are prime spots, but you obviously need to be extremely careful near livestock, *if* the landowner will give you permission to hunt around them. Irrigation ditches are likely places for deer to water, but it's tough to figure precisely where the deer visit the ditches.

Salt licks also attract deer, but be sure your state doesn't have laws forbidding hunting around licks. Many salt licks are in wide open places, with little opportunity to get close.

On farms and ranches where deer are lightly hunted, animals might be surprisingly tolerant of humans. This is logical, because deer often become conditioned to people. This is especially true when people are riding about in vehicles and farm machinery, but not when *Homo sapiens* leaves the machine and goes afoot. When that happens, deer that will stand around and look at a vehicle usually take off with no hesitation. They want no part of a person standing on two feet.

Although most mule deer don't use trails as extensively as whitetails, farm country muleys are an exception. Because their habits are fairly predictable and their habitat comparatively limited, they follow set patterns for feeding, drinking, and bedding.

This behavior has all the ingredients for a successful ambush. By knowing where the deer bed, you can waylay them as they travel to or from feeding areas. Tree stands are ideal where tall trees are available, but any kind of cover will suffice to make a blind. I know a small greasewood patch overlooking a wheat field in Colorado that produces bucks every year for a friend.

Because you can get close to your quarry along well-traveled trails, bowhunting is a fine option. Some of the best bowhunting for muleys is on farmland. The procedures are the same as for whitetails. Find a good vantage point as close as possible to a trail, and be sure there's enough open space to drive an arrow through. Be careful of the wind, and keep movements to a minimum. And make no mistake about it. A trophy mule deer buck sneaking along a trail is just as big a challenge as the super-intelligent whitetails you read about. Farmland muleys do not lack for brains.

Since farms and ranches are privately owned, they sometimes offer the best hunting for mule deer. This makes sense because the landowner may limit the number of hunters on his property, *if* he allows any hunting at all. Furthermore, agricultural areas offer everything a mule deer wants—plenty of feed, water, and usually adequate cover.

Farmers have been discovering that hunters are willing to pay for the privilege of hunting deer on their property, and many landowners sell a

These deer have moved onto a farm to feed. Private lands often offer good hunting, but sportsmen must get permission first.

trespass permit. The price varies, ranging anywhere from $10 a day to $100 or more. Some landowners sell a limited number of permits to hunters, and allow them to camp in designated places on their property. In some cases, the farmer or rancher runs a boarding house during hunting season, providing hot, home-cooked meals for hunters.

Most landowners don't advertise these services, because word of mouth usually takes care of it. However, there are ways to find out about trespass permit possibilities. Inquire with local chambers of commerce, Soil Conservation Service workers who deal with landowners every day, game wardens, or even county agents.

Some farmers sell trespass permits to groups of hunters who lease the entire property, or they simply lease the hunting rights to a hunting club or small group. Some farms and ranches have such good hunting that lease fees are extremely high.

But for all the popular expensive leased areas, plenty of others exist that budget-conscious hunters can afford.

There is an attitude in Western states containing a lot of public land that hunting should be free. I know plenty of hunters who vow they will never pay to hunt. All well and good, but the times are changing. I'm not in favor of paid hunting, but I can understand why landowners charge hunting fees, and I have no opposition to paying a fee. I don't want to see hunting become a rich man's sport as it is in Europe. On the other hand, I don't want to see private land locked up and made completely unavailable to hunters. If landowners allow hunting only because of vested reasons, then at least the sport continues.

Landowners consider wildlife a cash crop in many areas, just like the crops they grow and the livestock they raise. If they determine that deer hunters bring them some extra money to buy a new piano for the wife or put Johnny through college, then that's their prerogative. Hunters have no choice but to pay the fees or hunt elsewhere. If the fee is reasonable and there's a chance for a big old buck, I'll pay it.

Remember, though, lots of farmers and ranchers let you on with just a handshake. All you need to do is ask.

Hunting in
the Desert

Several types of deserts classified by amount of moisture, summer and winter temperature, and types of vegetation, are found in the West. For the purposes of this chapter, a desert is an arid region with little water and a combination of low-growing shrubs and a variety of cactus.

Many mule deer subspecies live in the desert, the two most important being the Rocky Mountain muley and the desert mule deer. The others are the California, the southern, and the peninsula mule deer.

Desert regions have a common denominator: water is scarce, and deer often concentrate near water sources. Precipitation in deserts usually falls in the winter months—as rain in the southern latitudes and snow farther north. Not only is precipitation low, it often does not last in water holes until it's needed in the hot summer months.

Drought years are particularly tough on desert-dwelling deer, and often causes severe die-offs. Drought affects deer by drying up water sources and by failing to replenish them, and also prevents proper plant growth. Deer depend on new shoots, buds, and grasses each year. If the vigor of preferred forage species is low, plant growth is insignificant or absent.

In an effort to distribute deer over larger areas, wildlife personnel construct water holes and guzzlers that collect and store water. The simplest water hole is an earthen dam built across a small drainage. Rainwater runs down the drainages and collects in the depression above the dam. These water hole developments work only when sufficient rainfall continues to keep the ponds replenished. In northern desert regions, melted snow fills the holes in the spring. Leakage of water from the holes is a common problem, and is overcome by sealing the depressions with bentonite clay or another form of sealant.

Guzzlers are becoming more popular in desert regions. They collect water and funnel it to underground tanks where evaporation loss is minimized. Water is piped to an above-ground pond or is simply made available at the collecting area.

Natural springs are the best sources of water because they're most dependable, but aren't abundant in many desert areas. Wildlife biologists often fence springs off to keep livestock from polluting and trampling them. Water is piped underground from springs to troughs by gravity pressure, and water is released into the troughs on a demand basis by float devices similar to the types used in toilets.

Desert mule deer graze in southern New Mexico. (*Photo courtesy of Jesse Williams.*)

In desert country with rock outcroppings and ledges, seeps trickle out of cracks and seams. I can remember discovering hidden seeps while hunting desert bighorn sheep in Utah's terribly rugged Dark Canyon Plateau. Deer tracks were evident at practically every seep.

Stockmen have been responsible for many thousands of water developments in desert regions. Cattle and sheep could not survive without water. Arid regions were completely inhospitable to livestock, requiring ranchers to either develop water or ignore the area. Deer have increased their desert territories enormously because of livestock water.

Obviously, hunters head for water because deer are concentrated in those areas. The strategy seems simple, but it seldom is.

Take, for example, the little water hole I found while hunting doves in the Utah desert. All sorts of animals used it, including coyotes, a herd of antelope, cottontails, a variety of birds, and a small group of deer, including a very fine buck. I saw the buck walking toward the water hole early one morning while I was waiting for doves. He caught my scent, wheeled about, and crashed through greasewoods up a canyon bottom.

I was confident the buck would continue to use the water hole, and decided to try for him during rifle season. Archery season was over, or I would have tried him with an arrow. Before I left the area that day, I found a good vantage point high in the rocks overlooking the water hole. The range was 200 yards, just right for my .30/06.

I parked a full mile away from the water hole and walked in to it the afternoon before the season. My plan was to sleep in the rocks that night and kill the buck from my sleeping bag on opening morning. But it didn't work out the way I expected.

That evening, I sat in my perch watching a herd of antelope feeding in the distance. I didn't dare start a fire because the smoke would probably spook the buck. As the last few minutes of light were slipping by, I was distressed to see the buck walk to the water hole and drink. I knew immediately that the morning hunt would be a lost cause. The buck no doubt would fill up and fail to return to the hole until the next afternoon.

Opening morning was a flop. All that showed at the water was a doe and two fawns, three antelope, and a coyote. I walked back to my rig, hunted pinyon-juniper country about 30 miles away, and hurriedly drove back to the waterhole in mid-afternoon to try for the buck again. I climbed up into my now-familiar stand and waited for dusk.

Again it was a fruitless vigil. I stayed until dark, but the buck didn't show. I was about to leave the stand when I caught just a trace of movement in the faint light. I raised my binoculars and barely saw the figure of a deer drinking. I couldn't be sure, but I swore I saw antlers reflected off the surface of the water. It was much too dark for a shot, in fact I couldn't determine which way the deer was facing, where its chest was, or even if it indeed was the buck, although I was sure it was.

I tried for the deer one more time the next day. I positioned myself a half mile up the canyon from where the buck originated each afternoon. By finding a stand farther up, I figured the buck might wander by me earlier when there was enough light to shoot.

Shooting light was just about over with no sign of the buck when I spotted an animal walking to the water. I was astounded to see the buck passing within yards of my original stand. I guessed the range to be 700 yards, and quickly ducked down and sprinted along the maze of rocks, hoping for a decent shot before darkness closed in.

It didn't work. The buck might have heard pebbles clattering as I moved along, or it might have seen me, but it was nowhere to be seen at the water hole.

I was out of time, and had to leave the little desert oasis for the season. I never saw the buck again on future dove hunting trips, but I'll never forget him. It was a memorable hunt, even though I didn't get a shot.

Studies show that mule deer in desert regions have a fairly small home range, and their movement patterns are related to water. From 1962 to 1968, Texas biologists conducted studies on desert mule deer of the Black Gap and Sierra Diablo Wildlife Management Areas to determine their dependency on water and the distance deer would travel to it.

The study was made by counting the number of deer around several water facilities, then turning the water completely off and counting the deer again, then turning the water back on, with another final count of deer. The study lasted 5 years, and deer were allowed plenty of time to adjust to the changes in available water. Before the study, when water facilities were full, 21 deer per section of land were around the water. During the years of no water, deer numbers dropped rapidly to as low as three per section. When water was again turned on, deer increased to the original level of 21 per section. The only time deer numbers increased during the study was when rain replenished the facilities temporarily.

A desert mule deer's home range has been estimated to have about a 1½-mile radius in Texas, which is comparable to other Western states.

Larry Gurr of Vernal, Utah,
glasses a vast desert area for
mule deer.

This behavior is both an asset and a liability to hunters. It is an asset in
that once a herd is located, they can be hunted in a relatively small area.
The liability is finding the herds, since many desert areas have few or no
deer at all.

Since water is the key to locating deer, the serious hunter should
locate as many water holes as possible to have several options. Water can
be pinpointed by obtaining maps and looking for springs and developments, or by carefully observing wildlife sign, or by putting a lot of
footsteps in the desert and looking for vegetation that spells water.

Much desert land is administered by the Bureau of Land Management.
The agency has maps of its lands, and water developments, springs, and
reservoirs are often shown. Personally, I prefer to buy topographic maps,
since they show more detail than BLM maps. With map in hand, start
looking in the desert and check for deer sign around water. Be certain
you don't confuse sheep and antelope tracks with deer.

Another way to find water, especially unmapped sources, is to watch
the behavior of birds and to look for an abundance of tracks. I located two
excellent desert oases by watching the flight paths of doves and following.

One water hole was in a small basin, impossible to see from any road. It turned out to be a bonanza for doves, but no deer were using it. Well-worn trails of any type in a desert environment usually signal the presence of water nearby. Antelope are highly visible in the daylight hours, and live most of their lives close to water. If you see antelope in an area consistently start searching for water. It's around somewhere, and perhaps a dandy buck deer is using it as well.

Once I was walking through the desert and spotted an unusual number of coyote tracks. I thought a den was nearby, and began looking around. I've always wanted to photograph a group of coyote pups playing in front of a den, and I happened to have my camera with me. The tracks seemed to be heading up a small arroyo, and when I walked up it 200 yards I came to a little pond brimming with water. A small buck deer and two does jumped out of nearby brush and hightailed it out of the country.

A sneaky way to locate water is to look for trees and shrubs that need more water than desert plants. You don't need to be a tree expert; just be able to recognize shrubbery that looks out of place in the desert environment. I like to get up on a vantage point where I can see for miles and carefully glass the surrounding landscape with binoculars. One day I was up on a ledge and saw a strange patch of green on a distant hillside. I investigated and discovered a seep that trickled out of a rocky seam. Deer tracks were everywhere. I told a buddy about the find, and he killed a modest buck later in the fall.

Another way to spot desert water holes is perfectly legal, but I'm not personally in favor of the method. That doesn't mean, of course, that it's unethical—just against my own set of beliefs. It involves chartering a small aircraft and looking for water from the air. This is the most effective technique of all, and the quickest. No water hole can hide from an airplane overhead. While flying in and out of Vernal, I often see little desert water holes around the outskirts of town that I never knew existed. I don't close my eyes, and in fact, have investigated several, but I don't believe in specifically going out to look for them in an airplane. I'd just as soon do it the hard way. It's much more fun and a challenge in its own right.

In many desert regions, an abundance of brush requires close-in hunting. The chaparral regions of the Southwest are often so dense it's difficult to walk through the vegetation. Desert plants are often unforgiving, with formidable thorns, spikes, and needles. All kinds of cactus, yuccas, and a myriad of well-armed thorny bushes are out to get the unsuspecting human visitor. One of the densest regions I've ever seen is California's San Gabriel Mountains. One summer I worked as a ranger naturalist on the Angeles National Forest just outside Pasadena, and learned how nasty the desert environment can be. I led nature walks along trails that wound through manzanita, yucca, and other horrid plants, and invariably had to rescue someone who wandered off the path and learned first-hand about the penetrating abilities of a yucca spike, or the density of a manzanita patch.

While I'm on the subject of southern California, I must describe an experience I'll never forget. After tourist season was over, I left the naturalist

A modest four-point Rocky Mountain mule deer buck in a desert environment. This deer lived near a small spring that provided water.

position and joined up with a Hotshot fire-fighting crew on the ranger district. When we weren't fighting the terrible brush fires, we routinely cleared firebreaks with hand tools. It was tough, hot work as we grubbed out the stubborn desert plants that invaded the firebreaks. One day, a fellow crew member shouted an obscene phrase as we worked a firebreak in Santa Anita Canyon. Although I was used to numerous epithets in the hot sun, I looked up from my axe and saw him pointing down to a paved highway below us. There, walking precisely up the center of a highway was an enormous buck mule deer with a spread that I judged to be 30 inches easily. I thought I was back in Utah, having had no idea the desert in southern California produced such bucks. Thinking I was suffering sunstroke, I alerted the rest of the crew, and we all watched the huge buck stroll along, finally disappearing into the brushy backyard of a handsome home where, of all things, people were swimming in a pool. I believe that buck had never been hunted, because no hunters suspected him to be in the country.

In densely vegetated desert areas, deer often travel on trails. Elevated stands are ideal for seeing into the maze of thick brush. Many times deer never fully expose themselves in openings, but feed and water in vegetation that swallows them entirely. Drives may work in such situations, but drivers could easily be repelled by impenetrable thickets. The best one can hope for is to find the intersection of well-used trails, check the wind, back off into the brush, and hope a legal deer strolls along.

Desert mule deer in the Southwest can often be spotted from long distances in mountain country. In the Trans-Pecos region in Texas, hunters often spot desert muleys on sloping hillsides with binoculars, then stalk into shooting range. In some desert areas, hunters can climb atop rocky knolls or sand hills and look down on the brush around them.

In the Rockies, mule deer often move out of the mountains in the winter and spend the cold months in desert regions. Many times, however, they don't get to the lowlands until well after hunting season is over, although early storms drive them out of the hills rapidly. If a hunter times it right, he might find a deer herd in a normally barren area that holds few or no deer on a year round basis.

Western deserts often have rocky, rugged outcroppings that run for miles in long fingers. These are favorite hideouts as well as feeding areas for mule deer. Vegetation often grows in the escarpments, and jumbles of boulders are convenient refuges. Big bucks often lie on the top edge of a desert ridge so they can see danger below. A workable strategy is to climb on the ridgetop and walk slowly, peering over the edges randomly as you sneak along. Don't be surprised to peek over a cliff and see a buck below you in his bed.

Desert hunting takes some preparation, and dangers are involved not associated with other habitats. First off, deserts can be exceedingly hot or extremely cold, from 20 degrees below zero or colder to 100 degrees or more. In hot weather you need plenty of water, and in cold weather you need energy and warmth. Always carry a lot of water when it's hot, enough to last several days. I take 10 gallons of water in an Igloo cooler, and store it in the back of my rig under a canvas wrap to keep the sun from warming it. When I hunt on foot, I carry a 1-gallon canteen on my back, or a 2-quart canteen over my shoulder. Hunting vehicles should be in good working order before heading into the desert. A breakdown could have serious consequences. At least in the mountains other hunters are apt to drive along if your rig is broken down, but in the desert, you might go for days without seeing another person. Wood is a problem in the desert if nights are cold and your vehicle quits. Survival manuals say to burn your tires one at a time to stay warm, but I'd just as soon not be in that type of situation in the first place. By keeping my rig well-maintained, I usually avoid those problems.

In hot deserts, rattlesnakes are often numerous. Snake-leggings are worn by cautious hunters in areas where snakes are known to be especially plentiful. Whenever in snake country, it's always a good idea to keep a wary eye to the ground, particularly when moving around rockpiles, clumps of debris, and other refuges where snakes take shelter from the sun.

Most Western deserts are public land, with Texas a notable exception. Almost all of Texas is privately owned, and hunters lease ranches from landowners. Most leases are sold on a seasonal basis, but there are some daily and weekly leases as well.

The desert, whether hot or cold, presents a unique challenge to mule deer hunters. Some surprisingly good bucks live in them, and many regions are underhunted in favor of mountains where "standard" hunting is practiced. The arid landscape offers a special setting, however, and much of it is still waiting to be discovered.

Getting in Shape for Mule Deer Hunting

Much of the information in this chapter was provided by Parker N. Davies, M.D., my neighbor, friend, and hunting buddy.

I was walking off a ridgetop in Wyoming when three small bucks bounced out of an aspen patch and trotted over the ridge. They walked into a little swale, dropped their heads, and started feeding. None of them were interesting, so I continued down the ridge to my truck where a sandwich and cold pop were waiting. I got close to the road and met a hunter slowly walking up toward the direction I had come from. I noted he was breathing heavily and sweating profusely.

"See anything?" he asked as he gasped for air.

"Yep. Three small bucks just over the top of the ridge. When I left they were feeding in a swale," I answered.

"Really?" the hunter exclaimed. "You really saw some bucks?" His eyes lit up and he smiled broadly. Obviously he was excited.

I pointed out precisely where I saw the deer, and watched the man climb the ridge. I doubted he would make it, at least not before the bucks wandered off out of sight. During our short conversation, the man said he was an accountant for an Eastern firm, and that he was out of shape. I judged him to be in his mid 30's, but he was paunchy and slightly overweight.

Later that afternoon I met the same hunter with his buddies. They were glassing a hillside from alongside their vehicle. I talked to the man a moment and learned he hadn't seen the bucks. He said he got dizzy and felt nauseous when he was midway up the ridge, and had come back down.

A few weeks later, in Utah, I met a hunter from the West Coast puffing up a cow trail in a quaking aspen forest. When he asked how far it was to the top and I told him, he said he'd forget it because his legs ached and he was too winded to continue.

Both of those hunters were suffering from overexertion. They were forcing their muscles to perform in a manner they were unaccustomed to, and their lungs and hearts were working overtime as well.

A hunter in poor physical condition has the odds against him if he's hoping for a crack at a big muley. As I said elsewhere in this book, you can kill a trophy whitetail in a farm woodlot or next to a corn field, but mule deer require you to put one foot ahead of the other for more miles and up more mountains than you'd like, unless, of course, you have the option of riding horseback.

Except for some desert regions, mule deer country is an up and down

Be prepared for cold weather by wearing adequate boots and clothing. Frostbite and hypothermia are constant dangers in the outdoors.

proposition. Although many deer are killed close to roads, the serious hunter heads out afoot to find a good buck. Sometimes muleys are nowhere to be seen near roads, and the hunter has no choice but to leave his vehicle and start walking. Much of that walking is just as liable to be up as down.

Writers commonly warn prospective mule deer hunters to get in shape before heading for the mountains where the slopes are steep and the air thin. I'll do so in this chapter with help from Dr. Davies, but first I'd like to offer advice not often given by writers to hunters who *can't* get in shape because of their physical condition. Some hunters carry nitroglycerine pills because of heart conditions, others have respiratory problems, and so on. They want to kill a muley just as much as the next guy, but they're handicapped and can't travel far. All is not lost for these hunters if some common sense is used.

I'll use some examples as to how handicapped hunters can increase their odds of killing a mule deer, and we'll use the name Harry to denote our man in the spotlight.

A good technique is to find a fairly gradual ridge where there is a road at the top and a road at the bottom. No problem there, since roads are established extensively in much of the West. Drive to the top of the ridge with Harry, drop him off, and tell him to meet you at a predetermined place on the road below. He can take his time and hunt downhill to the bottom road. If he kills a deer, you can set up a signal by having him fire a series of shots. The important thing is that Harry work his way downhill, which is admittedly rough on legs and ankles, but at least he isn't climbing steadily and overtaxing his physical capabilities.

Another place for Harry is as a stander on a drive. Put him on a ridgetop where he won't have to walk down into a drainage and then walk back up. Since mule deer like to run uphill when they're spooked, Harry will have just as good a chance as anyone.

Harry is a good candidate for sitting on a stand in the morning. Drive along a ridge in good deer country, let him walk off to the side of the road a few yards where he has a good vista into a canyon or sidehill, and let him sit quietly for a few hours. He might see more deer than the rest of the party put together.

Whatever you do, don't ignore mule deer hunting because you've heard it's only for the young and healthy hunter. While your chances are enormously improved if you can climb and walk the backcountry, you can still find deer if you use logic.

If you're a Harry and have booked a hunt with an outfitter, don't be a hero and be embarrassed to tell him you are physically handicapped. Be sure to tell him exactly what your limitations are, and don't be afraid to tell him if your guide is too fast for you or is climbing steeper hills than you like.

Let's say you're in reasonably good physical condition with no known ailments and you're planning a mule deer hunt. We'll assume you're a touch overweight and have a sedentary job which doesn't give you much chance to exercise. According to Dr. Davies, daily exercise in sufficient quality and quantity enhances your capability of dealing with the physical demands of a Western hunt. He suggests starting in on an active exercise program at least 6 months in advance of the hunt, and to ask your doctor's advice about the best type of exercise plan for you.

If you're over 35, Dr. Davies recommends you have a complete physical as well as a stress EKG if you're going to be involved in strenuous activity at high elevations. Before going on your trip, give your doctor some idea about the type of hunting you'll be doing. If you're hunting with an outfitter, ask him about hunting conditions and give the information to your doctor. If you take medication regularly, be sure your doctor prescribes enough for you to take on the hunt.

It makes good sense to begin a fitness program, not only for a mule deer hunt, but for your health as well. If you feel good while you're hunting, you'll hunt with much more enthusiasm and concentration. If you're only concerned with getting back to camp where you can relax, you're decreasing your odds of locating a buck. It often takes work to get to the midst of good deer country, and unless you're mentally and physically capable, you might as well figure on a poor hunt. You must work on your hunt if you want it to work for you.

Your hunting techniques and their effectiveness will be based on your ability to carry them out. For example, I like to stillhunt in the early morning, but I'm a wanderer the rest of the day. I'm always curious about the next ridge or canyon, and I commonly walk 6 to 10 miles a day. But when I'm not up to it, I take shorter walks and stay closer to roads. That's not to say bucks can't be killed near roads, but I've consistently seen bigger bucks the farther I got from people.

Dr. Davies related an incident he experienced during a 1980 Colorado hunt. While walking on a ridgetop, he met two Pennsylvanian hunters who were obviously bushed. They asked the closest way back to the road, because they'd had it with hunting. All they wanted to do was get off the mountain and rest. Deer sign was plentiful, and big bucks were in the area, but the two exhausted hunters didn't care. Because their bodies weren't up to the task of climbing and walking, they had given up mentally as well.

"It was a wasted trip for those hunters," Dr. Davies told me. "They were simply out of shape."

Of course, it's folly to push yourself if you're not in condition. If you become fatigued, adjust your pace accordingly. No one expects you to run around the hills like a mountain man. Use good judgment, and hunt within your capabilities. Dr. Davies has seen hunters die of heart attacks because they overexerted themselves. It's best to take it easy, rather than become a statistic.

According to Dr. Davies, more American males die of heart attacks than any other illness. Because hunting can be a strenuous activity, it's important to detect heart disease before going on a trip, thus the reason for a stress EKG for hunters over 35.

You should know the symptoms of a heart attack for your own welfare. Dr. Davies lists these symptoms: lower chest pains of a crushing nature unrelieved in any position, pain in the shoulders or arms, jaw numbness or pain, pain between shoulder blades, nausea, and cold clammy skin.

Several years ago, a hunting companion of mine took longer than usual to walk back to a road after shooting hours. Several of us waited, and we saw him coming, but he was walking very slowly up a mountain slope, taking frequent stops. He offered no explanation at the time, but later he had open heart surgery. He told us afterward he had had severe chest pains while walking up the hill, and had never experienced anything like it before. His surgery was a success, and he is in excellent shape.

There is a disease known as acute mountain sickness that affects humans in high elevations. The mildest form of the disease is a combination of trivial symptoms: headache, nausea, dizziness, sleeplessness, giddiness, and loss of appetite. More serious symptoms are headache not relieved by aspirin or codeine, vomiting, chest discomfort with shortness of breath, fatigue, malaise, and inability to coordinate muscular movements. Generally, recovery from acute mountain sickness is rapid if the afflicted individual descends to lower elevations. The disease can occur in any healthy person who travels rapidly from low elevations to elevations over 9,000 feet. The disease can't be predicted, it isn't related to an individual's phys-

I often pack 60 pounds of gear up a mountainside. One needs to be in shape to hunt muleys in mountain country.

ical condition, and its incidence increases in the young. The disease is more likely to occur if the individual climbs hard, fast, and high. Mountain climbers are the most common victims, but mule deer hunters who try marathon uphill treks should be aware of its existence.

Dr. Davies suggests that hunters carry basic items to prevent common illnesses. Aspirin is standard treatment for headaches and minor aches. It's a good idea to bring along an anti-diarrhea medication, as well as an anti-emetic (vomiting) medication. Lip balm is good to protect the lips from sun and wind, and sun screen lotion helps prevent sunburn, especially in the high elevations where increased ultraviolet radiation can cause severe burns. Dark glasses protect the eyes from bright sun, and a broad-brimmed hat keeps the eyes shaded. Moleskin is an excellent treatment for blisters, and should be carried by hunters who anticipate walking. Dr. Davies strongly advises that boots be well broken-in before the trip since there's no relief for sore feet.

If you're hunting in a hot climate, beware of heat exhaustion. Drink plenty of liquids, and take salt tablets to replace the salt that your body loses naturally through perspiration and urination. Salt is important for muscular function.

In cold regions, hypothermia and frostbite are constant dangers. Treatment for both is heat. Hypothermia can be prevented by staying as dry and warm as possible. It's especially dangerous if you become wet and the wind is blowing. Wool clothing is the best material to wear in wet weather, and a windbreaker or rainwear repels water. To prevent frostbite, cover extremities well, such as face, ears, and fingers. If your feet get cold, start walking to circulate the blood. When frostbite occurs, it often numbs the afflicted area and the individual isn't aware of the danger.

Foods with plenty of fats and calories are good in cold weather. Candy bars or other foods with a high sugar content are good for quick energy, because calories are readily available in sugar. Many sporting goods stores sell packets of high-energy foods with combinations of raisins, nuts, chocolate, and other ingredients.

Dr. Davies suggests you have a tetanus booster shot if you haven't had one in the last 5 years, particularly if you're hunting in a remote area.

If you're going to drink water that is suspect, boil it for at least 30 minutes to kill all harmful bacteria. Water-treatment kits do not destroy all bacteria, such as the giardia organism found in high country areas.

A first-aid kit with salves, bandages, gauzes, burn ointments, and other items is a must for every trip.

Finally, when you're out in the hills, get plenty of sleep. Poker games are great in camp, but you might regret them when the alarm rings the next morning. The more rest you get, the better you function in the outback. The same holds true with alcohol. Nobody enjoys a drink around the evening fire more than me, but use good sense in your drinking. You can enjoy liquor all year long. When you're in deer camp, remember the reason why you're there. You want to be clear-headed and well-rested every morning, ready for the big buck that can show at any time.

The Future of
Mule Deer

The graffiti on the bathroom wall in the Wyoming gas station said it all: "To hell with the Arabs; let's use our own oil." Most Americans agree with that statement, but the implications of producing our own energy will cause irreconcilable destruction of much of the West, and ultimately, of some of our best mule deer herds.

Some of our finest mule deer states—Colorado, Wyoming, Montana, Utah, and others, are underlain with incredible stores of coal. The world knows it, and this fossil fuel has suddenly become a valuable source of energy during these uncertain times of oil shortages and tenuous relationships with oil-producing countries. As you read this, Colorado ridgetops are being ravaged by enormous shovels and draglines that extract coal from the rich seams below. Prime game country in Wyoming is suffering a similar fate, as are countless acres in many other parts of the West.

In a 10-year forecast, the National Coal Association said U.S. coal production should climb to 1.35 billion tons by 1990. That compares to a production of 776 million tons in 1979. It also said that electric utility plants now on the drawing boards to convert coal into synthetic fuels will require 75 million tons of coal daily.

Reclamation laws require strip mines to restore the mined land back to its original character. Some companies are barely doing the minimum while others are sincerely reclaiming the land to the best of their abilities. I toured the area being mined by Energy Fuels, Inc., near Craig, Colorado. The company has a full-time wildlife biologist who directs reseeding operations and vegetation programs on restored lands. It was gratifying to see a company putting forth the extra effort and expense, but disconcerting to know that many other companies are not.

Coal is just the tip of the iceberg influencing the mule deer's future. Oil wells are being drilled throughout the West as higher prices make drilling more feasible in areas where oil is of low quality and formerly economically untouchable. To reach this oil, miles of roads are being constructed into prime deer country, allowing access in places that big bucks used for shelter. Besides the disturbance of drilling and opening up of new country, poaching by oilfield workers becomes a new problem. This is not to say oilfield personnel are, as a group of people, any worse than others, but any time humans work in the backcountry for long periods of time, deer poaching increases. Wildlife enforcement officers can verify that fact of life.

Natural gas is another resource extracted from prime mule deer country. As new gas wells are drilled, the distribution system must be expanded to pipe gas to Eastern consumers. Pipelines that are thousands of miles long are being laid through deer country.

Perhaps the greatest immediate threat to mule deer is the oil shale resource. Colorado, Utah, and Wyoming, in that order, have the most extensive and richest supplies of oil shale, but Montana has just announced new discoveries. Colorado's shale, which is the best of all, lies in the midst of the Piceance Basin, home of the continent's largest mule deer winter

Strip mining threatens some of the best mule deer country in the West.

Allan Whitaker of the Colorado Division of Wildlife looks over part of the Piceance Basin, home of the nation's largest wintering mule deer herd. Oil shale development will ravage a great part of this region.

range. Tales of gloom and despair persist for the future of this great deer
herd, and there are no bright solutions in sight.

Energy isn't the only factor affecting mule deer. The West is being developed rapidly, with unprecedented growth in the low-population Rocky
Mountain states. As communities are enlarged, more land and habitat is
lost to urban expansion. Foothill areas next to high mountain ranges
normally used by mule deer are quickly being converted from prime deer

wintering areas to housing subdivisions. Small towns are expanding their limits and encroaching on historically critical habitat.

The "people boom" brings with it another set of problems. More people means more hunting pressure. In Western states, residents are often given priority for deer licenses, and nonresidents must win a permit in a lottery or on a first-come, first-served basis. In Wyoming, for example, nonresidents obtain permits in a lottery, while residents have unlimited licenses. Since Wyoming is one of the fastest-growing "energy" states, wildlife officials say nonresident quotas will be lowered as resident populations increase and more demands are made for licenses. As the growth trend continues, Wyoming predicts even residents will need to apply for permits in a lottery system. In Nevada, residents are already required to draw for mule deer permits in a lottery. In Montana and Idaho, two top mule deer states, nonresident licenses are available on a first-come, first-served basis until quotas are reached. It's conceivable that those quotas will be lowered as resident hunter populations increase. What this all shakes down to is the increasing difficulty of getting nonresident permits in prime mule deer states.

Inflation continues to eat away at state wildlife budgets, requiring periodic license increases, especially for nonresidents. Worse, many states can't afford to buy critical mule deer winter ranges to save them from development. Most states buy lands and eventually turn them into wildlife management areas, but cutbacks in funding don't allow purchases, especially with soaring land prices. Inflation has also required many states to reduce their personnel force, and game warden positions are often the first to be cut or left unfilled. Consequently, law enforcement suffers, and poaching increases.

The Sagebrush Rebellion is one of the greatest long-term threats to the Western states in terms of wildlife and hunting. Remember those millions and millions of acres of land administered by the BLM that I've been talking about throughout this book? If the Rebellion is successful, those lands will be transferred back to state land boards which look at acres with only one motive: profit. Should state land boards get those BLM acres, mule deer will be in trouble, along with the rest of the wildlife in the West.

The Sagebrush Rebellion officially was born in Nevada on July 13, 1979, when the state legislature passed Assembly Bill 413. The bill claimed state ownership of almost 50 million acres of BLM lands. In one fell swoop,

Nevada's solons waved a magic wand and announced that the BLM was no longer in existence. The bill had no authority to transfer those lands from the BLM to state jurisdiction, but was intended to get the issue into the courts.

After Nevada's litigation, the impact of the Rebellion moved to Washington, D.C., as U.S. legislators introduced similar bills. President Reagan, who labeled himself a "rebel" and a firm supporter of the Sagebrush Rebellion, infused new life into the movement when he was elected.

Why the big fuss if the Rebellion is successful? After all, it would mean a return to smaller government rather than having public lands managed from the shores of the Potomac.

A Forest Service employee looks over heavy timber on the Idaho-Wyoming border behind the Grand Teton Range. Plans are to let some fires burn naturally. Wildlife cover will be improved.

There are two important reasons why the Rebellion would hurt mule deer. First, state land boards are profit-minded and see only dollar signs on those acres. Already Rebellion leaders have spoken of selling off those lands to private interests if the movement is successful, or of developing them to their fullest potential. That means the vast public lands that you and I enjoy hunting on could suddenly become a maze of fences and posted signs. The West would no longer be free and wild. The second reason is that the state land boards have a reputation as poor management agencies. Steve Gallizioli, a highly respected biologist with the Arizona Game and Fish Department, said: "Of all the overgrazed, abused, eroded public rangelands in Arizona, our state lands are without a doubt at the bottom of the barrel."

Another problem in the rapidly growing West—mule deer are frequently killed by vehicles. This busy highway in the oil shale rich Piceance Creek Area of Colorado is one of the worst for deer-vehicle collisions.

The Forest Service purposely burned this stand to improve big game habitat. Note the lush forage as a result of the fire. Government agencies are accelerating their wildlife habitat improvement programs.

It remains to be seen what will come of the Sagebrush Rebellion, and the fight will no doubt last several years. We can only wait and see.

So far this chapter has been rather depressing for the long-term outlook concerning mule deer, but there are bright spots as well. Mule deer are adaptable creatures, and are learning to live in harmony with man. Though not as tolerant as whitetails, mule deer can exist provided there is adequate winter range and other habitat needs.

Wildlife managers are studying mule deer intensively these days, and know more about their behavior patterns and needs than ever before. With this information, herds can be more effectively managed, and quality hunting holds much more promise.

As different hunting methods become popular, wildlife agencies provide specialized hunting opportunities for various advocates. Handgunning, muzzleloading, and bowhunting are enjoyed by sportsmen all over mule deer country. From all indications, states will continue to provide maximum recreational hunting opportunities.

All the Western wildlife and land management agencies, including state wildlife organizations, the Bureau of Land Management, and the U.S. Forest Service are engaged in intensive deer habitat improvement programs. Many agencies use fire as a management tool to promote deer forage. Logging practices are designed to improve deer habitat rather than destroy it. Livestock grazing is being keyed to wildlife needs by rest-rotation and deferred grazing programs. Winter ranges are being identified and protected. Predators are being studied and evaluated in their interaction with wildlife populations.

Generally speaking, the mule deer is being treated as he should be — as a marvelous creature that enchants hunters and spectators alike. Despite the obstacles ahead, and many are formidable, muleys will always be part of the Western scene. Long may they live.

Appendix

Venison Recipes

Lois Zumbo

Venison Smothered in Onions and Tomatoes

3½- to 4-pound venison roast
1 cup ketchup
2 cups sliced onions
1 cup tomato sauce
½ teaspoon salt
pepper

Place venison roast in crock pot or slow cooker. Add onions, ketchup, salt, pepper, and tomato sauce. Cook slowly all day or 6 to 8 hours. Check liquid level in pot periodically and add a little water if sauce mixture gets too low.

Steak in Wine

1 package venison steaks (2½ to 3½ lb.)
1 can condensed cream of mushroom soup
½ cup dry red wine
¼ teaspoon garlic salt
⅓ teaspoon onion salt
¼ teaspoon salt
pepper
cooking oil

Trim any fat from steaks. Place meat in a low casserole dish in single layer. Stir salts, pepper, soup, and wine together. Pour over meat. Bake in 325° oven for 2½ to 3 hours or until very well done.

Venison Ribs Oriental

4 pounds venison ribs
½ cup soy sauce
½ cup sherry
½ teaspoon garlic salt
3½ tablespoons brown sugar
½ cup water

Place ribs in large roasting pan. Combine remaining ingredients and pour over ribs. Cover. Bake 45 minutes in 350° oven, turning ribs several times. Remove lid and continue cooking, turning frequently until golden brown and well done. Baste periodically with sauce.

Venison in Milk

2 pounds venison steak
1 cup milk
½ cup flour
½ teaspoon salt
dash pepper
¼ teaspoon onion salt
¼ teaspoon garlic salt
2 tablespoons vegetable shortening

Arrange venison steaks in shallow bowl. Pour milk over the meat. Refrigerate for 1 to 1½ hours. Mix flour with salt, pepper, onion salt, and garlic salt in a small bowl. Rinse steaks well with cool water. Dredge in flour mixture. Sear meat on both sides in shortening over high heat. Reduce heat and cook, turning frequently, until meat is thoroughly cooked.

Venison in Foil

4 to 5 pound venison roast
½ envelope dry onion soup mix

Place meat on a piece of aluminum foil large enough to wrap the roast up generously. Sprinkle the dry soup mix on the meat and seal tightly in the foil. Place in shallow roasting pan and bake at 350° for 3 to 3½ hours or until well done. Serves 6 or 7.

Diet Lemon Steaks

2½ pound package venison steaks
1 lemon
garlic salt
onion salt
salt
pepper

Line a shallow baking dish with enough aluminum foil to be able to generously cover all steaks. Lay single layer of steaks on foil. Squeeze the juice from one-half lemon over meat. Sprinkle generously with garlic salt, onion salt, salt, and pepper. Turn steaks over and repeat using the other half lemon. Seal aluminum foil around steaks. Bake at 400° for 50 minutes. Uncover steaks and broil for 10 minutes. Serves 4 or 5.

Venison Pot Roast

3- to 4-pound venison roast
1 medium onion sliced
1 bay leaf
½ teaspoon dried rosemary
½ teaspoon pepper
½ teaspoon salt
4 cups white wine
4 tablespoons salad oil

Mix onion, bay leaf, rosemary, pepper, salt, and white wine together. Marinate meat in this mixture for 3 hours, turning frequently. Remove meat and pat dry. Brown meat in salad oil in large Dutch oven. Roast in slow oven (300°) for 4 hours or until well done. Baste with marinade every 15 to 20 minutes.

Low Calorie Venison

3½ pounds venison
½ medium onion, sliced
¼ cup ketchup
½ teaspoon salt
pepper
¼ cup lemon juice

Place venison roast in crock pot. Add all the other ingredients and simmer 6 to 8 hours.

Venison Stroganoff

1½ pounds venison round steak
¼ cup oil
1 cup sliced mushrooms
½ cup chopped onion
1 clove garlic
flour
salt
pepper
2 cups beef bouillon
¼ cup red wine
1 cup sour cream

Slice steak into thin strips. Roll in flour, salt, and pepper. Brown in oil. Add mushrooms, onions, and garlic. When everything is browned, stir in bouillon and wine. Cover and simmer for 1 hour or until tender. Stir in sour cream. Simmer 5 minutes more. Serve over hot buttered noodles.

Heart of Venison

1 deer heart
5 strips bacon
1 pint tomato juice
5 whole cloves
1 pint water
1 bay leaf
1 teaspoon sweet basil
¼ teaspoon cinnamon

Place the heart in the top part of a steamer kettle. Put bacon strips over meat. Add tomato juice, water, and spices in the bottom of the kettle. Cover tightly and steam slowly for 3 hours or until well done. Chill heart thoroughly. Slice thinly and serve cold.

Canned Venison

Roast venison slowly in oven at 350° for 15 minutes per pound of meat. Cut to desired chunks and place in quart jars to within 1 inch of top of jars. Add 1 teaspoon salt to each quart. Onion can be added if desired. Add 3 or 4 tablespoons broth from roasted venison. Clean rim of jar carefully and screw on cap tightly. Process 90 minutes at 10 pounds pressure.

Mountain Meatballs

1½ pounds ground venisonburger
2 large carrots, grated
1 large potato, grated
1 small onion, grated
1 egg
2 or 3 tablespoons flour
¼ teaspoon salt (or to taste)
dash pepper
1 can cream of mushroom soup
1 10½-ounce soup can of milk

Mix burger, carrots, potato, onion, egg, flour, salt, and pepper together in a large mixing bowl. Shape into balls about the size of ping pong balls. Fry in a heavy skillet containing sufficient cooking oil to prevent sticking. When meatballs are well browned and cooked through, place them in a greased casserole dish. Pour mushroom soup diluted with milk over meat. Bake in covered casserole dish at 350° for 35 to 40 minutes. Serves 4.

Texas Chili

2 pounds venisonburger
½ cup vegetable oil
1 cup chopped onions
2 cloves minced garlic
1 large green pepper, chopped
3 tablespoons chili powder
2 cups cooked kidney beans
2 teaspoons sugar
3½ cups whole tomatoes
1 cup tomato sauce
1 cup water
½ teaspoon salt
1 tablespoon flour mixed with 2 tablespoons water

Brown venisonburger in oil in heavy skillet. Add onions, garlic, and green pepper and brown for 5 minutes longer. Add chili powder, sugar, tomatoes, tomato sauce, water and salt. Simmer for 2 hours. Add the flour and water paste and cook until mixture thickens. Add the kidney beans and cook another 5 minutes. Serve hot with French bread or hot biscuits.

Smoky Jerky

venison
1 cup salt
1 quart warm water
2 to 3 cups liquid smoke
pepper

Freeze meat slightly for easier slicing. Slice venison strips 1¼ inches thick. Soak strips in brine of salt, water, and liquid smoke for 10 minutes only. Sprinkle with pepper to taste. Drain well. Put on racks and place in oven at 140 to 200° for 3 hours or until dry but somewhat tacky. Turn oven off and allow jerky to cool in oven.

Savory Roast

5 pounds venison roast
¼ cup wine vinegar
¼ cup chili sauce
1 tablespoon flour
1 teaspoon Worcestershire sauce
1 teaspoon dry mustard
½ teaspoon chili powder
2 teaspoons salt
¼ teaspoon pepper
2 teaspoons honey
4 strips bacon
½ cup margarine
2 cups hot water
flour

Dry meat well with paper towel. Make a mixture of vinegar, chili sauce, flour, Worcestershire sauce, mustard, chili powder, salt, pepper, and honey. Rub into meat. Place roast on rack in roasting pan. Lay bacon strips on meat. Dot with margarine and pour water in pan (not over meat). Brown in 450° oven, basting frequently with drippings. After about 1 hour, when meat is well browned, reduce heat to 350° and roast 4 hours longer if the animal was young. Add an hour if meat is from an older animal. Add more water if necessary. Thicken drippings and juice with flour for gravy.

Cantonese Steak

1 pound steak
½ teaspoon meat tenderizer
2 tablespoons cornstarch
3 tablespoons sherry
salt
4 to 6 big onions, sliced
2 tablespoons salad oil

Cut meat into strips ¼-inch wide and 2 to 4 inches long. Place strips in bowl. Add tenderizer, cornstarch and sherry. Sprinkle with salt. Mix and let stand at least 15 minutes. Separate onion slices into rings and fry in salad oil in a heavy skillet for 2 to 4 minutes, stirring constantly. They should be still somewhat crisp. Remove to heated platter. Place steak strips into skillet stirring constantly for 2 to 4 minutes. Add more oil if needed. Put onions back into skillet and mix with meat. Serve at once. Serves 3.

Venison Casserole

1 pound ground venison
½ package egg noodles
½ pound pork sausage
1 tablespoon chopped green pepper
1 medium onion, chopped
1 can tomato soup
1 can whole kernel corn
1 can mushrooms
¼ teaspoon garlic powder
pinch of ground oregano
salt and pepper

Boil noodles in salted water until tender. Drain. Sauté sausage, venison, green pepper, and onion in small amount of oil. Add other ingredients. Put noodles in casserole dish and pour the other mixture over them. Bake 30 minutes in 325° oven.

Venison Sausage

5 pounds lean venison
2 pounds salt pork
5 tablespoons sage
4 teaspoons salt
2 teaspoons cayenne pepper
1 onion
juice of 1 lemon

Grind meat and pork finely. Mix in all the other ingredients. Put into casing or fry as country sausage.

Campers' Venison

2 pounds cubed venison steaks
salt and pepper
flour
4 tablespoons margarine
2 cups hot water
1 4-ounce can mushrooms
1 medium onion, sliced
1 8-ounce can kidney beans
3 medium carrots, diced
1 6-ounce can tomato sauce
½ teaspoon dried oregano

Salt and pepper meat and dredge in flour. Brown in margarine. Add vegetables, water, tomato sauce, and oregano. Cover and simmer slowly for 2 hours or until meat is tender.

Picnic Swiss Steak

6 venison steaks
1 envelope onion soup mix
1 envelope tomato soup mix
3 tablespoons butter
aluminum foil

Dot aluminum foil with butter. Place venison steaks on individual pieces of foil. Mix soups together. Sprinkle half of soup mixture on meat. Turn meat over and sprinkle remaining soup mixture. Dot with butter and cook over open fire until done, or bake 1 hour at 350°. Serves 6.

Wine Patties

2 pounds ground venison
6 tablespoons red wine
8 strips bacon
melted butter
salt and pepper

Mix wine with meat and refrigerate 1 to 2 hours. Shape into eight patties and wrap a strip of bacon around each, securing it with a toothpick. Brush patties with melted butter and sprinkle with salt and pepper. Grill over coals, basting with butter. Serves 4 to 6.

Steaks à la Italienne

2-pound package venison steaks
1 package low-calorie Italian salad dressing mix
½ cup cornmeal
salt and pepper

Mix the Italian dressing according to directions on the package. Pour over well-trimmed steaks and turn with fork so that each piece is coated with dressing. Marinate for 1 hour. Remove from marinade with fork and dredge in cornmeal. Salt and pepper each steak. Sear in hot oil on both sides. Reduce heat and cook until meat is thoroughly done.

Tarragon Venison

8 slices cold, cooked venison (each about 6×4×½)
2 tablespoons butter
2 tablespoons flour
1 cup light cream
2 tablespoons fresh tarragon, chopped fine
1 tablespoon brandy
salt and pepper

Melt butter in heavy skillet. Stir in flour gradually until mixture is golden brown. Place skillet over low heat and stir in cream, mixing until smooth. When mixture thickens add salt and pepper to taste. Add remaining ingredients. Lay venison slices in this sauce and heat through over low heat. Serve with rice. Serves 4.

Western Hunter's Stew

2 pounds venison
½ teaspoon garlic salt
2 medium onions, sliced
3 tablespoons shortening
1 16-ounce can tomato sauce
2 green peppers, chopped
½ teaspoon salt
1 cup celery, diced
3 potatoes, diced
6 carrots, chopped
2 bay leaves
2 tablespoons taco sauce
flour
water

Sauté onions, peppers, and celery in shortening. Add meat chunks, garlic salt and salt. Brown meat, stirring frequently. Cover with tomato sauce and enough water to submerse meat. Add bay leaves and taco sauce. Simmer 3 to 4 hours. Thicken with a paste made from flour and water. Add carrots and potatoes. Add additional water if necessary. Simmer 1 hour or until meat and vegetables are tender.

Venison Curry

4 pounds cubed or ground venison
6 medium onions
2 tablespoons fat
1 cup beef bouillon
1 tablespoon salt
1½ to 2 tablespoons curry powder
4 tablespoons ketchup
1 tablespoon A-1 sauce
2 tablespoons Worcestershire sauce
1 tablespoon lemon juice
½ to 1 teaspoon turmeric
10 stalks celery
¼ cup margarine
1 4-ounce can sliced mushrooms

Brown onion in fat. Add bouillon and simmer 10 minutes. Add other ingredients except for meat and mushrooms. Bring to boil. Add meat and mushrooms and simmer 2 hours or until meat is tender.

Broiled Venison Steaks

2 pounds venison steak (¾-inch thick)
2 tablespoons melted butter
salt and pepper

Trim any fat from steaks. Coat top of steaks with half of butter. Broil 4 to 6 minutes. Turn. Coat with remaining butter and broil 3 to 5 minutes more. Season lightly with salt and pepper. Broil a little longer if meat is not cooked through. Serves 2 to 3.

Venison Meatloaf

2 pounds ground venison
½ pound loose pork sausage
1 large onion, chopped finely
½ teaspoon celery salt
¼ teaspoon parsley flakes
½ teaspoon thyme
1 cup dried bread crumbs
1 cup whole tomatoes, drained
1 egg
½ teaspoon salt
¼ teaspoon pepper
1 cup ketchup
2 teaspoons barbeque sauce

Place all ingredients except ketchup in a bowl. Mix well. Turn into buttered baking dish. Pour ketchup on top, spreading around to cover meat. Bake at 350° for 1 hour or until cooked through but still moist. Serves 6.

Venison Sauerbraten

3½ pounds venison roast
1 teaspoon salt
½ teaspoon pepper
2 medium onions, sliced
1 medium carrot, sliced
1 large stalk celery, sliced
4 whole cloves
4 crushed peppercorns
2 bay leaves
2 cups vinegar
½ stick butter or margarine
12 small gingersnaps, crushed
1 tablespoon sugar
2 tablespoons flour mixed with ¼ cup water

Season meat with salt and pepper. Place in crock or glass bowl. Add onions, carrot, celery, cloves, peppercorns, bay leaves and vinegar. Cover and refrigerate for 3 days turning several times a day. Drain meat. Reserve marinade. Wipe meat dry. Melt butter in Dutch oven and brown meat on all sides. Add strained marinade. Lower heat and simmer covered 2 to 3 hours or until meat is cooked through and tender. Remove meat to heated platter and keep warm. Bring pan juices to boil. Add gingersnaps and sugar. Stir over medium heat until thickened. If necessary, add flour and water mixture to thicken. Cook until desired thickness is reached. Pour sauce over sauerbraten and serve with potato dumplings.

Venison Pie

2 pounds venison cut into 1-inch cubes
flour
salt and pepper
1 stick margarine
2 cups beef bouillon
1 cup red wine
1 bay leaf
½ teaspoon dried rosemary
2 tablespoons parsley flakes
24 button mushrooms
1 large onion, chopped
2 packages frozen peas, thawed
3 cups whipped potatoes
1 egg yolk, beaten
1 tablespoon water

Dredge venison in flour and sprinkle with salt and pepper. Melt butter in Dutch oven and quickly brown meat. Add bouillon and wine. Heat until mixture boils. Lower heat and add bay leaf, rosemary, and parsley flakes. Cover and simmer for 1½ hours. Add mushrooms and onion; cook until tender. Add peas and cook until tender but still crisp. Remove from heat. Stir in 2 tablespoons of potatoes. Cover top of meat-vegetable mixture with thick layer of the potatoes. Swirl top and brush lightly with egg yolk thinned with tablespoon of water. Place in 400° oven until potatoes are golden brown.

Venison Nibbles

venison steak cut into pieces 3 inches long and 1 inch wide
salt and pepper
egg
cracker crumbs

Salt and pepper venison strips. Dip in beaten egg and then in cracker crumbs. Deep fry in hot oil like French fries until golden brown. Makes excellent family snacks or hors d'oeuvres.

Venisonburger Soup

1½ to 2 pounds ground venison
1 cup onion, diced
1 cup potatoes, diced
1 cup carrots, sliced
¾ cup cabbage, shredded
¼ cup rice
1 cup beef bouillon
1 bay leaf
½ teaspoon thyme
1½ teaspoons salt
⅛ teaspoon pepper
1½ quarts water
1 #2 can whole tomatoes

Brown meat and onion in large pot. (Add vegetable oil if venisonburger doesn't have enough fat to prevent sticking.) Add potatoes, carrots, and cabbage. Bring to a boil and add rice. Add the rest of the ingredients. Cover and simmer for 1½ to 2 hours. Add more water if necessary. Skim off fat just before stirring.

Quick Venison Dinner

2 pounds venison, cubed
1 10¾-ounce can cream of mushroom soup
1 envelope dry onion soup mix
1 cup canned tomatoes (stewed) or 2 fresh tomatoes

Place meat in a casserole dish. Add soups and tomatoes. Bake in preheated 325° oven for 2 hours.

Steak à la Soup

2 pounds venison steak
1 10¾-ounce can cream of mushroom soup
1 10¾-ounce can cream of chicken soup
½ cup dry red wine
¼ teaspoon onion salt

Mix all ingredients except meat together in a casserole dish. Place steaks in mixture, turning to coat all portions of meat. Make sure soup mixture covers meat. Add a little water if necessary. Cover and bake at 350° for 1½ hours. Serves 4 to 5.

Chinese Pepper Steaks

1 pound thin steak
3 tablespoons olive oil
½ teaspoon garlic salt
1 teaspoon ginger root, mashed (optional)
3 tablespoons soy sauce
1 teaspoon sugar
3 tablespoons cornstarch
¼ cup sherry, vermouth, or water
3 scallions, sliced thinly
1 can bean sprouts
2 tomatoes, peeled and sliced
2 green peppers, sliced thin
salt and pepper

Slice steak across the grain as thin as possible. Brown steak in oil, garlic salt and ginger root over moderate heat for 10 minutes. Add green peppers and tomatoes. Cover and cook over a low heat for 5 minutes. Add the bean sprouts, cover and simmer a few minutes longer. Mix cornstarch with wine and pour over mixture in the skillet. Season with salt, pepper and soy sauce. The pepper steak is done when cornstarch has thickened. Add the scallions one minute before serving.

Liver and Onions

1 fresh venison liver
¼ cup butter
2 medium onions, sliced thin
salt and pepper

Slice liver and skin slices, removing the veins. Cut liver into strips 1½ inches long by ½-inch wide. Heat butter in a heavy skillet. Sauté onions and add liver. Brown, stirring frequently for 5 to 10 minutes. Cover, steam for 15 minutes or until thoroughly done.

Venison and Beans

6 1-inch thick slices of leftover cooked venison roast
2 tablespoons olive oil
garlic salt
1 18-ounce can baked beans
1 cup mild barbeque sauce
4 strips bacon, fried crisp and crumbled

Brush oil on both sides of venison slices. Sprinkle with garlic salt. Grill over coals 8 to 10 minutes or until well browned on one side. In the meantime heat beans. Turn meat and spread beans carefully on browned side of meat. Drip barbeque sauce over beans, being careful not to knock beans into the fire. Cook until second side is well browned. Then carefully lift each piece onto warmed plates.

Venison Salami

4 pounds ground venison
1 pound ground beef suet
2 teaspoons black pepper
2 teaspoons garlic powder
5 teaspoons salt
2½ teaspoons liquid smoke
1½ teaspoons small red chilies

Mix all ingredients in a non-metal bowl. Refrigerate for 3 days, thoroughly mixing each day by hand. On the fourth day divide mixture into five parts. Knead and form into logs about 12 inches long. Place logs on cookie sheet and bake for 5 hours at 155°. Turn logs over and bake for another 5 hours. Remove from oven when cooking is finished. Wrap in paper towels to remove excess grease. Cool, wrap in foil. Store in refrigerator. Makes five 12-inch salamis.

Sweet & Sour Venison

1 package venison steaks or small venison roast
6 tablespoons olive oil
1½ teaspoons salt
1⅓ cups brown sugar
2 teaspoons mustard
2 tablespoons vinegar
¼ teaspoon cloves
½ teaspoon cinnamon

Brown meat in oil. Place in Dutch oven. Combine other ingredients to make sauce. Pour sauce over roast and baste frequently while roasting. Bake in oven at 400°; 20 minutes per pound.

Venison in Currant Jelly

1½ pounds venison diced into 1-inch pieces
salt and pepper
2 to 3 tablespoons butter
cayenne
2 tablespoons port wine
1 tablespoon currant jelly

Season meat chunks with salt and pepper. Brown quickly in butter. Sprinkle cayenne sparingly on all meat. Add wine and jelly and simmer until well done.

Venison Hawaiian Style

1 pound venison steaks
¼ cup flour
¼ cup butter
½ cup boiling water
¼ teaspoon basil
1 teaspoon salt
⅛ teaspoon pepper
2 to 3 pounds green peppers, diced
½ cup pineapple chunks

Cut steaks into cubes. Dredge in flour and brown in butter. Add water, salt, pepper and basil and simmer until tender. Add pepper and pineapple chunks and simmer 5 minutes. Mix sauce (below) and pour into mixture. Simmer 5 minutes and serve over Chinese noodles or cooked rice. Serves 4 to 6.

Sauce

2½ teaspoons cornstarch
½ cup pineapple juice
¼ cup vinegar
½ cup sugar
2½ teaspoons soy sauce

State-by-State Directory

Alaska

Our largest state is well-known for its fabulous hunting, but few hunters are aware of the excellent deer herds available. Sitka blacktails are thriving on Kodiak Island and along the coastal regions of southeast Alaska. Populations are growing rapidly, leading biologists to offer multiple permits in many areas.

According to wildlife officials, severe winter weather is the most important mortality factor, although areas with high wolf populations are slower to recover from deer declines than regions with low wolf numbers. Hunting pressure has little effect on blacktails. Current estimates place Alaska's deer population at about 150,000.

For information, write the Alaska Department of Fish and Game, Subport Bldg., Juneau, AK 99801.

National forests: Chugach National Forest, Pouch 6606, 2221 E. Northern Lights Blvd., Anchorage 99502 (907/279-5541).

Tongass-Chatham Area National Forest, Box 1980, Sitka 99835 (907/747-6671).

Tongass-Ketchikan Area National Forest, Federal Building, Ketchikan 99901 (907/225-3101).

Tongass-Stikine Area National Forest, Box 309, Petersburg 99833 (907/772-3841).

Arizona

With 300,000 mule deer, Arizona is a fine state to hunt in. Arizona has produced some giant mule deer over the years, and big bucks continue to roam in this magnificent southwest state. It is for a crack at a magnum buck that many nonresidents continue to hunt in Arizona.

Ten thousand to 15,000 muleys are killed each year by some 60,000 to 70,000 hunters. Although success is not high, usually about 20 percent, hunters who know the basic skills and are persistent often kill a big buck every year.

Arizona has the Rocky Mountain subspecies, the desert mule deer, and Coues whitetails. Roughly speaking, the Rocky Mountain deer inhabits the northern region while the desert muley lives in the central and southern areas.

When hunters talk of Arizona, the famous Kaibab area comes quickly to mind. This rugged land is in the north not far from the Grand Canyon, and is well-known for huge bucks. It was here that Teddy Roosevelt hunted extensively. Although the Kaibab isn't what it used to be in terms of many big bucks, there are enough around to attract trophy hunters. The old bloodlines are still in the herds, and big bucks isolate themselves in the incredible rugged canyons and arroyos.

The Kaibab, Prescott, Coconino, Tonto, Apache, and Sitgreaves national forests offer plenty of public acres to hunters.

Because the Arizona deer season is structured on a quota system, hunter pressure is carefully regulated.

This state has been one of the slowest to bounce back from the mule deer decline. Arizona's popularity with sun-seekers, retirees, and people with respiratory problems hasn't helped the deer situation. Vital habitat has been permanently erased or heavily impacted by the hectic pace of urbanization. Yet, deer hunting is good for hunters willing to expend some effort.

For information, write the Arizona Game and Fish Department, 2222 W. Greenway Rd., Phoenix, AZ 85023.

National forests: Apache-Sitgreaves National Forest, Federal Bldg., Box 640, Springerville 85938 (602/333-4301).

Coconino National Forest, 2323 E. Greenlaw Lane, Flagstaff 86001 (602/779-3311).

Coronado National Forest, 301 W. Congress, Box 551, Tucson 85702 (602/792-6483).

Kaibab National Forest, 800 South 6th St., Williams 86046 (602/635-2681).

Prescott National Forest, 344 S. Cortez, Box 2549, Prescott 86301 (602/445-1762).

Tonto National Forest, 102 S. 28th St., P.O. Box 29070, Phoenix 85038 (602/261-3205).

California

Our most populated state has a respectable deer population of 750,000, including Columbian blacktails, Rocky Mountain, southern, California, and desert mule deer subspecies.

Unfortunately, California is comparatively a poor state to hunt; hunter success percentages are about 10 percent. Between 300,000 and 350,000 hunters try their luck. Few are nonresidents, less than 2,000 annually.

The poor deer program is generally blamed on a conflict between politics and game management. A strict bucks-only law keeps the harvest restricted and prevents the necessary cropping of deer herds.

Although California has 18 national forests with almost 20 million acres of public land, some of the best hunting is on private land. Getting permission on these private holdings is almost impossible, since much of it is leased to sportsmen's clubs or groups, or is completely closed to hunting. However, some tracts, such as that of the Dye Creek Preserve, allow hunting on a fee basis.

This dismal picture shouldn't discourage ardent hunters, because excellent deer herds exist over much of the state. The problem is finding a legal buck. Hunters who penetrate the remote country away from roads have the best chances of scoring. Much of California's best deer country is incredibly steep. A hunter must be in good shape to negotiate this rugged terrain.

The northern counties give up the most deer. Mendocino and Trinity counties usually produce well each year. Plenty of national forest land allows public access. Modoc County in the extreme northeast is the place to go for Rocky Mountain muleys, but hunter success is not high.

Deer regulations are complex, and seasons vary with the unit. A very early August season allows hunters an extra period to pursue deer, but the days are blow-torch hot. Other seasons open later on and run as far as December in some units. Forked-horn bucks are legal quarry in some units, while three-point bucks (western count) are the minimum in others.

Permit availability is unlimited, and some zones allow the harvest of two deer.

For information, write the California Department of Fish and Game, 1416 Ninth St., Sacramento, CA 95814.

National forests: Angeles National Forest, 150 South Los Robles, Suite 300, Pasadena 91101 (213/577-0050).

Cleveland National Forest, 880 Front St., San Diego 92188 (714/293-5050).

Eldorado National Forest, 100 Forni Rd., Placerville 95667 (916/622-5061).

Inyo National Forest, 873 North Main St., Bishop 93514 (714/873-5841).

Klamath National Forest, 1312 Fairland Rd., Yreka 96097 (916/842-2741).

Lassen National Forest, 707 Nevada St., Susanville 96130 (916/257-2151).

Los Padres National Forest, 42 Aero Camino, Goleta 93017 (805/968-1578).

Mendocino National Forest, 420 E. Laurel St., Willows 95988 (916/934-3316).

Modoc National Forest, 441 N. Main St., Alturas 96101 (916/233-3521).

Plumas National Forest, 159 Lawrence St., Box 1500, Quincy 95971 (916/283-2050).

San Bernardino National Forest, 144 N. Mountain View, San Bernardino 92408 (714/383-5588).

Sequoia National Forest, 900 W. Grand Ave., Porterville 93257 (209/784-1500).

Shasta and Trinity National Forests, 2400 Washington Ave., Redding 96001 (916/246-5222).

Sierra National Forest, Federal Bldg., 1130 O St., Room 3017, Fresno 93721 (209/487-5155).

Six Rivers National Forest, 507 F St., Eureka 95501 (707/442-1721).

Stanislaus National Forest, 1977 Greeley Rd., Sonora 95370 (209/532-3671).

Tahoe National Forest, Highway 49, Nevada City 95959 (916/265-4531).

Colorado

This state is often considered to be the best of all for mule deer. Colorado gives up more record bucks than any other state, and deer herds are quickly building after the decline.

There are a number of reasons why Colorado gets top billing. First, about 500,000 mule deer of the Rocky Mountain subspecies lives within its borders. Second, permits are unlimited and can be purchased from any license vendor up until midnight before opening day. Third, 10 national forests and millions of acres of BLM land offer excellent public hunting.

Only Rocky Mountain muleys live in Colorado. A modest herd of about 2,000 whitetails lives in the northeast region, especially along the brushy river bottoms.

About 200,000 deer hunters head for the mountains each year, killing about 50,000 deer. Hunter success runs about 30 percent.

Colorado's mule deer country is generally in the western half of the state. This is the mountainous Rocky Mountain range that Colorado is so famous for. Much of the eastern region is flat farmland with little deer habitat.

Big bucks come from most of the forested mountains, but five counties seem to stand out for truly big deer. They are Grand, Summit, Eagle, Dolores, and San Miguel. The first three are west of Denver and an easy drive from this metropolitan area, while the latter two counties are in the southwest. It was in this region that Texan Doug Burris killed the number one typical muley in the San Juan National Forest in 1972. Many other grand bucks have come from this area.

Plenty of access roads provide penetration into good deer country, but the best areas are crowded throughout the season. Many outfitters are available to take hunters into remote mountain ranges.

Nonresident hunters often haul their own camps into prime deer country. Texans and Californians seem to favor this state among the others in the Rockies. Motor homes, pickup campers, camp trailers, tent campers, and tents blossom overnight all over deer country. Many hunters return year after year to favorite areas.

Colorado has two deer seasons. One is combined with the elk season and normally runs 11 days. The other is deer only and runs 5 or 11 days, depending on the unit. Several special seasons are held in certain units.

The Southern Ute Indian Tribe usually has a late-season trophy hunt on a limited permit basis. For information on this hunt as well as general regulations, write the Colorado Division of Wildlife, 6060 Broadway, Denver, CO 80216.

National forests: Arapaho and Roosevelt National Forests, Federal Bldg., 301 S. Howes. Fort Collins 80521 (303/482-5155).

Grand Mesa, Uncompahgre and Gunnison National Forests, 11th and Main St., Box 138, Delta 81416 (303/874-7691).

Pike and San Isabel National Forests, 910 Highway 50 West, Pueblo 81008 (303/544-5277).

Rio Grande National Forest, 1803 West Highway 160, Monte Vista 81144 (303/852-5941).

Routt National Forest, Hunt Bldg., Steamboat Springs 80477 (303/879-1722).

San Juan National Forest, Federal Bldg., 701 Camino Del Rio, Durango 81301 (303/247-4874).

White River National Forest, Old Federal Bldg., Box 948, Glenwood Springs 81601 (303/945-6582).

Idaho

Of all the big game in Idaho, mule deer are the most widely distributed and the most sought after. They live in every region, although whitetails are well entrenched in the panhandle. Only the Rocky Mountain subspecies of mule deer inhabits this state.

Biologists put the mule deer herd at one-quarter of a million, and expect it to reach 300,000 by 1990. Muleys are recovering nicely from the decline. Between 30,000 and 40,000 mule deer are killed by hunters annually. The hunter success percentage is decent at about 35 percent.

Idaho offers a varied environment for mule deer. The southern part of the state is a big, vast land that is surprisingly flat. It is here that the famous Idaho potatoes grow. The Snake River traverses the entire state from east to west, from Wyoming to Oregon. The Salmon River flows diagonally from the eastern border area into the interior in a southwesterly direction. Both these drainages are outstanding for mule deer, especially in the hard-to-reach breaks. My most memorable hunts have occurred along these famous rivers. Deer can be hunted from the tops of the river drainages, or the rivers can be floated in a raft. Both options are unique and rewarding.

The high desert near the Utah, Nevada, and Oregon borders is home to nice mule deer herds. This is a vast region with plenty of backcountry, yet several roads allow access into the hinterlands.

The Sawtooth, Wasatch, and Caribou national forests in the south central and southeastern regions are excellent for muleys. These mountains are lush, blanketed with aspens, ponderosa pines, and fir trees. Some of the biggest bucks in Idaho come from these mountains. The Targhee and Salmon forests are also favorites among mule deer hunters. The Boise National Forest receives heavy pressure from the heavily populated Boise area, but produces some dandy bucks every year. The Payette and Challis forests round out the prime national forests in Idaho's prime mule deer country.

Deer seasons vary with the units, but many begin the middle of October. In several units, a certain period is reserved for either-sex hunting, followed by bucks-only hunting.

Resident permits are unlimited, but 9500 are reserved for nonresidents on a first-come first-served basis. For information, write the Idaho Department of Fish and Game, 600 South Walnut, Box 25, Boise, ID 83707.

National forests: Boise National Forest, 1075 Park Blvd., Boise 83706 (208/334-1516).

Caribou National Forest, 250 S. 4th Ave., Pocatello 83201 (208/232-1142).

Challis National Forest, Forest Service Bldg., Challis 83226 (208/879-2285).

Clearwater National Forest, Rt. 4, Orofino 83544 (208/476-4541).

Idaho Panhandle National Forest, 1201 Ironwood Dr., Coeur d'Alene 83814 (208/667-2561).

Nezperce National Forest, 319 E. Main St., Grangeville 83530 (208/983-1950).

Payette National Forest, Forest Service Bldg., Box 1026, McCall 83638 (208/634-2255).

Salmon National Forest, Forest Service Bldg., Salmon 83467 (208/756-2215).

Sawtooth National Forest, 1525 Addison Ave., East, Twin Falls 83301 (208/733-3698).

Targhee National Forest, 420 N. Bridge St., St. Anthony 83445 (208/624-3151).

Kansas

Kansas has a very small mule deer population, less than 10,000, and most are along river systems in the western half of the state. The best hunting is along the Republican River, Sappa Creek, the Solomon River, and Prairie Dog Creek, all in the northwest area. A limited number of permits are authorized each year for residents only.

For information, write the Kansas Forestry, Fish and Game Commission, PO Box 1028, Pratt, KS 67124.

Montana

This largest Rocky Mountain state is endowed with plenty of big game. Mule deer are an important and favored big game species, although whitetails abound in much of Montana.

Montana is a land of varying landscapes. Western Montana is mountainous and rugged. The Continental Divide ribbons through lofty peaks and ridges here, and hunting is superb along its flanks. Southwestern Montana is considered to be prime mule deer country, but the rest of the state is good, too. The 1-million-acre C. M. Russell Wildlife Refuge in eastern Montana harbors plenty of mule deer, particularly in the backcountry breaks of the Missouri River where few hunters tread. The Custer National Forest in southeast Montana is excellent mule deer country and is commonly overlooked by hunters who drive to the western mountain ranges.

Considering Montana's size, hunting pressure is light in much of the state. As expected, areas close to large cities are crowded for a day or two around the season's opener, but in most of Montana, few people are afield at any given time. I've been amazed at the lack of shooting on opening weekend—and not because deer weren't present. Montanans simply bide their time and hunt whenever the mood strikes them. Hunting season is long—5 to 6 weeks, and many locals like to wait until snow falls in mid to late November before going after their buck.

About 140,000 people hunt deer each year, and success is good, usually running from 35 to 45 percent. The success rate would probably be much higher if nonresidents weren't forced to buy a deer-elk combination license. Many nonresident hunters come to Montana to hunt only elk, but since they're tallied as deer hunters as well, hunter success is lowered because they don't kill a deer.

Montana biologists don't have a handle on their deer population, but estimates put the deer population at 350,000 to 400,000. The annual deer kill averages out to about 40,000.

The state has a well-organized outfitter association; there are plenty of outfitters to choose from in the best deer country. When I hunt Montana, I like to book hunts through Jack Atcheson of Butte, an outfitter booking agent who works only with well-tried, reputable outfitters.

Nonresident deer permits are sold only in combination with elk licenses, although there are a few exceptions in eastern Montana, usually for antlerless permits. The state sets a quota of 17,000 licenses which are available on a first-come, first-served basis. They are usually sold out by early August.

Deer season usually starts in mid-October and runs through November.

For information, write the Montana Department of Fish, Wildlife and Parks, 1420 E. Sixth Ave., Helena, MT 59601.

National forests: Beaverhead National Forest, Box 1258, Dillon 59725 (406/683-2312).

Bitterroot National Forest, 316 N. 3rd St., Hamilton 59840 (406/363-3131).

Custer National Forest, Box 2556, Billings 59103 (406/657-6361).

Deerlodge National Forest, Federal Bldg., Box 400, Butte 59701 (406/723-6561).

Flathead National Forest, Box 147, 290 No. Main, Kalispell 59901 (406/755-5401).

Gallatin National Forest, Federal Bldg., Box 130, Bozeman 59715 (406/587-5271).

Helena National Forest, Federal Bldg., Drawer 10014, Helena 59601 (406/449-5201).

Kootenai National Forest, W. Highway 2, Libby 59923 (406/293-6211).

Lewis and Clark National Forest, Federal Bldg., Great Falls 59403 (406/453-7678).

Lolo National Forest, Bldg. 24, Ft. Missoula, Missoula 59801 (406/329-3557).

Nebraska

Mule deer populations have varied widely in this state over the last 20 years, running from 27,000 to 50,000. Generally, mule deer inhabit the western region, sharing the habitat with whitetails. Basically, the best regions for mule deer have been the Pine Ridge, Sand Hills, and Keya Paha units. The Buffalo, Loup, and Platte and Upper Platte also give up nice muleys. Much of the best hunting is on private land, but the Nebraska National Forest and Oglala National Grasslands offer public hunting.

Permits for mule deer are restricted, available through a lottery drawing. Seasons normally begin in mid-November.

For information, write the Nebraska Game and Parks Commission, State Capitol, Lincoln, NE 68509.

National forests: Nebraska National Forest, 270 Pine St., Chadron 69337 (308/432-3367).

Nevada

From major highways, casual tourists see Nevada as an arid, barren, wasteland. A look at the mountainous regions, however, reveals splendid deer country. The Rocky Mountain subspecies lives in this state. Biologists figure about 127,000 deer are wandering about, mostly on public land.

Nevada is a sleeper state when it comes to mule deer. Hunter success is very high—50 percent or better statewide, and much higher on certain units. The trick for the resident and nonresident hunter alike is to get a deer tag. A quota system established in the mid-1970's has restricted the number of hunters and has also served its purpose—to remarkably improve deer hunting. Usually, about 20,000 hunters kill more than 10,000 deer. Better yet, many of those deer are big. Wildlife officials say that about 40 percent of the harvest is made up of four-point bucks. Buck/doe ratios are excellent, about 25 to 30 bucks per 100 does.

The top traditional deer-producing counties are Elko, White Pine, Nye, Washoe, and Humboldt. The Humboldt National Forest has 2.5

million acres of good deer country. This forest, which lies in the northern and eastern regions, has nine separate tracts scattered widely. Most run in a long, narrow north-south direction. The 64,000-acre Jarbridge Wilderness north of Elko is a good bet for hunters who want to get into prime backcountry. In the central region, the 3.3-million-acre Toiyabe National Forest provides very good hunting in the four tracts between Austin and Tonopah.

The Bureau of Land Management manages more acreage in Nevada than in any other western state. Much of it is good mule deer country, especially on the sagebrush and pinion slopes that butt up against national forest boundaries.

Of the 20,000 or so deer permits, about 10 percent are reserved for nonresidents. Deer season usually opens in early October and runs into November. Apply for units of your choice by mid or late July.

For information, write the Nevada Department of Wildlife, PO Box 10678, Reno, NV 89520.

National forests: Humboldt National Forest, 976 Mountain City Highway, Elko 89801 (702/738-5171).

Toiyabe National Forest, 111 N. Virginia St., Reno 89501 (702/784-5331).

New Mexico

This lovely southwest state is well-known for mule deer, but hunter success in recent years has not been as high as it could be. It ranges about 20 percent, and that low figure is generally attributed to the mule deer decline and loss of habitat. Nonetheless, good deer hunting is to be had if hunters work a bit harder for their buck.

Both the Rocky Mountain subspecies and desert mule deer inhabit New Mexico. The Rocky Mountain muleys are residents of the central and northern regions, while the smaller desert deer lives in the southern areas. Whitetails also live in this state.

Biologists figure about 260,000 muleys live in the state. About 100,000 to 110,000 hunters kill some 20,000 deer annually.

In order to cope with hunter pressure, the state uses the so-called stratified hunt system. Seasons are very short, usually 3 or 7 days, depending on the region. Hunters may hunt only one season, regardless if they are successful or not. Obviously, it's imperative that hunters are familiar with the area they wish to hunt since they have only a few days to find their buck. For that reason, scouting is important, and a key to success.

New Mexico has abundant public land for deer hunting. Five national forests, the Carson, Santa Fe, Cibola, Gila, and Lincoln, offer public hunting on more than 8 million acres. The Carson and Santa Fe forests are favorites for hunters who want a shot at the bigger Rocky Mountain muleys. Millions of acres of pinyon-juniper forest administered by the Bureau of Land Management are excellent for big muleys.

Three mountain ranges, the Guadalupe, Sacramento, and Capitan, are good for deer hunting. Sportsmen who want to venture into the backcountry can try these wilderness regions: Wheeler Peak on the Carson National Forest, the Pecos Wilderness on the Santa Fe National Forest, and the White Mountains on the Lincoln National Forest.

The Jicarilla Apache Indian Reservation in northern New Mexico offers 758,000 acres of hunting on a limited permit basis. Many of New Mexico's biggest mule deer were killed on this reservation, but hunting is tougher now for a big buck. For information, write the Jicarilla Apache Tribe, Box 147, Dulce, NM 87528. The famous Vermejo Ranch also offers superb mule deer hunting on 400,000 acres. Write Vermejo Park, P.O Drawer E, Raton, NM 87740.

For information on hunting regulations, write the New Mexico Department of Game and Fish, State Capitol, Santa Fe, NM 87503.

National forests: Carson National Forest, Forest Service Bldg., Box 558, Taos 87571 (505/758-2238).

Cibola National Forest, 10308 Candelaria NE, Albuquerque 87112 (505/766-2185).

Gila National Forest, 2610 N. Silver St., Silver City 88061 (505/388-1986).

Lincoln National Forest, Federal Bldg., 11th and New York, Alamogordo 88310 (505/437-6030).

Santa Fe National Forest, Federal Bldg., Box 1689, Santa Fe 87501 (505/988-6328).

North Dakota

This state has a modest population of about 20,000 mule deer, most of which live in the southwest corner. The Little Missouri River and Bad-lands are the primary areas for mule deer.

Hunters normally draw for mule deer permits, and seasons and quotas are somewhat restrictive. Truly big bucks are scarce, but some respectable animals are taken each year.

For information, write the North Dakota Game and Fish Department, Bismarck, ND 58501.

Oklahoma

The few mule deer in Oklahoma live in the extreme western panhandle county of Cimarron, although efforts have been made to release muleys elsewhere.

Muleys will have to greatly expand their numbers and habitat before they're huntable to any extent in this state.

For information, write the Game Division, Oklahoma Department of Wildlife, 1801 N. Lincoln, Oklahoma City, OK 73105.

Oregon

Mule deer do well in Oregon, and live in all sorts of environments. The incredibly dense rain forests along the coast are home to Columbian blacktails, as are the timbered mountains in the Cascade range. Farther to the east, Rocky Mountain muleys live in the mountains and high deserts.

Biologists say mule deer in the eastern mountains are still not fully recovered from the decline, and are about 85 percent of what they could be. Nonetheless, the state has a population of about 300,000 Rocky Mountain mule deer and 460,000 blacktails.

Hunter success is modest, and runs 30 percent or so, far from the banner years of 60 and 70 percent before the decline.

Blacktail hunters do well up and down the coast and in the Cascade Range. The Siuslaw and Siskiyou national forests provide good deer hunting in the coastal range, while the Mount Hood, Willamette, Umpqua, and Rogue River forests allow public access in the Cascades. Many private timber companies own millions of forested acres in the western half of the state, and hunting is permitted on several of them. Blacktail hunters often concentrate their efforts in clearcut areas in this dense forested region because deer feed in them and visibility is better. In areas around large cities, hunting pressure is often heavy.

Despite the proximity of decent blacktail herds around urban areas, most Oregon hunters prefer the bigger Rocky Mountain bucks and drive long distances to get to them. Central Oregon is a favorite hunting ground for muleys, especially in Crook, Deschutes, Grant, and Lake counties. The Deschutes, Winema, and Fremont national forests offer about 4 million acres of deer country in this region.

Between 150,000 and 175,000 deer hunters try their skills at collecting Oregon bucks. There is plenty of company in the better areas. Hunters who want to increase their odds don a daypack and head for the hidden basins and distant ridges where fewer hunters go.

Blacktail seasons vary with the units, running from August into November. Mule deer season in the central and eastern regions usually begins in early to mid-October.

Permits are unlimited. For information, write the Oregon Department of Fish and Wildlife, PO Box 3503, Portland, OR 97208.

National forests: Deschutes National Forest, 211 NE Revere Ave., Bend 97701 (503/382-6922).

Fremont National Forest, 34 North D St., Lakeview 97630 (503/947-2151).

Malheur National Forest, 139 NE Dayton St., John Day 97845 (503/575-1731).

Mt. Hood National Forest, 2440 SE 195th, Portland 97233 (503/667-0511).

Ochoco National Forest, Federal Bldg., Prineville 97754 (503/447-6247).

Rogue River National Forest, Federal Bldg., 333 W. 8th St., Box 520, Medford 97501 (503/779-2351).

Siskiyou National Forest, Box 440, Grants Pass 97526 (503/479-5301).

Siuslaw National Forest, Box 1148, Corvallis 97330 (503/757-4480).

Umatilla National Forest, 2517 SW Hailey Ave., Pendleton 97801 (503/276-3811).

Umpqua National Forest, Federal Office Bldg., Roseburg 97470 (503/672-6601).

Wallowa and Whitman National Forests, Federal Office Bldg., Box 907, Baker 97814 (503/523-6391).

Willamette National Forest, 211 E. 7th Ave., Eugene 97440 (503/687-6533).

Winema National Forest, Box 1390, Klamath Falls 97601 (503/882-7761).

South Dakota

South Dakota has a respectable mule deer population numbering between 75,000 and 100,000. Most muleys are in the vast country west of the Missouri River. The West River Prairie Region, Custer National Forest, and Black Hills National Forest are inhabited by muleys. Stanley, Haakon, Jackson, Perkins, and Pennington counties are known to produce big bucks.

Hunting for mule deer is restrictive, since quotas are set each season and permits must be drawn. Much of the best hunting is on private land requiring permission from landowners.

For information, write the South Dakota Division of Parks and Wildlife, Pierre, SD 57501.

National forests: Black Hills National Forest, Box 792, Custer 57730 (605/673-2251).

Texas

Desert mule deer, some 200,000 strong, are thriving in Texas. Harvest is light, usually less than 5,000 annually, with hunter success about 39 percent. The Trans Pecos area of west Texas and the panhandle region are the places to go for muleys. However, almost all hunting is on private land, and most is leased. Daily hunting is available by paying trespass fees to landowners.

The season is usually less than 10 days, and normally runs in late November and early December. Since the standard Texas deer license authorizes the hunter to kill three whitetails and a mule deer, many hunters combine hunts to take advantage of the system.

Chambers of commerce often have information regarding available leases and daily fee hunts.

For information, write the Texas Parks and Wildlife Department, 4200 Smith School Road, Austin, TX 78744.

Utah

The Rocky Mountain mule deer subspecies lives in this state. The mule deer decline severely depleted herds, but populations are building nicely. An estimated half-million muleys inhabit Utah. Deer live in every part of the state, from arid deserts to tundra above timberline. The seven national forests offer more than 8 million acres of good hunting, and the BLM administers huge land masses as well.

Some of the best hunting is on private land, especially in the northern region. Permission is usually difficult to obtain. Strangers to the state do best by hunting public land.

Utah normally has an 11-day general deer season which begins in mid-October. About 200,000 people take to the hills for opening weekend, and the accessible hunting areas are crowded. Sportsmen who like to hunt in seclusion should head for the backcountry away from roads. After the first three days, most hunters head back to home and work, leaving plenty of room for hunters who remain afield for extended periods.

Hunter success in Utah is fair to good, running between 25 and 35 percent. Skillful hunters normally kill their buck every year. In some areas, antlerless permits are issued in order to thin burgeoning herds. Upwards of 20,000 permits are offered annually.

Although big bucks are killed in every region, the steep mountainous areas east of Salt Lake City and Ogden produce a disproportionate number of large animals. This is rugged country; a hunter must be in top physical condition to negotiate the terrain. Big bucks also come from the Wasatch National Forest near Logan, and the Manti-LaSal National Forest in the central region. The Book Cliffs in the eastern region was once a popular deer area, but hunting has been poor the last several years. Nonresident hunters, particularly Californians, favor the southern region where some huge bucks have been taken. The High Uinta Mountain Range on the Wyoming border offers wild, primitive hunting, but few make the effort to get into the heart of these mountains.

A new trophy ranch operated by the Deseret Land and Livestock Corporation is a place to watch. Range owners are managing this 200,000 acre spread for trophy deer and elk. I predict it will be one of the finest big-buck areas in the West by the mid-1980's. For information, write the Deseret Land and Livestock Corp., Box 38 Woodruff, UT 84086.

Utah deer permits are unlimited for residents and nonresidents alike, and may be purchased throughout the season. For information, write the Utah Division of Wildlife Resources, 1596 West North Temple, Salt Lake City, UT 84116.

National forests: Ashley National Forest, 437 East Main St., Vernal 84078 (801/789-1181).

Dixie National Forest, 82 N. 100 E. St., Cedar City 84720 (801/586-2421).

Fishlake National Forest, 170 N. Main St., Ritchfield 84701 (801/896-4491).

Manti-LaSal National Forest, 599 West 100 South, Price 84501 (801/637-2817).

Uinta National Forest, 88 West 100 North, Provo 84601 (801/584-9101).

Wasatch National Forest, 8226 Federal Bldg., 125 S. State St., Salt Lake City 84138 (801/524-5030).

Washington

This state is a diverse land of opportunity for mule deer hunters. From coastal rain forests to timbered peaks and lowland deserts, it produces blacktails of the Columbian subspecies and Rocky Mountain mule deer. A healthy herd of whitetails lives in the northeast corner. Most of the blacktails inhabit the southwest region. The Mount St. Helens eruption destroyed a significant part of the herds, but plenty of deer remain. The Gifford Pinchot National Forest is in the middle of prime blacktail range and offers 1.2 million acres of hunting. Lewis County is one of the best for blacktails, and so are Grays Harbor and Cowlitz counties. These are all in the southwest area within easy driving distance of the heavily populated Seattle-Tacoma area.

Many millions of acres of good blacktail country is owned by timber companies. Deer hunting by permission is allowed on much of this land, and special regulations are often in effect. The state wildlife agency has information on these large timber holdings.

For the bigger Rocky Mountain mule deer subspecies, hunters head to the central and eastern regions. Okanogan County in the north-central region on the British Columbia border is considered the best mule deer country. The Okanogan National Forest has 1½-million acres of public hunting land. Chelan County to the southwest is also a top-ranked mule deer area. Many millions of deer hunting acres are available on other national forests scattered across the state.

Many of the accessible regions are overcrowded by hunters. About one-quarter of a million hunters take to the hills each year. The answer to hunter competition is to head for hidden drainages and ridges far from any roads.

Washington's hunter success is modest, running about 25 percent or so. Each year, 50,000 to 60,000 deer are killed, of which 20,000 to 25,000 are Rocky Mountain muleys. Blacktail harvests could be higher, but most hunters show a preference for the big-racked bucks of the more open mountains.

Biologists estimate there are about 240,000 blacktails and 181,000 Rocky Mountain mule deer.

Permits are unlimited for deer. Seasons usually begin in mid-October and run to late October or into November, depending on the unit.

For information, write the Washington Game Department, 600 North Capitol Way, Olympia, WA 98504.

National forests: Colville National Forest, Colville 99114 (509/684-5221).

Gifford Pinchot National Forest, 500 W. 12th St., Vancouver 98660 (206/696-4041).

Mt. Baker and Snoqualmie National Forests, 1601 Second Ave., Seattle 98101 (206/442-5400).

Okanogan National Forest, 1240 2nd Ave. S., Okanogan 98840 (509/422-2704).

Olympia National Forest, Box 2288, Olympia 98507 (206/753-9534).

Wenatchee National Forest, 301 Yakima St., Wenatchee 98801 (509/662-4323).

Wyoming

With an estimated 350,000 mule deer of the Rocky Mountain subspecies, Wyoming is an excellent state for muleys, and big ones, too. About 100,000 hunters take to the hills annually, bringing home some 55,000 deer or so. Hunter success is very high, often 60 percent or better.

Unfortunately, getting a permit in the best deer areas is tough for a nonresident, since licenses are awarded via a lottery drawing. Deer tags in popular regions such as D, E, F, G, and H are often difficult to obtain because of competition from other hunters. Be aware that application deadlines are very early in this state—March 1. Some regions have non-resident permits left over after the lottery, and are available from the Wyoming Game and Fish Department after the deer drawings are held in mid-May.

Mule deer are scattered around the state, but much of the interest is focused on the western half. The huge Bridger-Teton National Forest has plenty of great deer country, with almost 3½-million acres of public hunting land. The Shoshone National Forest that borders Yellowstone Park is also excellent for mule deer. The Medicine Bow and Bighorn National Forests are set apart from the others, being in the southeast and north central regions respectively. Both are good for mule deer, and permits are often left over after the lottery drawing for the country around the Bighorn Forest.

My favorite Wyoming mule deer area is in the Greys River drainage near the Idaho border. Other favorite spots are in the Gros Ventre and Hoback areas near Jackson. Outfitters are available in all of this top-notch game country.

There is also a great deal of BLM land to hunt around the state. I prefer the southwest region where aspen-covered mountains and sagebrush slopes support plenty of mule deer.

Wyoming offers a number of deer units that restrict harvest to four-point-or-better bucks. Some units are structured in this manner because deer are scarce and a light harvest is desired by biologists. Other units are excellent for trophy bucks, especially when early opening dates allow hunters to pursue deer in the high country.

There is no general deer season in Wyoming, since dates vary with the units. However, mid-October usually marks the opener of most.

Because of the extraordinary hunter success and abundance of public land, Wyoming will no doubt continue to be one of the top mule deer states. Deer herds are on the increase in practically every region, and a bright future is anticipated, although the energy boom will continue to cause problems with deer habitat.

Because Wyoming is my favorite big game hunting state, I apply for a permit each year. If I'm fortunate, I consider it a lucky bonus to be able to chase muleys around the rimrock. Many hunters are in agreement with my opinion on this fabulous state.

For information on hunting regulations, write the Wyoming Game and Fish Department, Cheyenne, WY 82002.

National forests: Bridger and Teton National Forests, Forest Service Bldg., Jackson 83001 (307/733-2752).

Bighorn National Forest, Columbus Building, Box 2046, Sheridan 82801 (307/672-2457).

Medicine Bow National Forest, 605 Skyline Dr., Laramie 82070 (307/745-8971).

Shoshone National Forest, West Yellowstone Highway, Box 2140, Cody 82414 (307/587-2274).

Note: Black Hills National Forest is listed in South Dakota.

Alberta

Mule deer are fairly well established in Alberta at about 100,000. They range throughout the province, except in the northwest corner. The best mule deer hunting is in the southwest region, in the forests of the Rocky Mountains, and in the parklands of the central region. The eastern slopes of the Rockies, particularly in the foothill areas, are often considered the best mule deer environments.

For information, write the Alberta Department of Lands and Forests, Natural Resources Building, 109th Street at 99th Ave., Edmonton, Alberta, Canada.

British Columbia

Both the Rocky Mountain mule deer and the blacktail live in this large Canadian province. The larger Rocky Mountain deer inhabits the interior while blacktails live along the coast. The Columbian subspecies of blacktail is found on the lower coast and on Vancouver Island as well as adjacent islands. The Sitka blacktail dwells along the northern coast, Queen Charlotte Island, and other islands in the north sector. B.C. has about 500,000 blacktails and 100,000 muleys.

Hunting for deer in B.C. is surprisingly good, with very high hunter success in many units. Most deer hunters are residents, since nonresidents visit the province chiefly for moose, caribou, goats, sheep and bears.

Seasons are long, and multiple bag limits are permissible in some units, usually in the blacktail areas.

For information, write the British Columbia Department of Recreation and Conservation, Fish and Wildlife Branch, Victoria, British Columbia, Canada V8V 1X4.

Saskatchewan

Mule deer are in the minority here, with whitetails the most plentiful species. What muleys there are live in the southwest corner, although there are scattered populations in whitetail country as well. Only about 5 percent of the total deer harvest here is mule deer. The southern half of Saskatchewan is reserved for resident hunting only, effectively eliminating mule deer hunting for nonresidents.

For information, write the Wildlife Branch, Department of Natural Resources, Government Administration Building, Regina, Saskatchewan, Canada.

Index